Business and Personal Wisdom

A Wise King's Advice

by Bob Biles

DORRANCE
PUBLISHING CO
EST. 1920
PITTSBURGH, PENNSYLVANIA 15238

Dorrance Publishing Co
585 Alpha Drive
Suite 103
Pittsburgh, PA 15238
Visit our website at www.dorrancebookstore.com

ISBN: 979-8-89027-992-7
eISBN: 979-8-8902-7548-6

Business and Personal Wisdom

A Wise King's Advice

Contents

Introduction

Don't we all aspire to be wise? And wouldn't it be great if we acquired that wisdom at an early age? Experience may be the best teacher, but it is also possible, and a lot less painful, to learn from others. If possible, wouldn't you want to learn living skills (wisdom) from a very wise person?

There was such a person three thousand years ago. Rather than keep his wisdom to himself, he preserved for posterity much of that wisdom in the book of Proverbs.

In this book, you'll find the first nine chapters of Proverbs, Solomon's letter to his son, broken into 34 sections. That follows the breakout in the 1985 New International Version Study Bible by the Zondervan Corporation. Considering these smaller sections of the letter allowed me to gaze intently upon it and explore the wisdom Solomon is offering to his son and us. Because this is a letter from Solomon to his son, references to other books in the Bible have been minimized. The intent was to study the letter as Solomon constructed it. Where references to other parts of the Bible have been made, they are intended to help you understand historical events Solomon may have had in mind as he wrote his letter. Rather than insert long passages from other parts of the Bible, you'll find summaries of the events. If you want to read these passages to get the full story, you may want to have a Bible, especially one with references, close by.

Each chapter in this book uses the same format. After providing the Proverbs verses to be considered, the chapter includes:

- **Background/Circumstances** – More background on the chosen Proverbs section, along with explanations of terms and to what Solomon may have been referring.
- **Business Application** – How the section applies to companies and those who run them, as well as those who work for others.
- **Personal Application** – What Solomon is telling each of us as individuals.

In Appendix 1, Business Application Questions, you'll find a list of questions intended to help you explore, discover, and retain the business applications in each chapter. In Appendix 2, Personal Application Questions, you'll find a list of questions intended to help you explore, discover, and retain the personal applications in each chapter. These questions are intended to jumpstart your consideration of or discussions about Solomon's teachings and instructions.

As you go through the book, you'll find Solomon had a lot to say in his nine chapters, chapters often passed over to get to the pithy proverbs that start in Chapter 10. Yet it is a mistake to pass over these chapters or to read through them too quickly. When you carefully explore the wisdom being offered, you'll find a treasure trove of thoughts and insights. Solomon understood life, people, and the forces at work in the world. While outward things like transportation (cars instead of camels) have changed, nothing has really changed about life, people, and the forces at work in the world. Solomon's Proverbs are just as valid today, maybe more so than they were at the time Solomon wrote them.

Throughout the book, I've used examples from my business career and personal life to illustrate some of the topics Solomon brought up three thousand years ago. Please be aware these examples are based on my understanding of the situations being described. While others may have differing opinions about or a more complete knowledge of what took place, I have done my best to accurately describe events as they actually took place.

This book is the result of a question I asked myself one early October morning: "I wonder what business wisdom there is in Proverbs?" Little did I know then that question would lead to a year-long search to understand the first nine chapters of Proverbs. During that search, I came to appreciate the value of taking time to ponder the truth being presented in each section before moving to the next section. While you can give this book a quick read, I believe the greatest value to you will come from reading one chapter at a time, struggling to find and understand the truth Solomon is providing, and cementing the truth and understanding in your mind and heart through discussions with others.

I truly hope you will be blessed by reading and contemplating Solomon's wisdom, as well as my thoughts on his words. As you'll learn, reading and contemplating are good but the real challenge is to put Solomon's words into practice. And the place to start is where Solomon started in Chapter 1, Verse 7: "The fear [loving reverence] of the LORD is the beginning of knowledge." For whoever finds this knowledge moves along the path to gaining wisdom and finding true life.

Proverbs

Chapter One

Chapter 1

Four Types of People and Their Weaknesses
Proverbs 1:1-6

The proverbs of Solomon son of David, king of Israel: For attaining wisdom and discipline; for understanding words of insight: for acquiring a disciplined and prudent life, doing what is right and just and fair; for giving prudence to the simple, knowledge and discretion to the young—let the wise listen and add to their learning, and let the discerning get guidance—for understanding proverbs and parables, the sayings and riddles of the wise.

Background/Circumstances

The author of the book sets forth the reasons the book is being written. So many important things are included in this introduction, let's make sure we cover them in some detail.

First, the author clearly states these sayings are those of Solomon. He is not talking about any old Solomon. Rather this Solomon is the son of David, the king of Israel. In many ways, David was the ideal king. Although he failed many times, he kept a close relationship to the LORD and always came back to the things of God. This Solomon was the son whom David chose to be his successor and ensured that he became king. Although other sons were older and could have been named king, David chose Solomon for a reason. There must have been something special about Solomon that David recognized. If you know the story, you know that specialness shows up when God asks Solomon what he would like to have as a gift. Rather than riches or long life, Solomon asks for wisdom so he can lead the nation of Israel wisely. And God abundantly gives him wisdom, so much wisdom that Solomon is recognized as the wisest person who has ever lived. So the author, in one short sentence, is telling the reader these proverbs are worth reading and understanding because they are from THAT Solomon, the wisest of the wise.

From there, he lists the benefits from reading (and understanding) the proverbs. They include:

1. **Attaining wisdom and discipline.** There are two ways to obtain wisdom, with the school of hard knocks being one of them. But that can be a painful way to learn. How much better to sit and learn from someone who is wise! But we learn right away that wisdom isn't enough; one also has to attain discipline. It is quite possible that Solomon was looking back over his life and thinking about how his lack of discipline, especially with women, affected his decision making.
2. **Understanding words of insight.** Even though one sits at the feet of the wise, listens all day, and takes great notes, if the person doesn't understand the insights it's wasted time. It's like me listening to Beethoven's Ninth Symphony; I know the music is really good but I don't at all understand why it is great music. But others who really understand music listen to his Ninth Symphony, come away understanding what Beethoven was saying in this symphony, and can talk about it with others who understand. So it is with insights. One can hear and not understand.
3. **Acquiring a disciplined and prudent life (which entails doing what is right and just and fair).** Attaining wisdom and discipline and understanding words of insight are the first two parts of the author's trilogy. The third part is to acquire a life

that is disciplined and prudent. For what good is it to have the first two parts if it doesn't show up in your life? Apparently, the truly wise take what they learn and live a life that revolves around doing what is right, just, and fair.

After talking about these benefits, the author of the book identifies four different kinds of people. Understanding who they represent is crucial for understanding this section as well as other proverbs to come. The kinds of people are:

- **The Simple** – Those who are going through life without giving a lot of thought to what is happening. They appear to not be young, wise, or discerning. In light of the other three groups, this category likely represents the vast majority of people.
- **The Young** – Those who are yet to be exposed to knowledge and discretion. Because they are candidates for gaining knowledge and discretion, they must be between the age when we would expect a young person to be capable of gaining these two things and adulthood. Whether they turn out to be simple, wise, or discerning (or as we'll see in the next proverb, fools) is yet to be determined.
- **The Wise** – Those who know how to take care of situations. They have escaped being simple and are likely no longer young.
- **The Discerning** – Those who feel a situation is developing that needs to be addressed. They, too, have escaped being simple and are likely no longer young.

Just in case you think this is going to be easy, the author lets us in on a little secret: The Wise speak in proverbs, parables, sayings, and riddles that aren't always easy to understand. It is going to take work on the listener's part to grasp what the Wise are truly saying.

Business Application

Over the years, I have lost track of the number of times I saw presentations on the four types of people. Isn't it interesting that Solomon, over three thousand years ago, compiled his list of the four types of people? As we go through Proverbs, we'll find that Solomon talks a lot about each of these groups. It's his intent to help his son, and us, understand how each of us and those we meet fit into these groups.

What's even more interesting is he identifies what each of these groups is lacking. Yes, even the Wise and Discerning have areas of weakness! No one is exempt from needed improvement. Let's take a closer look at each group and what they need:

- **The Discerning.** Most of us have a person on our team who has the ability to see an opportunity or know that something is wrong (if you don't have anyone, get one as soon as you can). Often, this person will have some degree of responsibility. While they carry out their responsibilities well, they can become stymied when certain matters arise or decisions need to be made. For them to do their best, they need guidance. Otherwise, problems will worsen, opportunities will be missed, or things will just stall. Because these folks see what is happening, wise organizations will make it easy for the Discerning to bring problems up—even though the problems may be very uncomfortable or one's superiors or peers don't want to hear about them. If you give them enough encouragement, these are the folks who will tell you that the "emperor has no clothes on"—that the business deal being proposed has large gaps that are being ignored or missed.
- **The Wise.** Often, this person will be sitting in a job where his knowledge and experience come to bear when key decisions need to be made. But as this person rises in the organization,

their knowledge can become stale. Processes, people, product, and the market may have changed from when they were doing the actual work. Unless this person takes steps to stay current, the risk for making poor, maybe even disastrous, decisions increases every day. The person most likely to know what is going on, and thus the person most likely to be able to help him, is the discerning person.

A codependency seems to exist between the Discerning and the Wise. Each group is missing something without the other. Only the Wise can help the Discerning and vice versa. Thus, their ability to prosper as teammates within the company will yield great results. Further, their ability to work together is key to developing the other two groups. So the wise employer will seek to ensure their teams always include a wise person and a discerning person.

- **The Young.** Consider those who are just coming into the workforce—the Young. Because they are new to the business, they have much to learn. In order for them to do their jobs well, they have to be given the knowledge needed. Most companies have some sort of initial training that helps the totally new employee learn the technical skills they initially need to do their job. But that isn't enough; they also need to learn discretion which, according to the New Oxford American Dictionary, takes two forms:
    - **Quality of behaving or speaking in such a way as to avoid causing offense or revealing private information.** If you think about yourself when you were younger, you likely can think of some things you said that offended others. The "truth" had to be told, so you took it upon yourself to speak the "truth," not particularly caring how it would impact others. While it might have felt good at the time, it probably was not the best way to handle the situ-

ation. One can deliver truth in a way that doesn't create chaos or hard feelings. It's a good skill to learn and one that is invaluable for the Young to learn quickly. While that is one thing to guard against, the other is a tendency for the Young to "spill the beans" too easily. In an effort to show how much they know, it's only too easy for the Young to divulge more than they should to others. To a question about how business is going, a young person can be led into talking about business prospects, company financial information and strategies, or even company secrets. If you're a young person reading this and want to be trusted, you have to develop discernment in these areas.

- **Freedom to decide what should be done in a particular situation.** Most businesses want to push decisions down to the lowest level in the organization that they can. However, it isn't always easy to do that when the positions that could have the authority to make the decisions are populated by younger people who may not have the knowledge or discernment to make consistently wise decisions. Standard operating procedures and rules are developed to provide consistency. But be aware they can chafe those young people who do have the ability to make wise decisions and delay development for those who lean on the rules and standard operating procedures too much.

  In this area, it is important to understand that transferring knowledge is a completely different challenge compared to teaching discretion. Most employees can pass on knowledge to a new person but a relatively few can teach discretion. Those who have discretion in your organization are the Discerning and the Wise. As you look at your company, are your wise and discerning folks actively involved in teaching your young discretion? Don't be surprised if the answer is "not nearly enough." Don't despair. Your wise and discerning groups can pull together a plan to teach the Young this skill. While a talented and motivated person can achieve discretion on their own, success is more certain if you take charge and are actively involved.

- **The Simple.** I would have preferred a different name than "Simple" for this group. They aren't necessarily simple. Most likely, they just want to come in and do a good job for you. They have the skills and knowledge to do the job but may lack prudence (good judgment or good sense). It is up to the Wise and the Discerning to help them learn. This can vary from setting specific rules that cover as many contingencies as you can think of (e.g., if there is a water spill, here are the actions you take) to establishing some general rules (we want a safe workplace and expect you to look out for your fellow employees). If you want to get the best from them and improve your bottom line, make sure you have helped this group learn to be prudent in their work.

The benefits from taking the time and making the effort to meet the needs of each of these four groups is astounding. Your employees will attain more wisdom and understanding and become more disciplined and prudent. They will do what is right and just and fair and turn your company into one that does what is right and just and fair. A company like that will have a loyal and dynamic workforce and a terrific reputation.

Are you ready to do what is needed for you and your company?

Personal Application

In the business world, we spent lots of time, and different four-point tools, evaluating our employees and ourselves. We gained broad understanding of how each of us fit into certain behavior sets, as well as how to communicate with each other and avoid pushing each other's hot buttons. We did all of that work because we felt the time and money spent would benefit us in the end. Although all of this got a little old, I can attest to having several "ah-ha" moments in one session. What I learned about my boss helped me understand him better and dramatically changed how I worked with him. That new understanding on my part led to a stronger and more productive relationship.

Think about it. We spend less than 30 percent of our lives at work, but we spend a ton of time and energy figuring out how to understand others and communicate well with them. If businesses consider it that worthwhile, shouldn't we consider doing the same in our personal lives?

Fortunately, we don't have to go through the expense of hiring consultants to help us figure this out. Rather Solomon, within the first few verses of Proverbs, starts describing the four types of people and then spends the rest of Proverbs telling us about the characteristics of these four types. Where he differs from the corporate world is the criteria: His classifications are based on what is important to God (more on that in an upcoming section). But he doesn't stop with just identifying the four types of people; he also lets us know what a person in each different group needs to do to become one who does what is right, just, and fair. In Solomon's thinking, a person who does what is right, just, and fair is leading a "disciplined and prudent life." No matter how much we might want to take shortcuts to get there, Solomon makes it clear that kind of life only comes from attaining wisdom, discipline, and understanding. In Proverbs, Solomon is going to tell us how to go about it.

So the initial challenge thrown at us is to consider the four types of people and then consider in which category you fit. If you have any question about where you fit, or if you want confirmation, ask a good friend to help you. It's only too easy to place ourselves in a category to which we think we belong rather than in the one we do. Once you have a good feel for the group to which you belong, then you can start considering the advice that Solomon provides. In these few verses, he points to the primary need of each group. Here is a quick summary:

- **If Simple** – You need to be cautious in your dealings with others. They can see that you may lack judgment (prudence) and try to take advantage of you.
- **If Young** – You need to gather knowledge and discretion. Discretion means behaving or speaking in such a way as to avoid causing offense or revealing private information. It also could mean gaining judgment skills (prudence) so you can have the freedom to decide what should be done in a particular situation.
- **If Discerning** – You need a wise advisor who can help guide you in your decision making.
- **If Wise** – You need to be humble enough to ensure you have current information (knowledge) before using your wisdom to help others.

Enough about you for now. How about the people in your life? Do you know what category to which they belong? Knowing their category and considering what they need to attain a disciplined and prudent life, and acting upon it, will benefit you and them as you go through life together. You'll take fewer false steps, enjoy life more, and have more satisfying relationships.

Chapter 2

Enter the Fool
Proverbs 1:7

The fear of the LORD is the beginning of knowledge, but fools despise wisdom and discipline.

Background/Circumstances

In the first six verses of Proverbs, the author introduced us to four types of people: 1) the Simple, 2) the Young, 3) the Discerning, and 4) the Wise. Although he talked about the Young, as we'll see, the Young eventually take their place in one of the other categories. Now, Solomon turns our attention to a fifth type of person, who we will see more fully described in subsequent proverbs. This person is the Fool.

Before getting into the basic characteristics of the Fool, we need to understand the phrase "The fear of the LORD." From a religious understanding it means "a loving reverence for God that includes submission to his lordship and to the commands of his word." For the purposes of this discussion, I want to define it more narrowly as "a loving reverence for the truth." Thus, a substitute reading of the first phrase in the proverb would be "a loving reverence for the truth is the beginning of knowledge."

With that in place, now let's take a look at the Fool. He is astounding:

- **He doesn't seem to care about knowledge that is based on truth.**
- **He despises wisdom.**
- **He despises discipline.**

Consider how different the other four types of people are from the Fool. They can see and understand that knowledge, wisdom, and discipline are intertwined in their journey to completeness. Hope exists for them if they will take Solomon's advice and apply the remedies he recommends. While the Fool also sees all these things, he *purposefully* takes another direction. Truth doesn't matter to him at all. Neither does wisdom. He may well recognize good advice as wisdom, but he rejects it. The same with discipline. The Fool may understand more discipline would be good for him, but that cramps his style. So the Fool throws discipline to the side, too. You can almost feel how incredulous Solomon is that a person could be so completely and totally deceived.

Business Application

Beware of the Fool! While you probably have gathered that already, let's take a deeper dive into why.

Because the Fool doesn't care about knowledge based on truth, he can cause lots of mischief. You may get some reports from the Fool that are perfectly fine. But other reports will be inaccurate because:

- **The Fool may not be careful in his research.** Because he doesn't have a loving reverence for truth, he may make some simple observations and call it good enough. He is careless in his work. If you've been a boss for very long, you will have come across the Fool. I certainly have. Because I worked in the world of government finance, lots of financial reports were based on financial records as well as budgets and financial projections based on spreadsheets. Over the years, I had staff who were careful in preparing these reports. While I trusted them—because the results would be provided to the governing board and other interested parties—I still reviewed their work just to be sure the results were close to what was expected. Although staff had been careful, there would be times when the results didn't look quite right. When I would bring it to their attention, often the staff members would know exactly what they had overlooked. Now, the staff I'm thinking of here weren't Fools; they had only missed something.

Other staff, however, were much less careful in their work. While they could do good work, they had the tendency to not think through their work or their assumptions. When reviewing their work, I was much more careful and usually had to take a deeper dive to find their mistakes because they were stuck on the assumptions and processes they used to prepare the reports. In assigning work to them, I had to be much more explicit with directions and things they should consider.

- **The Fool may have no problem with falsifying information to present the truth as he wants it to be presented.** But this isn't carelessness. Rather, this is a purposeful effort to mislead. I've also run into this way too many times. Rather than tell the truth about a situation, some will spin the "facts" or point to other things to distract from the truth. Somehow they thought the truth wouldn't come out if they could only ignore it or paint a different picture for others to look at. Although it often failed, it worked just enough that people would still give it a go. You especially see this at a national level. Too many elected officials spin events to meet their current political needs. This is so prevalent that reasonable people (who I believe make up the majority of the country) are having a hard time understanding what the facts actually are.

It's bad enough that the Fool can cause problems because of his disregard for knowledge, but he creates even more chaos by despising wisdom. What does that look like? Most commonly, this person won't listen to reason. In its most extreme form, this person will come off as a "know-it-all" who won't listen to anyone else. You can use all of the logic you can bring to bear and talk until you are blue in the face; it won't make any difference. He has a jaded perspective and he isn't going to change that perspective.

I would come across this kind of person during the annual budget preparation. In one situation, I had an employee who always wanted us to be ultra-conservative when estimating revenues. While that might have benefitted me (actual revenues would always be above budgeted revenues; little criticism for the Chief Financial Officer (CFO)), the direct result of purposefully underestimating revenues is the government has to restrict its service levels well below what it could have provided to its citizens. That is a bad thing. Each year in our staff meetings and presentations to my peers, I had to resist this person's appeal to take the ultra-conservative approach. In the one internal budget meeting I missed in my tenure there, this person presented such a dire financial picture the executive team spent their budget session talking about the drastic cuts that would have to be made. Some walked out and told their staff drastic budget cuts were coming. The day I got back from my vacation, one staff member called me to tell me what had happened in the last budget meeting. She recommended I address it at the next executive meeting, which was taking place in thirty minutes. At that meeting, I was able to show the executives more realistic financial projections using the more realistic assumptions. While we had some work to do to balance service and capital requests with revenue projections, it was not nearly the catastrophic picture that had been painted in the previous budget session.

Our first approach to dealing with the Fool is to use logic and reasoning (wisdom). If things are just explained well enough to them, surely they will come around to your way of thinking. Unfortunately, this doesn't work with the Fool. They despise any attempt at giving them wisdom. Because that doesn't work, the next approach is usually discipline. Guess what? The Fool also despises discipline and will refuse to learn anything from it. And because that is his attitude, he is likely to continue with, or maybe even exaggerate, his behavior. Pay attention and you'll sense his defiance to correction.

Did anyone you work with come to mind in the last three paragraphs? If so, you have a dangerous person in your midst. Why would you want to keep anyone around who provides bad information, won't listen to good advice, and refuses to respond positively to discipline? It's bad enough they are behaving this way. Even worse, if the Fool can act this way and get away with it, he may be raising other Fools within your organization.

To prevent this, you need to identify the Fools in your organization as quickly as you can and provide them with an early exit path. If you don't, you are playing with fire. For example, if the Fool works with the Young, the Young won't acquire knowledge and discretion. It is wishful thinking to think the Fool will teach the Simple how to be prudent. The Fool will provide false wisdom to the Discerning and inaccurate information to the Wise. And if you should happen to have two or more Fools together in key positions, what a mess! In the final analysis, the Fool is bad news and you don't want to be associated with him. As we continue reviewing the proverbs, Solomon will explain in greater and greater detail what you need to know about the Fool.

Personal Application

Were you surprised that the fear of the LORD is the beginning of knowledge? It's a fascinating thought and one we shouldn't go past too quickly. It means that as much as one may know now, unless he has this loving reverence of the LORD in place, he really can't begin to have knowledge.

On the face of it, this seems to be a ridiculous claim. We all know people who are experts in their field and who wouldn't ever be described as having a loving reverence for the LORD (in fact, it may be just the opposite). We all know others who are knowledgeable of a lot of things, some whom would scoff at the idea of having a loving reverence for the LORD. It is possible for those who ignore or reject the LORD to have quite a bit of knowledge. So what is Solomon talking about?

I think it comes down to this: If you don't recognize there is a Supreme Being who carefully and lovingly put the universe into place, you have missed the most important piece of knowledge there is. Without it, your life and this world are just accidents and anything goes. But with that knowledge, the world and your life have a new and eternal meaning. Shaking your fist into an abyss and shouting, "Why am I here?" feels a lot different than turning to this loving LORD and asking, "God, why am I here?"

And this begins to explain why the Fool is such a fool. Even though the evidence is abundantly clear a loving Supreme Being for whom he should have reverence exists, the Fool refuses to revere this Supreme Being. And that sets him on his path to the next two things the Fool does: despising wisdom and discipline.

Most of us go through a young and foolish period. For me, it was a three-year period spanning my last two years of high school and my first year of college. During that time, I heavily discounted anything an older person, especially my parents, told me. Although they were offering wisdom that could have benefitted me, because they were of the older generation and couldn't possibly understand or know what my generation knew, I played the Fool and despised the gems of wisdom they had gathered from their life experiences and were offering me. As I look back at those three years, my treatment of my parents during that time was really despicable. Then, one day early in my sophomore year in college, I woke up and realized my parents were actually pretty smart and had a lot of wisdom to offer me. It was like the fog of foolishness that had settled over me three years before had suddenly lifted.

Now I wish I could say from that point on I unerringly walked the path of the Wise. Let's just say it can take a while to move from playing a fool most of the time to seeking wisdom most of the time. It can be a two-steps-forward, one-step-back journey. And, on some things or in certain circumstances, I can zoom right back to the foolish ruts I set during those three years. What saves me now is I no longer despise wisdom or discipline. Not to say that it is always easy to receive wisdom or discipline; sometimes it has stung for a while. But that pain was nothing compared to the benefits I received from harkening to the wisdom and discipline I received.

As you ponder this verse, there are a few things to consider:

- **How do you respond to wisdom and discipline?** If you welcome them and make it a point to learn from them, then you are behaving wisely. But if you find yourself thinking nasty thoughts about the person who offered the wisdom or imposed the discipline, you may well be playing the Fool. It may be hard for you to accept this advice, but here goes: Stop right now and take a hard, honest look at yourself and what you are doing. You are only hurting yourself.
- **Have you taken the first step to knowledge**? It's pretty plain what the first step is; Solomon doesn't pull any punches. It comes down to developing a loving reverence for the LORD. Almost all of us have a relationship like this in our lives, one where we have a loving reverence for another. For many of us, it has been a parent or other adult who loved us deeply enough to lead us toward what is right, just, and fair. That leading likely included giving us wisdom and a fair amount of discipline. At the time, we may have resented it. But as we matured, our feel-

ings toward them turned into admiration, thankfulness, and love for whom they were and what they did for us. That's close to the idea of loving reverence, except here the object of that reverence is a magnificent LORD who cares even more deeply than that adult who changed your life.

- **How would you categorize those with whom you associate?** It's a question worth considering. If you want to be wise, it's best to associate with those who are wise and learn from them. And to be fair, it may not always be easy. The Wise person who cares for you will challenge you in those areas of your life that you don't want to change but need to in order to be wise. Even then, it's better than being in the company of Fools. Because, if your friends are Fools, they will have no interest in anything except leading you to be as foolish as they are. What a waste.

And it is a true waste. While we all have done foolish things, most of us learn from our experiences and become wiser. We go on to live good lives, meaning we become more concerned about doing what is right, just, and fair. But the Fool's life is completely different. Rather than becoming wiser, he becomes more foolish. Rather than accepting correction, he despises it and learns nothing. The picture is pretty bleak—once a Fool, always a Fool.

Though he doesn't say it, can't you hear Solomon earnestly telling you to, at all costs, avoid becoming the Fool?

Chapter 3

Value of Instruction and Teaching
Proverbs 1:8-9

Listen, my son, to your father's instruction and do not forsake your mother's teaching. They will be a garland to grace your head and a chain to adorn your neck.

Background/Circumstances

In the first seven verses, the author described the five basic types of people that he will explore in greater detail in the rest of the book. Here Solomon starts the next section talking directly to his son.

First, he directs his son to listen to his father's instruction. The term used for "listen" is a strong command. It means to gaze intently and understand. It's easy to imagine that Solomon has written some instructions and wisdom for his son to follow. It might even be the book of Proverbs to which Solomon is referring. Whether it is written or verbal instructions, or both, this son is being told he needs to spend time contemplating the truths within these instructions. While reading them may be easy, understanding them is another matter. It is going to take concentration and focus.

Why is Solomon pointing this out right at the beginning of his message to his son? If Solomon is as wise as we understand him to be, he has given a great deal of thought to the things his son needs to know if he is to be wise and a good king. As we'll see, his instructions will cover those things the son should become, as well as those things he should avoid.

But Solomon understands that another person has been, and will be, critical in his son's development—his mother. While Solomon provided instruction, the mother provided teaching. This is quite a distinction and we shouldn't miss it. "Teaching" refers to underlying principles the son has been taught, likely from a young age on his mother's knee through his current age. These teachings are so strong within him that in order to go another direction in his life he would have to *forsake* them. This would mean a willful rejection of the good things his mother worked so hard to instill in him.

Because the mother has provided the underlying principles for the son, Solomon's instructions delve into how to apply those principles in everyday life. Solomon takes the work of the mother and expands on it. The clear message is both are needed.

But giving the son these two commands—to listen to his instructions and not forsake his mother's teachings—isn't enough. The son needs to know why these commands are so important. It turns out, the quality of his kingship will be determined by the son's willingness to listen and not forsake. If he does as Solomon directs him, the people will recognize him as a good king (garland on his head). Besides being a good, and popular, king, his life as king will be one of beauty (chain to adorn his neck). Everything around him—family, country, and kingship—will be a thing of beauty. If he will only listen and not forsake, he can have a reign just as magnificent as Solomon's reign.

The stage has been set and the questions hanging at the end of the ninth verse loom: "Will the son listen to Solomon's instructions?" "Are his mother's teachings embedded so deeply that the son won't forsake them?" "Is the promise of a popular and wonderful kingship a strong enough incentive to keep the son from straying?"

Business Application

It's interesting that Solomon, after describing the types of people, paints a picture of a father and mother giving their son teaching and instruction. Each one has something different to offer.

So it is in business. Those who are older and wiser have a responsibility to teach and instruct those who come after them. We often see "teach" and "instruct" as the same thing but the wisdom in these verses provides a much different perspective. It's one that you, as the leader of your company, need to grasp if you are going to be effective in bringing your employees along to the maturity you would like them to have. As related here, teaching is about providing those bedrock principles that govern how you and your company do business. Common examples include:

- The customer is always right.
- Employees are our most valuable asset.
- Quality is our middle name.

You probably have developed some bedrock principles that drive how your company operates. If you haven't done so already, it is worthwhile to write them down. It forces you to articulate them in a way that makes sense to you, your employees, and even those you deal with on a regular basis. It also forces you to think through how the principles should be applied or could be misapplied. Then you can communicate your bedrock principles to your employees. It's up to you how you do that, but it should be in a way that is impactful and consistent. It takes a while to imprint principles; therefore, you have to keep after it much like a mother does when her child is ready to learn.

But we have to go beyond teaching our basic principles and get into instructions. For instance, knowing the basic principle of "The customer is always right" doesn't give the employee any sense of what to do from there. Imagine one of your customers comes into your business and tells your employee that the product she bought yesterday broke and is a piece of junk. You might think your employee would know what to do, but you might be surprised because businesses can, and do, handle this situation differently. Examples include:

- Companies that take all products back with no questions asked.
- Businesses that want to ask a few questions before deciding how to handle the complaint. Usually these involve the possibility that the customer grossly misused a product they purchased and damaged.

Unless you have provided instructions on how to apply the basic principle of "The customer is always right," your employee could think he is to take the product back and either give the customer a new one or her money back when you would rather have had the employee ask a few questions first. You might have even wanted this employee to seek out a more experienced employee, maybe the onsite manager, who has the authorization to handle product returns. While the basic principles provide an outline of what you want, the instructions fill in and color the picture in such a way your employees can grasp and understand how you want things to be done.

It's important to complete that picture for them, especially if you are interested in seeing your employees excel and mature. Your ability to provide a foundation of good guiding principles and timely instructions will make all the difference. Besides making your business prosper, a well-deserved pride results from helping an employee grow into a leader who is admired by his fellow employees and deserves all the accolades he receives. Done well, the company will produce an outsized number of employees who are honored by the community for their principled way of living. They will be sought after to be leaders. These employees also will do well in other areas of life.

But it is only too easy to do one thing well and miss out on the other. For instance, the partners at the regional office of the international accounting firm I worked for straight out of college often quoted the founder's principle of "think straight, talk straight." In the accounting world, that is a pretty good principle: Make sure you are 1) adhering to accounting and auditing standards in your work and 2) being honest with peers and clients. I've always remembered that principle and it proved to be useful to me. What I don't remember as well are the instructions on how that principle was to be applied in our work. There might have been more than the prepared audit procedures; I just don't remember. Some twenty years later, when the firm was in the news over Enron's fraudulent financial reporting, I had to wonder how a different regional office of the firm that had the underlying principle of "think straight, talk straight" could have missed the boat so badly that it led to the dissolution of the firm.

So you have to provide teaching *and* instruction and both need to be done well. Teaching without instruction lets employees decide how to implement your underlying principles. You may not be happy at all with how that turns out. Instruction without the underlying principles leaves employees without any understanding of the "why." While they may do what you want, employees will tend to develop into rule keepers and you'll have trouble developing your employees into the vibrant, thinking employees who can advance in the company.

If you can provide teaching and instruction well, your company benefits tremendously. For starters, because they are on the same page, have wisdom beyond their years, and are dedicated toward meeting and exceeding goals, your staff will accomplish amazing things. Others within the company will see what this group accomplishes and will want to learn their "secrets." Several on your staff will become community leaders and your company will be recognized as one that has an abundance of great people. Because of that reputation, you'll get first choice of the very best of the next generation and you can repeat that success with this new group. You'll win on the bottom line as well as contribute to the good of your community.

Personal Application

Like me, you have likely daydreamed about accomplishing great things and being honored by those around you. Whether it was hitting a grand slam to win the baseball game in the bottom of the ninth (of course with two outs and facing the other team's best pitcher); sinking the desperate, unlikely shot to win the championship basketball game; standing tall as a firefighter or policer officer to protect others; or changing public opinion through your never-to-be-matched speech and actions, at some point in your life you have likely had a thought, however fleeting, that you were worthy of the adoration of others. Also like me, you have probably had that daydream about what it would be like to have a beautiful life. That life could be defined differently for each of us, but in our daydreams it usually includes wealth, a wonderfully perfect family, and a peaceful setting.

There's nothing wrong with any of those daydreams. As we see in these verses, Solomon paints a similar daydream for his son. He can have "a garland to grace your head and a chain to adorn your neck." Yes, he can be honored and have a beautiful life, if he will only do two things:

- **Listen to his father's instructions.**
- **Not forsake his mother's teaching.**

Although the son is going to be king when Solomon passes away, whether he will be honored and have a beautiful life depends entirely on the son's attitude toward these instructions and teachings from his mother and father. If he forsakes his mother's teachings, his life will not be beautiful. If he refuses to listen to his father's instructions (something he already has and is getting more of in Proverbs), he will not be honored even though he becomes king. If I could say it a different way,

"Son, if you don't listen to us, it will really suck to be a king without honor and you will live a terrible life."

Is it any different with us? I think not. There is a good and right way to prosper, one that others will honor and leads to a beautiful, not a perfect, home life. It comes from following the high-quality teachings and instructions we receive from loved ones. Those loved ones are preferably a mother and father living a high-quality life together. Absent of those, there are others, including Solomon in Proverbs, who are willing to provide you with the teachings and instructions Solomon is talking about.

Depending upon your age, you may think the die is cast for you but let me disagree with that. As we'll see in Proverbs, one can choose to take a different path in life.

While we tend to think about ourselves a lot, let me turn your attention to the young ones around you. This could be your kids, nieces or nephews, or other children with whom you are in close contact. Have you given much thought to the teachings and instructions you want, and need, to give them? If you haven't, I hope you will now. We have a responsibility to provide those young ones around us with a good foundation of principles (be honest all the time, care for others, etc.). These principles have to be taught in a way that they become a way of life. Once these are laid down, instruction is layered upon it so that not only will they know what to do but also why they are doing it.

If you have been around children much at all, you'll also know that each child is different. Knowing that, you'll want to adapt your teaching and instructing style so it best matches the child's learning style. It can be frustrating when the child's learning style is the opposite of your learning style. However, remember your goal is to equip the child with underlying principles and instructions that will serve him well for the rest of his life.

Think about how important it is to have the underlying principle in place. Let's use honesty for our example. Once someone has made honesty one of their underlying principles, no matter the situation or what it might cost her, she will be honest. The decision to be honest has been made once and for all. If you've ever had someone display honesty to you, especially if it cost that person dearly in time, effort, or money to make things right, you'll never forget her.

But consider the sorry situation of the person who hasn't made honesty one of their underlying principles. Every day, as events take place, she has to decide whether to be honest or not. Circumstances, feelings, or something else may color her decision. Deep down, she knows she isn't an honest person and, guess what, others will soon know that she isn't a person to be trusted.

Solomon almost begs his son to take the good instructions and principles offered and hold tightly to them. After all, what good parent would teach their child bad things? But he also quietly reminds parents (and loved ones who help out) that a child may not listen to their instruction and may forsake the good principles they have been taught. And that is the truth. No matter how devotedly you have worked toward doing your best for your child, he may turn away from you and your guidance. What heartbreak for the parents and misery for the child!

While this turning away can happen at any time, the transition period between childhood and adulthood is a common time for this to happen. A child wants to be independent and feels like he needs to question or reject, at least on the surface, everything you have taught him. In many ways, it's a scary time as you never know whether he will take a real turn for the dark side. Hopefully, after a while, he will have achieved his "independence" and realize what he was taught actually works. He will have a new appreciation for his parents and be on the way to a good life.

But there are those children who take a deeper turn away from their parents. When this happens, the parent must consider the nature of their child before doing anything. What the parent has done in the past isn't going to work now. A new plan and new wisdom are needed. (You may want to seek out advice from others who have had a similar experience and a successful outcome.) Whatever you do, don't force the child into a corner where he has to fight you desperately to get out of the corner. That is a recipe for disaster. Avoid it! Instead, when you are getting close to backing him into a corner, always leave enough room so he can escape the corner without losing face. He will have heard your arguments and will, at some point, appreciate that you didn't keep him in the corner pounding away at him. That tends to crush a child's spirit and make him want to get away from you, and what you believe, as soon as he can.

So, parents, you have a tough job but take a hint from Solomon: Do your best to provide teachings and instructions on how they can lead a beautiful life with honor. And, if you need help with those teachings and instructions, just pay attention as we continue on in Proverbs.

Chapter 4

Watch Out! Enticers Ahead!
Proverbs 1:10-19

My son, if sinners entice you, do not give in to them. If they say, "Come along with us; let's lie in wait for someone's blood, let's waylay some harmless soul; let's swallow them alive, like the grave, and whole, like those who go down to the pit; we will get all sorts of valuable things and fill our houses with plunder; throw in your lot with us, and we will share a common purse"—my son, do not go along with them, do not set foot on their paths; for their feet rush into sin, they are swift to shed blood. How useless to spread a net in full view of all the birds! These men lie in wait for their own blood; they waylay only themselves! Such is the end of all who go after ill-gotten gain; it takes away the lives of those who get it.

Background/Circumstances

Having talked about the mother's teachings and father's instructions and their value, Solomon now turns to other reasons why his son should listen and not forsake their counsel; he will run into people who will try to entice him into doing evil. Their advice is "Forget what you have been taught, let's be thieves and murderers so we can have all the valuable things we want." It's a startling contrast to Solomon's advice in the prior two verses: "Faithfully follow our teachings and instructions and you will be honored and have a beautiful life." Solomon makes it clear his son will have to make a choice. There are several things Solomon points out that need more discussion:

- **Those doing the enticing are "sinners."** As defined in the New Oxford American Dictionary, "sinner" means "a person who transgresses against divine law by committing an immoral act or acts." And look at what they want to do. They want to attack, possibly murder, and take what isn't theirs because they covet it. That's breaking at least three of the Ten Commandments (don't murder, don't steal, don't covet). Worse, they have no remorse at all; they truly are sinners.
- **It's fascinating how the enticing is stated.** Nowadays, we likely would start off with a "Would you like to make some money or get rich?" and once the person says yes, then we would get into the details of what they have to do to get their money. But that isn't the approach here. Instead, they start with what they want the son to do (hurt someone he doesn't even know) and then talk about the valuables he can obtain. It's a straight appeal to do evil. It makes me think Solomon was very concerned his son would, in fact, be enticed by such an appeal.
- **Knowing the son might be very tempted by this evil enticement, Solomon provides some instructions to his son.** The first is to "not give in to them." Solomon sees the enticers are appealing to his son to forsake his mother's teaching (i.e., those basic principles of being good, honest, etc., that he has been taught from childhood). Rather than forsake them, he should hold fast to what he has been taught and reject their enticements. The second is to "not go along with them." It's not enough to just reject their enticements; the son needs to stay away from them. By hanging out with this group, the son will inevitably be drawn into their schemes and start down a path that leads to disaster.
- **These sinners have it out for "some harmless soul."** If you remember Solomon's descriptions of the types of people, this

could either be the Simple or the Young. Neither one will realize they are being stalked or being targeted as victims.

While the sinners think they will succeed and get away with it, Solomon says their adventures will end quite differently. While he doesn't come right out and say it, Solomon's short rebuttal makes it very clear these people are Fools. They think they are being smart, but he gives two reasons why they aren't:

- **They are in a hurry to do their evil deeds.** Unlike others Solomon will talk about later on in Proverbs, these folks rush into their evil. There doesn't seem to be a lot of planning going on except they will hang out someplace (doesn't say they even hide) and attack someone (anyone who looks like they might have something they want). When they see a favorable target, they launch their attack (maybe even without checking to make sure no one else is around).
- **What they are planning to do is so obvious that few people, if any, will fall into their trap.** It's interesting that the comparison is spreading a net in full view of all the birds. If birds are smart enough to observe and comprehend what is happening when someone spreads a net to capture them, then those who are watching these sinners will be able to recognize the danger before them.

While these sinners have big plans, they end up stumbling into their own net and getting caught in it. Whatever their evil plans might be, they just aren't able to carry them out. In their rush to do evil, they screw it up every time. As a result, they fail at getting the valuables they sought and they place their very lives at risk. While this may be referring to physical death, the best reading seems to be "their lives will continue to degrade and become even more miserable."

Business Application

Although it's been decades ago, I vividly remember the office supply salesman who contacted me about ordering office supplies for our city government. After a quick introduction, he started talking about the "special offer" he could give me with an order of a certain dollar amount of office supplies. The "special offer" was a brand-new TV delivered directly to my house! The thought going through my mind was "He's trying to bribe me!" Needless to say, that conversation and our relationship with that vendor ended pretty quickly.

At about the same time, another person in that city government was buying water treatment chemicals in amounts that didn't make sense. It became a news item when someone at the water plant talked about how many chemicals were at the plant, too many to store properly, and how some of them were being ruined before they could be used. The manager explained away the large purchase of chemicals based on a special price for buying quantity, but there were undertones he may have personally gained from the city's purchase of chemicals. Nothing was ever proved but the manager's reputation was severely damaged.

In the scheme of things, those two instances seem minor but they serve as examples of how others try to entice us. Like we were, you may be in a meeting where someone is talking about a business deal and he suddenly slips in a comment about how you could personally benefit from doing business with them. It may not be as blatant as the offer of a bribe or kickback, but his suggestion has a tinge of impropriety about it. And you may think, "Was he kidding?" Let me assure you, it was anything but kidding.

Rather, the other person was putting out a feeler to determine whether you are open to doing something shady. If you call him on what he suggested, you'll likely get a very quick denial (but, importantly, not an apology for the suggestion) and he will move on to regular business. At some later date, that person may try again but it is unlikely. Once you've shown you aren't interested in trading company business for personal gain, the other person will move on to seek others who might be willing to compromise their standards.

On the other hand, if you give any indication you would be willing to entertain personal gain, don't be surprised when the stakes, and what you can personally gain, ramp up fairly quickly. It may never get to the point of physically attacking and murdering someone but the financial implications can get very close to that. Squander enough company funds, and others get hurt through layoffs, lower pay, or reduced benefits.

I find it very interesting Solomon is cautioning his son, who is going to become king, to beware of those who will try to entice him. That tells me a couple of things:

- **No matter what your position in a company, others are going to try to entice you to do something wrong.** Wouldn't you think the sinners would be cautious about trying to lead the king's son astray? A livid father and what he might do is one thing. A livid king is something else. These sinners could actually lose their heads! But these kinds of enticers will look for anyone in your company who will listen to their proposals. If someone at the top, even better.
- **Their enticement will be aimed at the place where they think you are most vulnerable.** In their appeal, Solomon has the sinners targeting at least three areas where his son might have weaknesses: 1) Let's hurt somebody, 2) Let's get financial gain, and 3) We'll be a team. (All three areas come into play when the son becomes king and has to make a fateful decision.) The clear message is we all have one or more points where we are vulnerable, and enticers will seek them out.

What enticers try to do is to get you to forsake your underlying principles and the good you have been taught. In today's language, we might say, "Are your values for sale?" It's a question you need to consider. You, and I, want to quickly say, "Of course they aren't." But the reality is, if the right button is pushed, too many of us would be willing to fudge on, or abandon, those values.

In this section, we learn there are only two ways to go on this: 1) Hold on to your values or 2) Give up your values and head toward all kinds of trouble, remorse, and a miserable existence for the rest of your life.

Does the second way seem too harsh? Let me encourage you to think of a time when you compromised and have mentally kicked yourself since then for making that compromise. If it's a minor value violation, those reminders may not come back often or have much of a kick. However, the more serious the value violation, especially if it was one you knew you were making at the time, the more it is seared into your memory, comes back into your thoughts, and comes with a deep remorse for selling yourself short. Bad memories and remorse are awful enough, but compromising your values can lead to financial, physical, and legal troubles— troubles that, if you had known how bad they were going to be, would have kept you on the straight and narrow.

Rather than go through any of that, Solomon advises us to use our underlying principles and instructions to brush off those who try to entice us into doing wrong. No matter how good they try to say the deal is, giving in to them only leads to disaster. Staying true to those good things you have been taught lets you sidestep those who try to entice you.

Personal Application

We are bombarded with messages intended to sway our thinking and behavior. Think of the messages in the various advertisements you see or hear every day. Here are a few of them:

- You deserve to have my product.
- You can save money if you'll buy my product.
- Our product is better than everyone else's product.
- You'll look great using my product.

It's a rare industry that focuses on just one type of message. For example, fast-food restaurants have used each of the messaging examples above in one form or another. One would tell you that "You deserve a break today" while others would talk about how much you could buy for just five dollars. One would spend most of its commercial time talking about the quality and quantity of their meat, and another would run an entire series on how you could lose weight and look good by eating their sandwiches.

The advertising must be effective. Otherwise, these companies wouldn't spend so much money on them. Whether the advertising relates to cars, gasoline, tires, furniture, insurance, attorneys or whatever, those paying for the advertising realize, with the right message, you may be willing to change your preference from the product you currently use to their product or be motivated to use their product when you first buy that product.

If advertising, which comes from a company or a person we don't know, can influence us, then we need to consider how easily we can be influenced by those we do know. We are getting messages from them all day, too. Most of them are harmless (e.g., "Have you tried the new restaurant down the block?"). But mixed in with those messages may be a few enticements, which are inviting you to do something that is not right, fair, and just (the goal Solomon set in Verse 3).

And while we would like to think those enticing messages will be easy to resist, and many are, Solomon makes it clear there are those who will target their messages to reach you in an area where you may be willing to compromise. If you doubt that, think of those around you. You have probably seen the following happen:

- An honest person who ended up being dishonest getting caught and going to jail.
- A spouse's friendship with a member of the opposite sex turns into an intimate relationship that ruins two marriages and negatively affects their kids.
- A nice guy gets caught up with others and ends up destroying property or others (e.g., placing a chain on a police car axle in *American Graffiti* and Tony killing Maria's brother in *West Side Story*).

Let's be honest; enticers are good at their messaging. But you don't have to be lured into their schemes. You know many of the tipoffs already. What they propose has to be done in secret or at night. Or they use language like "No one needs to know," "No one will find out," or "This can be our little secret." When you hear these tipoffs, run away as fast as you can!

But other times, these enticers will lure you in, especially if you haven't developed prudence. You'll be living life with this person and, suddenly, you'll find yourself in a situation you never intended, or wanted. Kind of like the frog in the water that slowly heats up to boiling; by the time the frog realizes his danger, it's too late. Suffice it to say, you don't want to get into that position, so you have to cling strongly to the wisdom provided here:

1. **Keep to your underlying values and instructions.**
2. **Don't give in to those who want to lead you astray.**

Chapter 5

Wisdom's Plea and Predictions
Proverbs 1:20-33

Wisdom calls aloud in the street, she raises her voice in the public squares; at the head of the noisy streets she cries out, in the gateways of the city she makes her speech: "How long will you simple ones love your simple ways? How long will Mockers delight in mockery and fools hate knowledge?

"If you had responded to my rebuke, I would have poured out my heart to you and made my thoughts known to you. But since you rejected me when I called and no one gave heed when I stretched out my hand, since you ignored all my advice and would not accept my rebuke, I in turn will laugh at your disaster; I will mock when calamity overtakes you—when calamity overtakes you like a storm, when disaster sweeps over you like a whirlwind, when distress and trouble overwhelm you.

"Then they will call to me but I will not answer; they will look for me but will not find me. Since they hated knowledge and did not choose to fear the LORD, since they would not accept my advice and spurned my rebuke, they will eat the fruit of their ways and be filled with the fruit of their schemes. For the waywardness of the simple will kill them, and the complacency of fools will destroy them; but whoever listens to me will live in safety and be at ease, without fear of harm."

Background/Circumstances

The father has already warned his son to beware of those who want to entice him. Now the father points out there is another person, Wisdom, who also speaks. Rather than the secrecy employed by the enticer, Wisdom shouts her message. She has to because she is trying to be heard above the noise of everyday life.

Her message is addressed to three groups of people: 1) the Simple ones, 2) the Mockers (who appear to be a subset of the Fools), and 3) the Fools. Each group rejects Wisdom's advice for a different reason:

- **The Simple ones –** They love their simple ways and don't want to change their lives at all to align with Wisdom's advice.
- **The Mockers –** They choose to ridicule and make fun of whatever Wisdom says. And they revel ("delight") at how well they are doing it. No doubt, they believe they have true wisdom.
- **The Fools –** Once again, we see the Fool despising knowledge. This group may see Wisdom is offering something to them but they are so set against knowing real truth, they not only reject it but they also despise it.

After explaining why these groups won't listen to her, Wisdom laments over what they have missed and tells them there are consequences coming. Those consequences are:

- **Disaster, calamity, distress, and trouble are heading their way.** These four things will overwhelm them like a storm or whirlwind.
- **Wisdom will treat them the way they treated her.** They laughed at and mocked Wisdom, so Wisdom will laugh at and mock them as disaster, calamity, distress, and trouble befall them.

- **After they suffer from disaster, calamity, distress, and trouble, these groups will decide to call out for Wisdom.** But it is too late for that.
- **Wisdom will not answer them.** Because they 1) hated knowledge, 2) willingly chose to go their own way, 3) refused to accept Wisdom's advice, and 4) spurned her rebuke (some sort of warning after they refused to listen), Wisdom turns away from their cries.
- **Instead, they have to suffer the consequences of their actions.** The waywardness of the Simple results in their death. The Fools' false sense of security ends up destroying them.

Finally, Wisdom assures those who listen to her they will live in safety and be at ease, without fear of harm. But for those who don't listen to her and suffer disaster, Wisdom will laugh at them because they were so foolish.

As with those who rush into sin (Verses 10-19), those who fail to listen to Wisdom have a tragic end. But Solomon points out that those who listen to Wisdom will live in safety and be at ease, without fear of harm. Once again, the contrast is stark. If his son will only listen to Wisdom, he can have a life befitting a king; he can live a life of safety and be at ease. And he won't have to be afraid that harm will come his way. But if he fails to listen to Wisdom, like the Simple, the Mocker, and the Fool, his life will be dominated by disaster, calamity, distress, and trouble.

It should be an easy choice, but as we'll see, Solomon knows he needs to give his son more directions and cautions in order for him to be prepared for living life.

Business Application

It's a noisy world out there, isn't it? There is no shortage of information vying for your attention. In fact, the sheer volume can be overwhelming and it comes from everywhere—internal reports, business meeting communications, phone calls, impromptu visits, electronic messages, social and business media, and so on. All this comes from a variety of groups, too—bosses, owners, peers, subordinates, competitors, sales representatives, contractors, reporters, influencers, and so on. It's an ongoing challenge to find the golden nuggets buried in all this information that will make a difference to you and your business.

In this passage, wisdom is held up as the golden nugget. Typically, you would think we all seek wisdom when we enter into our work. But that isn't the case. Several types of people reject wisdom. Let's take a look at them and explore their reasons for rejecting wisdom:

- **Some are comfortable where they are and don't want to change.** You probably have some of these folks on your staff. They will resist almost any change, no matter how big or small. Back in the day when we issued payroll checks, we decided issuing checks at 2 P.M. on payday made it hard for employees to get their checks in the bank that day unless they left work or, like some street employees, drove their dump truck to the bank on the way to their final job of the day (definitely not the image we wanted to portray). We asked the payroll clerk who prepared the checks if we could instead issue payroll checks at noon. Hearing that it could be done, Human Resources let employees know their next paycheck would be available at noon.

  When payday arrived, the payroll clerk said something had come up, and rather than the checks being ready at noon, the checks would be available at 2 P.M. The result was a lot of upset people, but the payroll clerk assured us the next payday checks would be available at noon. The next payday came and, wouldn't you know it, the payroll clerk had something else come up and the checks were not ready until 2 P.M.

The next business day, the city manager had every city employee who had anything to do with payroll called into a meeting where the group outlined on a whiteboard all the steps, and their timing, to produce payroll. In a forceful statement, he made it abundantly clear that if an employee became aware the payroll process was running behind, it was that employee's responsibility to bring it to management's attention immediately so corrective action could be taken. He also made it abundantly clear that if the noon distribution was ever missed again, he would find out when the payroll timing first went offtrack and everyone in the process thereafter, if they didn't raise an immediate alarm with management, would be subject to stern discipline. Thereafter, paychecks were always ready at noon! All that hassle, just because a payroll clerk didn't want to change.

- **Some will laugh at, mock, and dismiss wisdom.** There are multiple examples of companies that derided or ignored new ideas (rejection of personal computers by IBM, Kodak and digital cameras, etc.) and missed out or suffered setbacks.
- **Some will fail to gain the knowledge, or hire people with knowledge needed to make their idea succeed.** Developing the first working airplane is a good example. Although others were working to develop a workable airplane, the Wright brothers succeeded well before the others because they excelled at gaining and applying the knowledge needed for flight (wing lift, engine development, etc.). We all know who the Wright brothers are but would be hard pressed to name any of their contemporaries.

So, to be successful, one has to resist succumbing to those voices, including the one in your own head, who say, "We've never done it this way before," "That is a stupid idea," "There's no way to make that work," or similar defeatist comments. This isn't wisdom; it's common reactions from certain types of people. While it might not be obvious at the beginning, listening to these voices eventually ends in ruin. Rather than go that way, Solomon urges us to listen to Wisdom and gain the benefits of "living in safety and ease without fear from harm."

One further note, if you somehow take the bad advice from this crowd, early in the work you may have a sense you are going down the wrong path. Rather than dismiss that hunch, explore it. Often, Wisdom is trying to talk to you before the point of no return and hoping you'll reconsider and turn back. But if you dismiss this sense and plunge ahead, don't be surprised when disaster comes.

Even more, don't be surprised when others shake their heads and laugh at the disaster you willingly brought on yourself by spurning good advice and following bad advice. It's one thing to have tried to pursue a good idea with good intentions and fall short. People understand that and are usually very forgiving and willing to give those folks another shot. But those who fail after ignoring good advice and choosing to follow bad advice are seen quite differently. If the failure is spectacular enough, that person becomes a laughingstock in his day and goes down in history as an example of a foolish person.

But it doesn't have to be that way for you. As we go through Proverbs, you'll learn more about wisdom and how to avoid those who want to drag you down.

Personal Application

How long? How long before you realize that what you're doing isn't working for you? That's the basic question Wisdom asks these three groups of people.

- **For the Simple one, the question is about how long he will love his simple ways.** His simple ways are allowing him to be easily persuaded to do things that aren't right, just, and fair. His lack of judgment, immaturity, and inexperience allow him to be taken advantage of on a regular basis. He was, and continues to be, naïve. Although at some level the Simple one recognizes he needs to do something different, he chooses to stay where he is. You can hear the frustration in Wisdom's voice. Wisdom knows she is offering the prudence the Simple one needs but won't lift a finger to gain. How sad.

- **For the Mocker, the question is how long he will delight in mockery.** Because he is proud and arrogant, he isn't about to accept what Wisdom has to offer. Rather, he will spew insults and hate and cause as much strife as he can. He is too busy enjoying the role of a Mocker. If he listens at all to what Wisdom has to say, he does it so he can ridicule and make fun of it. Nothing Wisdom has to say will penetrate very far into his brain.
- **For the Fool, the question is how long he will hate knowledge.** There is a subtle distinction being drawn here. This person may know a great deal about a lot of things. He is happy to have that knowledge and is probably willing to let others know how much he knows. But the knowledge he rejects—wisdom and discipline—comes through loving reverence of the LORD. He wants to lead the kind of life he wants to lead based on his own knowledge with no restraints. If he can come up with a justification for whatever he wants to do in his life, no matter how stupid or evil, he is going to do it.

Although Wisdom is speaking directly to these three kinds of people, she also is speaking directly to you and me. How long? How long before you get tired of trying to live life your way? How long before you turn and seek Wisdom?

While you have to seek Wisdom, finding her is easy. In that day she was crying out everywhere the people would be—in the street, the public squares, the noisy streets, and the gateways to the city. Today, she still cries out everywhere. If you listen well, you can hear her speaking to you whether you are listening to a faithful pastor (very likely) or at a wild, wild party (remote but it does happen). A faithful pastor speaks God's truth from the Bible every week; it's laid before us, but we have to grab on to it and let it affect our life. A similar thing can happen at that party. An inaudible voice may place a clear thought in someone's head: "There's more to life than this." It's a startling thought out of nowhere, the voice of Wisdom. But now that person has a choice: Grab on to it and let it affect his life or reject it.

When you hear Wisdom, you, too, have a choice. Solomon tells us that if you respond favorably to Wisdom, she will pour out her heart to you and make her thoughts known to you. By opening the door wide to Wisdom, you can understand her heart and thoughts and they will become your heart and thoughts. With her heart and thoughts filling you, you truly can live in safety and be at ease, without fear of harm.

Those who choose not to listen to Wisdom are doomed. Even though Wisdom cried out, they rejected her cries. Even though Wisdom held out her hand to rescue them, they refused to even acknowledge it was there. Though Wisdom came to rescue them, they were happy being the Simple, the Mockers, or the Fools. Accordingly, they get to eat the fruit of their ways: disaster, calamity, storms, and whirlwinds.

So why would you, or anyone for that matter, refuse to listen to Wisdom? Why would you choose death and destruction over life? Why would you choose disaster and calamity over safety and ease?

Although we think we always would choose life, safety, and ease over death, destruction, disaster, and calamity, if you want to be honest with yourself, you can see characteristics of the Simple, the Mocker, and the Fool in yourself. For to respond to Wisdom, you have to be willing to change, stop ridiculing wisdom, and accept her knowledge on how to live life.

So Solomon puts a question directly in front of his son, and us: "How long will you resist, ridicule, and hate what Wisdom offers?" Your response to that question will determine whether you live a life under God's protection (safety and ease) or a life full of distress and disasters leading to destruction.

Think about it and choose well!

Proverbs

Chapter Two

Chapter 6

Searching for Wisdom
Proverbs 2:1-8

My son, if you accept my words and store up my commands within you, turning your ear to wisdom and applying your heart to understand, and if you call out for insight and cry aloud for understanding, and if you look for it as for silver and search for it as for hidden treasure, then you will understand the fear of the LORD and find the knowledge of God. For the LORD gives wisdom, and from his mouth come knowledge and understanding. He holds victory in store for the upright, he is a shield to those whose walk is blameless, for he guards the course of the just and protects the way of his faithful ones.

Background/Circumstances

In Chapter 1, Solomon has warned his son about those who seek to entice him into wrong pathways. He also warned him not to reject wisdom. Now Solomon tells him to seek out wisdom. His mother's teaching and Solomon's instructions, while they may be sufficient to handle the enticer, will not be enough to get him through all of life. While their teaching and instructions are good, the son needs to gain the wisdom the LORD gives.

Being a realist, Solomon lays out the amount of work it takes to gain wisdom. As a start, the son has to:

- **Accept his father's words.** This is the crucial first step for the son. If he doesn't accept his father's instruction, he won't be able to gain wisdom. If he won't accept Solomon's wisdom, he won't be willing to accept God's wisdom either.
- **Store up his father's commands.** Besides accepting his father's instructions as being good, the son must internalize these instructions. Rather than fumbling to remember what the father's instructions were, he needs to have them imprinted so deeply they will come to mind when needed.
- **Turn his ear to Wisdom.** Next, he has to direct his attention to Wisdom's voice by tuning out the other voices vying for his attention so he can clearly hear what Wisdom has to say.
- **Apply his heart to understand.** Hearing Wisdom isn't enough; his heart, not just his mind, has to be engaged to really understand it. And that implies quite a struggle will occur in order for him to wrap his mind and heart around some of the wisdom coming his way. He needs to be prepared for that.

But there are two other conditions. The son also must:

- **Call out for insight and cry aloud for understanding.** The son has to desire wisdom. His whole substance has to yearn for it, to the point of saying aloud how much he wants it.
- **Look for it as for silver and search for it as for hidden treasure.** Though he yearns for it, that still isn't enough. The son is going to have to work to find it. Like he would look for silver and hidden treasure, he will look for wisdom in the most likely places to find it and doggedly dig and search for this wisdom.

If the son faithfully does all of these things, he will understand what it means to have the fear (loving reverence) of the LORD and find knowledge of God. If he will do all of these things, the LORD will give him wisdom, knowledge, and understanding—all the things the son will need to be a successful king. Finally, if the son will be upright, blameless, just, and faithful, the LORD will give him victory, shield him, guard him, and protect him.

Solomon leaves us hanging again: Will his son do it?

Business Application

In the business world, you can conduct yourself in any number of ways. May I suggest following the best path? The results of following this path are what most of us want: 1) victory and 2) protection. Other benefits include gaining a loving reverence for truth, finding true knowledge, and gaining what one wants. Sounds a bit like nirvana, doesn't it? Who wouldn't want to take this path?

Let's take a closer look at this path and what it involves. To do that, we start at the end of the section with Verses 7 and 8. One key is to "follow the course of the upright, blameless, just, and faithful." What does that mean and how does it apply? We'll start with the applicable definitions:

- **"Upright" (New Oxford American Dictionary) –** (Of a person or their behavior) strictly honorable or honest.
- **"Blameless" (New Oxford American Dictionary) –** Innocent of wrongdoing.
- **"Just" (New Oxford American Dictionary) –** Based on or behaving according to what is morally right and fair.
- **"Faithful" (Wikipedia) –** The concept of unfailingly remaining loyal to someone or something, and putting that loyalty into consistent practice regardless of extenuating circumstances.

These four bulleted qualities describe how one should conduct himself.

We begin with being upright. We all understand telling the truth is what we should do. But it isn't always easy, especially if it causes loss to your business or to you. Consequences may make it hard to tell the truth, but it is still the best policy. Accepting and acting on the truth saves so much pointless, unproductive effort. But being upright involves much more than telling the truth; it includes acting in a way to honor others and yourself. Let me give you an example from my college days.

To get a break from studying, I would go to the gym to play a game of pickup basketball. Of all the games I played, one still sticks in my mind. It was during a holiday break. We happened to have only ten players there, and we were all of about the same ability and height. That made for a good contest. But it became memorable when a defender fouled an offensive player and called the foul on himself. (For those not familiar with pickup basketball games, the offensive player usually calls the foul. It can become very contentious, especially if a player claims they were fouled on every shot they missed.) For two wonderful hours, guys who previously didn't know each other used an honor system for calling fouls.

I've thought about that game so many times because of how the ten players honored each other. It was the only basketball game I've been in like that. It was an unusual and special game.

Something that special doesn't have to be limited to a pickup basketball game. If you want to create an unusual and special company, strive to be one where the company and its employees strive to be upright.

Which leads us to blameless. Following up on the basketball analogy, fouls fall into two categories: 1) Intentional and 2) Unintentional. As the name describes, intentional fouls are those which a player decided beforehand to commit. Many of those fouls have higher penalties associated with them, because the offensive player can be severely injured (a hard foul while the offensive player is in the air). The player committing the foul had every intention of doing so.

However, most fouls are unintentional. The defensive player was doing his best to compete but committed a foul. In this case, the player was blameless; he did wrong but didn't intend to do it. Such it is in business. It is certainly okay to compete but if you want to be blameless, you can't be planning to do wrong to another party. Those actions lead to penalties, often stiff ones. It is much better to compete without intending to harm anyone else. But it is important to note here: Even the blameless person, like a basketball player, can harm others without intending to do so. Truly, no one is perfect, so don't confuse being blameless with being perfect.

Because we aren't perfect, we will wrong someone, even though we had no intention of doing so. Once we are aware we have wronged someone, we face the choice of whether we will be just. One way of being just is having a policy whereby an unsatisfied customer can return his purchase within a certain amount of time and receive a full refund. That is certainly right and fair. But take doing wrong to its extreme: You know your product damaged someone's health, now what do you do? Deny that your product caused the damage? Seek to assign the blame to others? Lawyer up to fight to the bitter end? Of course, you can do any of those things, but a much more effective route is just to make things right.

How does it work? You contact the injured party, assure him you will take care of his immediate needs (medical and otherwise), and offer to make things right. It's easy to understand this. If you were the injured party, how would you react to a company that won't acknowledge you were hurt and throws up every possible roadblock to your claim? Wouldn't you want a pound of flesh, and more? Wouldn't you tell everyone how the company mistreated you? But consider how you would react if a company contacted you as soon as it knew about your injury, said it would do everything it could to take care of you and then did what it said it would do. Wouldn't you be very appreciative and more gracious in coming to a final settlement? Thus the admonition to be just.

The first three steps to the course of wise conduct—act honorably, avoid wrongdoing, and do what is morally right and fair—are followed by one more: Be faithful in practicing these steps. So what is involved in being faithful? One has to: 1) unfailingly remain loyal to someone or something, and 2) put that loyalty into consistent practice regardless of extenuating circumstances.

There is the challenge for those in business. We can talk all we want about our code of ethics and policies and how they are linked to the concepts of being upright, blameless, and just, but if we or our employees won't be faithful to them, no matter what the circumstances may be, they are only talk or words in a policy manual.

Which means those in the company haven't spent enough time, effort, and maybe agony to understand what it means to be upright, blameless, just, and faithful within the context of your business. Someone may have demonstrated those qualities before, but if the current crop of management and employees haven't gone through the process of getting to that same level of understanding, it's only a matter of time before their behavior will start to veer away from the company's ethics.

If you're fortunate to have an upright workforce, your employees will come forward and fess up about where they fell short of company expectations. Employees who do that also are likely to be blameless and want to make things right (be just). Dealing with an employee like this, though the circumstances may be difficult, usually ends in matters resolved and a wiser and more valuable employee.

How different it is if you have employees who, rather than fess up when they fall short of company expectations, try to hide what they've done or seek to blame others. It takes a much greater effort to identify and resolve these matters. You have to spend time trying to find out who is telling the truth. Then, you get to deal with the employee who didn't fess up (and may still not fess up, even when confronted with evidence of their misdeed). Internal investigations, attorneys, human resource professionals and, if you have them, union representatives are likely to be involved in the development of the facts, performance agreements, corrective actions, and discipline.

When you stand back and consider these two outcomes, it makes you wonder why companies, maybe even your company, avoid taking the time and effort to ensure new employees grasp and internalize the concepts of upright, blameless, just, and faithful. While it may well take more time upfront, in the long run, imprinting these concepts in your employees' minds and hearts will shield, guard, and protect your company and ensure your company will be one of the unusual and special places where people want to work.

Personal Application

Wouldn't it be fabulous if everyone we met was upright, blameless, just, and faithful in all of their dealings with us? There would be so many fewer hassles. Problems that did occur would be resolved quickly and fairly. I'll sign up for that!

Of course, Solomon's instructions aren't for "them"; they are for each of us. (I know, now he is meddling.) It's a direct challenge. Do you have the courage to follow this path? This road is one with lots of twists and turns and some steep elevation gains. Rocks and other obstacles may get in the way. You may have to get your hands dirty as you dig through what is worthless to find what is valuable.

You have to want to find wisdom, knowledge, and understanding. As a parched and thirsty man looks for and desires to find water to quench his thirst, so you have to thirst and hunger to find wisdom, knowledge, and understanding. This search has to be the topmost thing on your mind, almost an obsession.

When you find the wisdom, knowledge, and understanding of which Solomon speaks, you need to ponder what it is. This consideration first takes place in your mind; you have to think through what is being said. For instance, in this passage, what does it mean to "accept my words"?

Today, we say, "I accept what you said," but all that really means is "I heard what you said." That isn't what Solomon means. Today, we also say things like "I accept that those are the facts as you see them." We are willing to acknowledge something can be true for you but not necessarily for me. Again, that isn't what Solomon means. Instead, "accept my words" means the son is to understand those words just as his father does and to believe in their meaning just as deeply as his father.

Even that isn't enough; the son has to apply his heart to understanding them, too. Mentally agreeing is the easier part; taking it to the heart level is harder. For instance, you can mentally agree that stealing is bad and still steal, because the mind will let us justify actions that we mentally know to be wrong. But if you have wrestled with the concept of stealing and come to feel the total wrongness of it deeply in your heart, you will never steal again. When tempted, you will be repulsed by the thought of stealing from someone else.

That is why it takes a while—days, months, or years—to align our minds and hearts with the wisdom, knowledge, and understanding Solomon introduces to us. To be aligned, you have to come to believe—mind and heart—the best path for your life is to seek to be truly upright, blameless, just, and faithful. Then you can start the journey toward becoming the person God wants you to be.

Let me encourage you to start the journey. Begin by considering Solomon's advice and determining you want to follow his path to wisdom, knowledge, and understanding. Listen to, accept, and apply your heart to understanding this wisdom. When struggles come, call out for insight (wise counsel) and keep seeking. Accept and live out this wisdom day by day. As you become upright, blameless, just, and faithful, your life will show it. And, in case you don't think anyone will notice, Solomon says the LORD himself sees and takes care of those who choose to live life His way.

If you've been on the path to wisdom, knowledge, and understanding but took a wrong turn somewhere, don't think it's all over. Just call out for insight, cry aloud for understanding, and seek for wisdom as seeking for silver or hidden treasure. For the LORD gives wisdom, knowledge, and understanding to those who call out for insight, cry out for understanding, and seek His wisdom. Do that and He will show you the way back to the good path you were on.

Chapter 7

Wisdom's Protective Shield
Proverbs 2: 9-11

Then you will understand what is right and just and fair—every good path. For wisdom will enter your heart, and knowledge will be pleasant to your soul. Discretion will protect you, and understanding will guard you.

Background/Circumstances

In the prior verses of this chapter, Solomon laid out the steps to be followed if the son was to seek wisdom and understanding. To get through those steps, the son needed to make it the great desire of his life to gain wisdom and understanding from the LORD. He also needed to strive to be upright, blameless, just, and faithful. If the son will do his part, Solomon assures him God will give him what he desires. Having experienced getting what he most desired himself, Solomon could assure his son the LORD would do the same for him.

What Solomon desired most and received was great wisdom. With these verses, Solomon describes how attaining wisdom will reveal itself in his son's life, but let's keep in mind that Solomon is speaking from his personal experience with the LORD. This wisdom will show up in his son's life in three areas:

- **Understanding what is right, just, and fair.** As you may remember, in Chapter 1, Verse 3, one of the purposes of Proverbs is to help the reader learn how to do what is right, just, and fair. But Solomon sets the goal a bit higher. His son will *understand* what is right, just, and fair. This is important. One can do what is right without knowing why he is doing it. How much better it is to see a situation and be able to determine the right thing to do. It's a higher skill that benefits the one who has it.

- **Having wisdom enter his heart.** Not only will he have the head knowledge of what is right, just, and fair, he also will have that knowledge at the emotional level, too. He will be able to balance the demands of the head and heart as he rules over the kingdom.
- **Having knowledge be pleasant to his soul.** Because he will have great wisdom, he will be able to see how new knowledge fits within the big scheme of things. It's like finding a jigsaw puzzle piece and putting it into a place that makes it much more obvious where other pieces go. There will be excitement and satisfaction at each new discovery.

While this is all good, Solomon points out why having this wisdom and knowledge will be important. They will protect and guard the son from the next two groups who are going to try to lead him astray.

Business Application

Have you ever wondered how fine upright business people you know suddenly became news over a startling ethical lapse? This section explains it; one may act right, just, and fair without embracing them. Without going through the hard work described in the prior verses, a person can put on a pretty good show, but there will be a weakness. He won't understand *every* good path. Because he doesn't understand every good path, he inevitably will walk down one or more paths that lead to his demise.

To prevent that from happening to you or your company, you have to gain an understanding of what it means to be right, just, and fair. More than that, it has to become part of your DNA. Let me encourage you to stop right here for a few moments to do a quick evaluation. Can you say, without a doubt, you are devoted to doing what is right, just, and fair? Would you be crestfallen if you failed in one of these areas? How about your company? Is being right, just, and fair the heartbeat of the company? Would there be remorse, and an overwhelming desire to make things right, if the company failed in one of these areas?

Hopefully, you were able to affirm you and your company understand what it means to be right, just, and fair. That wisdom will serve you well, because:

- **It guides you in finding good paths to follow.** Using those three standards will prevent you from taking actions that will cost you (money, reputation, etc.). Want some examples?
    - **Lying about your product.** Look at what happened to Volkswagen when the company decided to cheat on its diesel emissions testing. According to a July 8, 2021, *New York Times* article, total fines and legal settlements have exceeded $20 billion. Rather than do what was right, VW chose to lie, and it paid the price for it.
    - **Failing to be just.** When you buy something that is defective, would you be happy if the salesperson acknowledged he sold you a defective product and only apologized for it? Of course not. You have an expectation the company will be just in their dealings with you. They would either give you an equal replacement or your money back. You would expect to be made whole as the just (morally right) thing to do.
    - **Discriminating when hiring or promoting within the company.** You would think companies would strive to promote those who most closely match the skills and abilities

they need in a position. It would give them the best results. But too often these decisions are based on friendship, race, gender, or some other characteristic that has no bearing on whether the person can do the job. It isn't fair. Almost every day, you can read about a company or agency forced to pay a large amount due to their discrimination in hiring, promotions, or how rules were applied.

We all could avoid lots of problems if, before we acted, we asked, "Is this action going to be right, just, and fair?"

- **The knowledge you gain will be more useful.** I'm intrigued by the wording "knowledge will be pleasant to your soul." It made me think about my career and when I could make the claim knowledge was pleasant to my soul. As I've thought about it, it always comes back to those situations where I was trying to find an answer to a problem and I found it. It's hard to describe the sensation, but "pleasant to the soul" is a good one. But I would only get that sensation when the answer solved all of the issues associated with the problem *and* it met the right, just, and fair criteria. That's easy to understand, too. How can an answer that harms someone else end up being pleasant to your soul?
- **Wisdom leads to discretion and understanding.** Before passing by this too quickly, we need to note the distinction between how discretion and understanding function. Discretion protects; understanding guards. We make the distinction but don't really think about it. For example, suppose Alice was ready to sign a deal with Bertha, who has a history of bad faith. As Alice is about to sign the agreement, she has a nagging feeling something isn't right, so she decides to read the agreement one more time. Sure enough, Bertha changed the wording in one section, resulting in Alice now taking on outsized liability or costs. As soon as Alice reads this section, she questions why

she ever tried to reach an agreement with Bertha. By having questions about Bertha at the beginning, Alice was demonstrating understanding. If Alice had paid attention to this, she never would have started the process. But Alice opened the gate to Bertha and started working with her. From then on, Alice had to apply discretion to protect herself.

In the business world, constant, forceful pressures are going to push against you. It is best to prepare for them by becoming a right, just, and fair person. Those principles and your love for the truth will guide you in making great decisions. Some will guard you; some will protect you. Let them!

Personal Application

One of the big challenges in life is finding the path we are supposed to follow. There are so many choices, and outcomes from those choices often are unknown. As an example, think of some of the major choices that a young adult gets to make between the ages of seventeen and twenty-two:

- Do I go to college or enter the workforce now? Do I work for someone else or start my own business?
- Which college should I attend? What course of study do I pursue? Should I take extra schooling to get a Master's or Doctorate degree?
- Do I want to get married? Is my significant other the person I want to marry?
- Where do I want to live?

Each choice will have a bearing on the starting path of a young adult. Young adults who make a series of good choices will start on good paths. Other young adults will make choices that aren't the best for them (e.g., going to college when they shouldn't have). However, they can exchange their poor choices for good choices and get back on a good path. A few young adults will be stymied by all of the choices before them, refuse to make some choices, and end up in limbo.

Life choices don't stop at the age of twenty-two; they keep coming and coming. Although the topics may be different for these later choices, the outcomes are still unknown. Here are a few my wife and I have faced:

- **Family –** How many children do we want to have? How do we want to raise our children? What school do we want them to attend? Do we want to homeschool them?
- **Work –** Do I seek promotion or stay in my current job? Should I change employers? Should I start my own company? Do I want to be the boss?
- **Financial –** How do we handle our family finances? What is important to us? Do we want to adopt, and follow, a budget? How will we invest any surplus? How much should we contribute to our church and other organizations?
- **Location –** In what region of the country do we want to live? How do we determine the kind of house to buy or rent? What amenities do we want nearby?
- **Church and friends –** Which church do we want to join? Where will we volunteer? With whom of our friends do we want to have a closer relationship?

As you would expect, the combination of choices we made led us down a unique path. While most of our choices were good, some choices were not and made life more difficult for us. When I look back on those decisions and do an honest assessment, I can see where I went wrong. Many of those decisions failed to do what was either right, just, or fair. If I had held to those criteria, I could have avoided most of the potholes I hit.

It's why Solomon places so much attention on learning to do what is right, just, and fair. It's the most important decision one has to make. Solomon knows those who seek and come to understand deep in their hearts and minds what it means to be right, just, and fair consistently will make choices leading to "every good path" in their lives. In addition to the wisdom that comes with seeking to do what is right, just, and fair, three protections will become evident.

Gaining knowledge is the first protection. The wise person learns and his learning helps him when he has to make choices. Discretion is the second protection. The wise person thinks before he talks and says what is appropriate for the occasion. He also knows what is within his purview and stays within those boundaries. Finally, he has an ability to grasp and understand situations as they unfold around him. He can see where things are heading, and he can make decisions that keep him on "every good path."

As he was writing this passage, I expect Solomon was thinking about some of the poor choices he made in his life and how he wished he had stayed true to doing only what was right, just, and fair. Those of us who have been parents a while understand from where Solomon is coming. None of us want our kids to make the same mistakes we made, so we try to show them a better way.

That is exactly what Solomon is doing here. He is pleading with his son—and you and me—to become a person who is right, just, and fair. Solomon knows the person who makes that choice, especially when they are young, will escape all those who seek to drag them down paths of destruction. Rather than go down those harmful paths, they will follow all the good paths laid before them.

If we were honest with ourselves, we know the advice Solomon is giving us is true. No matter how young or old we are, all of us have made decisions that didn't pass the right, just, or fair test, and we probably suffered the consequences for those poor decisions. As we get older, those consequences become more and more severe. As a child, we might have received time out, a talking to, or a spanking. (Today, spanking is out, loss of a privilege is in.) By the time we become adults, the consequences for our worst decisions ratchet up to jail time, judicial oversight, or capital punishment. If we all understand this is true, why don't we jump at the opportunity to take Solomon's advice?

As we move along in Proverbs, Solomon is going to tackle this very question. Earlier in this chapter, he gave a reason: One has to have a determined devotion to find wisdom. Too many want wisdom but fall away when the going gets a little tough. That is the challenge for those who want to continue studying Proverbs. Do you have a determined devotion to dig in and discover the valuable wisdom Solomon, and the LORD, have for you?

I hope you do, because the "sinners" in Chapter 1 are not the only ones who seek to bring you down. In the next two sections, Solomon describes two other groups who want to ensnare you. And you'll need the knowledge, discretion, and understanding wisdom brings to see and reject their entreaties.

Chapter 8

Saved from Wicked and Wayward People
Proverbs 2:12-19

Wisdom will save you from the ways of wicked men, from men whose words are perverse, who leave the straight paths to walk in dark ways, who delight in doing wrong and rejoice in the perverseness of evil, whose paths are crooked and who are devious in their ways.

It will save you also from the adulteress, from the wayward wife with her seductive words, who has left the partner of her youth and ignored the covenant she made before God. For her house leads down to death and her paths to the spirits of the dead. None who go to her return or attain the paths of life.

Background/Circumstances

Remember in Chapter 1, Solomon warned against those who would try to entice. To ward them off, the son needed to "listen to his father's instruction and not forsake his mother's teaching." While those are sufficient to reject the sinner's enticements, Solomon knows more difficult challenges are ahead. His son needs more tools in his toolbox. Wisdom is the answer—a wisdom that understands what it means to be right, just, and fair. Along with wisdom, his son will gain discretion and understanding, which will, respectively, protect and guard him.

The son will need wisdom, discretion, and understanding to deal with the next two groups seeking to lead him astray: 1) wicked men and 2) the adulteress. Like the sinners in Chapter 1, these wicked men and the adulteress are like the Fool, because they reject truth and despise wisdom and discipline.

The description of wicked men and their ways is thorough. They:

- **Have speech that is perverse.** According to Merriam-Webster, the definitions of "perverse" are: "1) turned away from what is right or good; corrupt, 2) contrary to the evidence or the direction of the judge on a point of law, and 3) obstinate in opposing what is right, reasonable or accepted; wrongheaded." They know what is right and good but purposefully oppose it.
- **Choose to leave straight paths to walk in dark ways.** Because these folks oppose what is good and right, it is no surprise they would reject good ways and choose to behave in dark (illegal, unethical, etc.) ways.
- **Delight in doing wrong.** Most people's consciences bother them when they have done something wrong. Not this person! He experiences pleasure when he has wronged someone.
- **Rejoice in how evil they are.** Not only is he delighted in the wrong act, but he also is joyful at all the wrong acts he has done and how evil he is.
- **Take crooked paths.** These people are willing to go to extremes to get what they want. They will be quick to engage in violence, up to and including murder.
- **Are devious in their ways.** Because they are all of these things, they will put on an act to deceive others. They will pretend to be one thing but are exactly the opposite.

Next, Solomon warns about the adulteress. In many ways, she is like wicked men. Her characteristics are slightly different as she:

- **Uses seductive words.** While the wicked man tricks people into following him, the adulteress is straightforward about what she is proposing. "This is wrong, but it will be so great that you won't care."

- **Leaves her partner.** Notice that she isn't divorced; she is a wayward wife. While still in the marriage relationship, she has, for all practical purposes, left the marriage.
- **Ignores covenants she has made.** Because she has emotionally left her partner, she has no problem breaking her marital covenant and sleeping with other men. She has become an immoral woman.

I find it interesting that Solomon lets the son assume the results of following wicked men are bad but has to spell out the exact results for following the adulteress. If the son succumbs to her charms, he will be led to places of death and destruction and never get back to where he was before or attain paths of life.

Business Application

Did you notice the difference between the enticements in Chapter 1 and the enticements here in Chapter 2? In Chapter 1, the enticer tries to get the son to change his mind or join him. The son can dodge the enticements if he adheres to his solid foundation and follows good instruction. That is the application we learned earlier. A business with solid foundations and excellent training can avoid sorrow and loss. But in Chapter 2, the enticer's methods, and the preparation to ward them off, are different. Let's take a closer look at these two dangerous enticements.

It shouldn't come as any surprise there are people in this world who want to deceive you. Their claims about their product or service may be embellished. Their resumes might have some exaggerations. Their proposed agreements may have wording more favorable to them. As an experienced business person, you know to keep your antennae up and active so you can spot false pitches.

But this section is talking about a higher level of deceit. These people are devious with a capital "D." They will develop their plans of deceit and go to great lengths to mislead you. They have to do this; otherwise, you would spot them a mile away and reject their agendas. To get what they want from you, their attractive proposals to join forces will come all wrapped and topped with a big bow with some extra incentives for you to accept it. When you get one of those "too good to be true" proposals, beware!

Before you break open the proposal to read it, you need to use your understanding as a first filter by looking at the big picture. What is this company's history? Are its leaders reputable? Are there any red flags that give you pause? By doing this high-level review, you are gauging whether the proposing group is "right, just, and fair." If the group fails this review, you can simply pass on its proposal.

But suppose your review doesn't provide enough information to say no and you decide to open the proposal and consider it. Now is the time to exercise discretion to avoid causing offense or revealing private information while thoroughly evaluating the proposal.

Yes, you have to be careful when dealing with a proposal like this. Sometimes they are trying to obtain proprietary information from you that they can use if you reject the deal. It doesn't have to be a data dump of all your customers, your detailed financial statements for the last three years, or some other formal ask. They may be trying to find out what your new product or expansion plans are. Just a casual conversation over lunch and snooping questions in an unguarded moment can be the vehicle for undermining you. While you will be asking your own probing questions, understand these folks have probably planned the moment, will be on high alert for probing questions, and will have a consistent story to tell. If you can during your conversations with them, try to find out what they delight and find joy in. That may well tip their hand.

If they don't tip their hand in conversation and behavior, you thoroughly have to evaluate the proposal, especially if it is "too good to be true." I think back to a proposal made to our city from a company wanting to buy the future revenues from the leases telecommunications companies had with us to place their equipment on our water towers. These leases ran for as long as twenty years and had fixed annual payments with moderate increases every five years. In their mid-2000s proposal, they stressed how the telecommunications industry was changing dramatically and how those revenues would be uncertain. Out of the bigness of their hearts, they would pay us cash now and take the risk on the lease revenue.

As you might expect, a one-time cash payment of several million dollars was attractive—until one looked under the hood. Doing some simple cash flow discounting of the future lease payments showed how one-sided their proposal was. Yes, we would get cash now, but they would break even within three to four years and enjoy up to seventeen years of gain. Once the Board of Directors saw the numbers, they saw what was right, just, and fair to the taxpayers and rejected the offer.

While this simple analysis created enough information for us to understand the long-term effect of the lease proposal above, your evaluation may need to be much more detailed and rigorous to understand a proposal you receive. It may entail a very thorough reading of agreements to understand short-term and long-term impacts, legal advice, background checks, financial analysis, and any number of other checks due diligence requires. Finally, you will want to do a gut check on whether this is the right thing to do for you and your company. Are these the people you want to be tied to? Watch out for the devious business person!

But there is another person of whom you have to beware. Rather than using devious methods, this wayward person will use seductive words to bring you into partnership with him. Here are a few reasons why this person is so dangerous:

- **He is completely unmoored from any restrictions.** He is going to do his own thing no matter the consequences. He has no problem completely ignoring agreements, rules, or moral codes. He also has no problem with being duplicitous in his dealings with partners. He is going to go after whatever looks good to him at the moment and dump everyone else.
- **His talk is much more than smooth; it is seductive.** His talk has to be seductive because he doesn't try to hide what he is proposing. He is openly inviting you to ignore your agreements, rules, or moral codes. But he does it in a way so alluring you are severely tempted to go along with him.
- **The results for you will be disastrous.** If you choose to team up with this person, you can never go back to whom you were before. Once you have compromised, the next compromise becomes easier. Even worse, following this person weaves you into his waywardness so tightly you can't really get out of it. You will be implicated and tied to whatever bad behavior he and you did while you were in partnership. It's not unlike being a cosigner on a loan when you know the other signer is a bad risk. There is a high likelihood you will get to pay off the loan plus penalties, additional interest, and court fees in full. Because this person is unmoored from moral restrictions, his acts may be so serious that you will be in jeopardy of losing your freedom. How? Any number of ways. You can become so tainted that no one wants to do business with you anymore. You can lose all your friends and family. You can be saddled with crippling restitution and lose all you have worked so hard to obtain. And, yes, you could end up in jail for a long time, possibly for the rest of your life.

As with the wicked man, understanding and discretion can save you from the wayward person. Having understanding means you'll ask straightforward questions about the person who is making the proposal from the outset. Because he doesn't try to hide how he behaves, you should be able to identify this is a person to avoid. But their pitch is so seductive, you may ignore those warning signs and start to listen to their proposal. Because of the emotion of the moment, you'll be tempted to dispense with your due diligence. Don't! That careful review will point out the folly of the proposal and save you from untold heartache.

Personal Application

Have you ever dealt with a devious person? How long did it take before you learned they had completely misled you? While we would like to relegate this activity to those who want to sell us something, the truth is we have family and friends who fall into this category. They want a "partner in crime," and they will do what they can to get you to come along with them. One example is being invited to a meeting supposedly about a cause you believe in, but it turns out the meeting is about a completely different cause, one with which you do not agree. That is probably a mild example—but not necessarily if it exposes you to being identified with a cause you oppose. Extreme examples have had families plunged into ruin by following the devious person's lead.

The wayward person tries to entice you in a completely different way. Their words drip with honey and it all sounds so good. You might have a momentary thought, "This isn't right," but the appeal is so strong you may bury that thought. While the devious person takes you down paths you wouldn't normally go, he isn't attacking your morals; he is only deceiving. But the wayward person? He strives to get you to abandon your morals, agree with him, and go down awful paths with him. Adultery is the example given, but it can apply just as easily to other areas where we can abandon our morals to pursue things (fame, fortune, power, etc.). If you have only been deceived, you can admit you were deceived, make things right, and return to where you were. But if you abandon your morals and follow (agree with) the wayward person, it is much harder to go back. We see that with friends and family who have taken a wayward path and refuse to leave it. So many times, they run their lives into the ground and they don't seem to care if they do. It is so sad to watch as they destroy their lives.

We do need to recognize that some people will admit their error(s) and fight their way back. But they will be the first to tell you their lives aren't as good as before. They have to be on guard all the time to avoid falling into the same temptation again.

How do we avoid being taken in by the wicked or wayward person? Solomon tells us to use the wisdom, understanding, and discretion gained from following his guidance at the end of Chapter 1 and beginning of Chapter 2 (being upright, blameless, and just). Once you have done the work to put those in place, you have to exercise them in your dealings with others. Understand the situation and people you are dealing with by asking yourself big-picture questions like "Is this person trustworthy?" or "Why am I being presented with this?" Once you are okay with the situation and the people, exercise discretion by asking the right questions about what is being proposed and why it's being proposed until you are completely satisfied. After that, do a final check. Often your gut, or a small voice, will let you know whether what you are about to do is the right thing to do. If it screams "no," you might want to listen to that voice and turn away from what they want you to do.

Chapter 9

Living in the Land
Proverbs 2:20-22

Thus you will walk in the ways of good men and keep to the paths of the righteous. For the upright will live in the land, and the blameless will remain in it; but the wicked will be cut off from the land, and the unfaithful will be torn from it.

Background/Circumstances

In the first three pages of the book of Proverbs, Solomon has provided quite a bit of instruction to his son. A quick summary could be:

- **There are four kinds of people in this world – the Simple, the Young, the Wise, and the Discerning.** All of them have weaknesses to address.
- **Then there is the fifth kind of person, the Fool.** He has irredeemable attitudes.
- **Your mother and I have taught you well.** Hold to what we taught you.
- **Some people will try to entice you by persuasion or getting you to come along with them.** Our teaching and instruction will save you from them and their end.
- **Listen to Wisdom and enjoy the benefits of wisdom.** Those who reject her are headed to disaster.

- **There is a path to gaining wisdom, a wisdom that is worth a great deal**. Work for it!
- **By gaining this wisdom, you will understand what is right, just, and fair**. Your understanding and discretion will guard and protect you from those described in the next bullet.
- **Wicked people may use two methods.** One will go to great lengths to develop a devious plan to get you to go along with him. It's a bait-and-switch game. The other person will entice you via seductive words and ideas in an effort to get you to abandon your morals and follow him.

He covered a lot in just a few pages. Now, Solomon provides a summary of the benefits of following good men and being upright and blameless compared to the outcome for those who are wicked and unfaithful. The first group will "live and remain" in the land, while the second group will be "cut off and torn" from it.

Before talking about the outcomes, let's get an understanding of why the land is the focus of the outcomes. The land being discussed is the land that had been promised to Abraham, the father of the Israelite people, nine or ten centuries before Solomon's time. Possessing and living in the land is seen as proof of God's blessing. A lot has happened since that promise:

- Abraham's grandson Jacob and Jacob's small family leave the promised land and go to Egypt to escape famine.
- The family grows exponentially and is enslaved.
- Moses delivers the nation and brings them back to the land they possess.
- The nation goes through a few centuries with cycles of prosperity and turmoil, which are, respectively, directly related to its following good or wicked men.
- Israel adopted a kingship governance model about one hundred years earlier, with Solomon being the third king.

- Israel possesses the land now, and it is a time of prosperity and peace. Because of this, it is obvious to all, especially to the Israelites, that God's blessing is upon the nation.

So life is good! But from past history and his understanding of people, Solomon knows it will be easier for his son and the nation to follow the ways of the wicked and unfaithful than it will be to make the effort to be upright and blameless. Accordingly, Solomon foretells what will happen based on the choice his son makes. First, what happens if he chooses to be upright and blameless? They will get to *live* and *remain* in the land. Thinking about "living" in the land, I get a picture of people who are enjoying life without any threats. There is peace and tranquility. It truly is a fabulous time to be alive! "Remain" means they can live securely there for the foreseeable future. Nothing can change it—unless they make a different choice. The fact they will be "in the land" completes the picture. They are in alignment with God and truly blessed. They are who they are supposed to be.

But if the son chooses the second, easier path, they will be *cut off* and *torn* from the land. As I think of this, being "cut off" from the land means they are living on the land but they don't control it anymore. It is quite likely they will become subservient to the new owners and not have much say in how they live. The next step is being "torn" from the land. That sounds very painful. The two outcomes are awful. They forcefully will be removed and taken elsewhere, losing all they have. Their emotional anguish will be worse. They know they will never see their home again. They screwed up a good thing by being unfaithful.

Solomon makes it clear there are only two paths to take. The son should take the one leading to great things rather than the one leading to certain disaster.

Business Application

Here we are again at a choice between two ways of doing business. Solomon has talked about this before, so the temptation is just to skip over this section. But we do so at our own risk. Why? Because the stakes have been raised. Up to now, the consequences from choices made have accrued to the individual. Now we find out the consequences affect your organizations and, depending on your station in life, maybe your country. Because of that, it becomes extremely important that you and your company "walk in the ways of good men" and "keep to the paths of the righteous."

As we've learned from the earlier portions of Chapter 2, the pathway to becoming a good man (or woman) can be quite a struggle. It involves developing one's character (upright, blameless, just, and faithful) as well as forming a foundation of teachings and instructions on which one adds wisdom, understanding, insight, and knowledge. To be the good man involves full development of both aspects. In addition to high moral character, he will have great business acumen. He will do the right things, the right way, at the right moment. That is truly the way of a good man.

But the good man is not infallible. He is going to make mistakes. When that happens, he will be the one who presses to make sure the matter is corrected by doing what is morally right and fair to any injured party. Turns out, those things make for good business.

Wouldn't it be great if all of the people in your company, or with whom you deal, meet the definition of being good men? But that isn't what we typically find. While we like to praise those who show great character, we often reinforce other behaviors without really thinking about it. How often have you heard someone say something like "Business is business" or "All is fair in love and war"? The meaning of those sayings is clear—you can't be successful in business, or love and war for that matter, and stay true to high moral character.

Part of the problem is we tend to see high moral character and high business acumen at the opposite sides on a linear scale. In reality, they are more like the "X" and "Y" axis on a graph. For one can have low to high moral character and low to high business acumen.

The challenge is twofold:

- **How do we find people who are high in moral character and business acumen?** It's a real challenge. No matter how much I refined my interview process (a multiple interview process with many others involved, which took about six hours per candidate), from time to time, I could be fooled as to where a candidate fit on a moral character/business acumen graph. But usually, even if I had to go through multiple searches, the person we hired scored high in both areas.
- **How do we develop people who are high in moral character and business acumen?** The challenge here is finding those who are as motivated as Solomon says one has to be to become a good man. Many employees are willing to take courses about business acumen or personal development. Most are willing to use what they learn, as long as it doesn't require a lot of changes in their work or behavior. These folks never aspire to become "good men." But there are those few who are driven, who want to become the best they can be, to become a "good man." When I identified someone like that, I followed a piece of advice I had been given: "Work with the willing!" I made time and invested resources in helping that person learn and grow.

If you keep your eyes open, you can find these individuals; they are around. While you may find good men and those who are working on becoming good men, they won't stay around very long if you are less than serious about being a good man and having a good company. In addressing those concerns, Solomon lays before you two questions: Are you willing to do what it takes to become a good man? Are you willing to do what it takes to have a good company?

If so, there are blessings in store for you. Besides the protections discussed earlier in Chapter 2, there will be a special blessing. In Solomon's day, that was living and remaining in the land of Israel, the land of promise. What the blessing will be for you only time will tell, but it will give you a sense of fulfillment and rest. That is the path to take. Embrace it, walk it, and become a good man.

Personal Application

With GPS and online driving assistance available nowadays, we go from one place to another without worrying about whether we are taking the right path. We can follow the directions from our GPS with a high degree of confidence we will get to our destination quickly and efficiently. Consequently, we have lost an understanding of how difficult traveling used to be. It wasn't that long ago in history when maps were inadequate, if they were available at all. To get to a destination, one had to follow unmarked roads and paths often using verbal descriptions (turn left at the big rock) or rely on one's ability to find their way to the right place. Even with the best instructions, it wasn't unusual to come to a place where the road split into two roads and the directions were unclear on which one to take. Now the traveler was in a quandary: Which of the two roads was the correct road? It wasn't a question to be passed over lightly. If he chose the wrong road, he would, at a minimum, make his journey hours or days longer. But that wrong choice could also expose him to a series of dangers to his cargo, his animals, and himself.

With all of our travel aides today, and our much better road and signage systems, we have minimized potential dangers. Traveling from point A to point B is so much easier than it used to be. While those "fork in the road" traveling problems are mostly solved, we hardly can say the same about life. You and I come up against "fork in the road" decisions quite a lot, and often in ways we don't realize at the time.

Take, for example, the decision to drive when under the influence of drugs or alcohol. Too many times, the one under the influence makes the decision to drive. When he makes that decision, he has no intention of running into another vehicle and injuring or killing others. But he is taking a sizeable risk. The odds he will have an accident are much, much higher. He exposes himself and others to dangerous outcomes.

That is one extreme example; there are many more, such as taking drugs, joining a violent gang, getting intimate with someone who isn't your spouse, or other similar "big" forks in the road. While Solomon certainly talks about those kinds of less-frequent big forks in the road (wicked men and the adulteress), his focus always comes back to choosing a life course that will serve you well:

- **Walk in the ways of good men.**
- **Keep to the path of righteous.**

While these may seem like Solomon is saying the same thing, I see a difference. With the first bullet, I picture an apprentice who is working beside an accomplished tradesman, learning the trade and getting regular pointers on doing good work. As he spends time with the tradesman, he gets better and better at his work and eventually reaches the point where he can go out on his own. With the second bullet, our apprentice, now an accomplished tradesman himself, has a choice of whether he will continue to perform excellent work or start turning out an inferior or uneven product.

So it is with wisdom. To gain wisdom, it works best if you can find good men who have wisdom to share. How do you know if you have found a good man? If his ways lead you to become upright, blameless, just, and faithful and to understand what is right, just, and fair, that man is a good man and you should listen to him, learn his ways, and seek to understand wisdom. If a man is heading you into other directions, get away from that man as quickly as you can!

Learning the good man's ways is only part of the battle. Having learned them, the real battle plays out in our daily lives. Here are a few situations to consider:

- I'm having a bad day and my mood is sour. How do I express that when my family comes in?
- My young child keeps making mess after mess today. What is the right way to handle this (scream at him or realize he is a young child and needs help)?
- Another driver cut me off in traffic. Do I teach my kids new curse words or let it go?

Choosing the journey Solomon recommends makes all the difference. You will understand the good paths to follow. You will develop the character that will keep you on the good path. With those in place, you can sidestep the tragedy the wicked and the adulteress bring and enjoy the good life that the LORD has in store for you.

By following the teachings and instruction in the first two chapters, you might think you are well prepared to face the world. As we'll find out in Chapter 3, Solomon has several commands for his son and us to follow if we want to receive all the benefits wisdom offers. It's quite a list, and you'll want to get them all!

Proverbs

Chapter Three

Chapter 10

Gaining Favor and a Good Name
Proverbs 3:1-6

My son, do not forget my teaching, but keep my commands in your heart, for they will prolong your life many years and bring you prosperity. Let love and faithfulness never leave you; bind them around your neck, write them on the tablet of your heart. Then you will win favor and a good name in the sight of God and man. Trust in the LORD with all your heart and lean not on your own understanding; in all your ways acknowledge him, and he will make your paths straight.

Background/Circumstances

Chapter 2 ends with Solomon encouraging his son to "…walk in the ways of good men and to keep to the paths of the righteous" so his son and the nation would live and remain in the land of promise. Now, Solomon shifts to a series of teachings and commands that, if followed, will prolong his son's life many years, bring him prosperity, and provide many more benefits. Who wouldn't want to have that list? We'll discuss two of six commands in this section and cover the others in subsequent chapters.

1. **Let love and faithfulness never leave you.** I find it interesting Solomon doesn't feel a need to define "love" and "faithfulness." The underlying assumption is his son already understands what

it means to love and be faithful. The son may have demonstrated by his previous actions he understood or Solomon may have talked about it so much already he feels his son understands the two concepts well. Although he may have some understanding about these two concepts, Solomon's first command to his son is to never let love and faithfulness leave him. By starting here, Solomon shows great wisdom:

- **Love and faithfulness form the basis for the other teachings and commands to come.** If the son can't love and be faithful, nothing else will matter.
- **He is to bind love and faithfulness around his neck, much like one would wear a beautiful necklace.** He is to display openly his love and faithfulness for all to see. While outward displays are good, Solomon knows necklaces can be taken off as well as put on. If the son isn't careful, his commitment to love and faithfulness will turn into one of only outward appearance. His love and faithfulness will come to depend upon circumstances.
- **Solomon tells the son he has to have a deep, emotional commitment to love and faithfulness**. It's more than a core belief; love and faithfulness define him. If he makes that commitment, the son's heart will be of the same nature as Solomon's father, David.

If he does as Solomon commands, his son will win favor and a good name in the sight of God and man. Notice how these are paired. His son will get a good name with others by displaying consistently wise outward actions. However, God looks at what is written on the heart. If these commands to be deeply committed to love and faithfulness are written on his son's heart, the LORD will favor—look out for—him.

2. **Trust in the LORD with all your heart.** Another assumption is the son has seen or heard enough to know about trust. Maybe he leapt into Solomon's arms from a high place when he was younger or heard Solomon talk about how his grandfather, David, trusted in God. Whatever the past, the son knows what it means to trust. Rather than leaving it as a general command to trust, Solomon becomes very specific:
   - **The son must trust in the LORD.** This refers to the personal and covenant name of God. It emphasizes His role as the nation's redeemer and His covenant relationship with it. The nation's history was full of examples showing the LORD was worthy of its trust.
   - **He must trust the LORD with all of his heart.** As with love and faithfulness, the son has to be all in. Partial trust isn't really trust. If you really trust someone, you trust them all of the time and in every circumstance.
   - **He must avoid leaning on his own understanding.** The son would have known stories of his ancestors who trusted the LORD as they went through difficult circumstances. Here are some well-known ones:
     - After receiving God's call, Abram leaves his home and travels to the land to which God told him to go. God looks after Abram and promises him: 1) The land he sees will become the land in which his descendants will live, and 2) he will have a huge number of descendants. Approximately twenty-five years later, when Abram is 99 years old, the LORD appears to him again. The LORD changes his name to Abraham, which means "father of many nations." A year later, God tells Abraham to change his ninety-year-old wife's name from Sarai to Sarah and promises him she will bear a son. Because Abraham laughs at the idea of having a child at his and

Sarah's advanced ages, in one of the many humorous moments in the Bible, God tells Abraham to name his son Isaac, which means "laughter." Years later, after a multi-day journey to a mountain in Moriah, God directs Abraham to sacrifice his teenage son as a burnt offering. Abraham prepares the sacrifice and is ready to plunge the knife into his son when the angel of the LORD intervenes. Abraham has proven he trusts the LORD completely!

- When Joseph was a teenager, Joseph's eleven envious brothers sold him into Egyptian slavery. Over the next few years, Joseph serves his master well. The only problem is the master's wife, who tries to seduce Joseph. After she tries to trap him in her bedroom, Joseph runs out of the room but leaves his cloak behind. Upset by Joseph's rejection of her advances, she accuses Joseph of raping her. The master reluctantly puts Joseph into prison. Joseph prospers there. While imprisoned, he interprets the dreams of two fellow prisoners, the wine steward and the baker. Based on their dreams, Joseph tells them the wine steward will go back to Pharoah, while the baker literally will lose his head. Within three days, the wine steward is taken back to serve Pharaoh and the baker's life ends.

  Joseph languishes in prison for two more years. When Pharaoh has a dream no one can interpret, the wine steward remembers Joseph and tells Pharaoh he knows a guy who can interpret dreams. Joseph is cleaned up and called into Pharaoh's presence. In addition to interpreting Pharaoh's dream (seven years of plenty followed by seven years of famine), Joseph tells Pharaoh how to prepare for the coming famine. Be-

cause Joseph was the only one who could interpret his dream and provide a plan of action, Pharaoh determines no one else is as wise as Joseph and immediately makes him the second-highest official in Egypt. Furthermore, Pharaoh places Joseph in charge of famine preparations. Because of his position, Joseph saves his father Jacob, now called Israel, his eleven brothers, and their families from the famine.
    - David, though a young teen and relatively small, knows God will be with him as he takes on and defeats a gigantic and experienced warrior. He knows the God who had been with him to fight off bears and lions to protect his sheep will be with him as he takes down Goliath.
- **He must acknowledge the LORD in all his ways.** According to the New Oxford American Dictionary, "acknowledge" means to "accept the existence of," "recognize the fact or importance or quality of," "express or display gratitude for or appreciation of," "accept the validity or legitimacy of," or "show that one has noticed or recognized (someone) by making a gesture or greeting." As his son lives his life, he is to be ever mindful of the LORD and trust Him.

When he trusts as Solomon commands, the son can be assured the LORD will make his paths straight—remove obstacles from his pathway and bring him to his appointed goal. Abraham sojourned in the land and believed God's promises about the land and his descendants. Joseph endured thirteen years of slavery and prison. All that time, he knew God was with him, because God kept putting him in positions where Joseph's abilities were noticed. Eventually, he became second only to Pharaoh and saved the young Israel nation. David, using the simple tools of the shepherd—a sling and a stone—takes down the man who dared to defy the nation and its God. Because of his heart-filled trust, God makes David the king of Israel. Abraham, Joseph, and David knew God was worthy of their trust and readily told others God was responsible for their success. As Solomon looked out on the country of Israel and its people, he knew God had kept his promises.

When you trust in God completely, be prepared to see things happen!

Business Application

A good name, favor with those in charge, obstacles removed, and reaching the goal—all of us would like to experience them. But the path to get to these experiences isn't always clear. Solomon is going to tell us how to get there. While his advice is straightforward, Solomon never says it is easy.

If you and your business want to have a good name and obtain favor, you have to have a 100-percent commitment to love and faithfulness. Before going on, let's recognize what a 100-percent commitment really is and think through some of its implications. For instance, how would love and faithfulness come into play in these situations?

- A recession hits and revenues aren't going to be high enough to support current payroll. How do you determine which actions are best for the company and its employees?
- You become aware one of your products has a defect that could result in injuries to your customers. What actions do you take to protect your customers and preserve your reputation?
- One of your employees makes a mistake that will cost the company a fair amount of money. What is your approach with that employee? Bonus question: Does it matter if the employee was a good versus an average employee?
- Customers are having a hard time reaching the company and getting answers to their questions. How do you improve customer service while minding the store?

It's easy to talk a good game, but carrying it out can be hard. Let me pick on customer service systems for a minute or two. Almost every business has some sort of customer service system. These range from great—"I can get the answers I need quickly and they are correct!"—to awful—"How many buttons do I need to push to talk to someone who can't answer basic questions?" The main difference between those two extremes is how the companies think about their customers. If you really want to love and be faithful to your customers, you'll make sure your customer service system is built with the customer in mind—easy to use, most answers readily available and, when needed, a knowledgeable person readily available. After I use a system like the one just described, I gain confidence in the company and will choose to do more business with them.

But some companies have awful customer service systems—answers are hard to find, options are geared toward sales rather than service, and when you can talk to someone he can't take care of you. I'm trying to use a system like that right now. I need a replacement part for insulation I put on the inside of my garage door. While I like the product and the benefit I achieved from installing it, the clips holding the insulation in place keep losing their tightness and popping off. Although the company knows about this problem, replacement clips are not available anywhere at any price. By refusing to make the replacements available, the company has turned this previously satisfied customer into a dissatisfied customer. Next time, my business is likely to go elsewhere.

As you think about your company's problem areas, can you say you and your company are being loving and faithful to your customers? Nothing says you have to be. But if you want a good name and favor with your customers, you have to love your customers and be faithful to them in all aspects of your interactions with them—product, sales, and service.

As we try to reach our goals, we often come upon obstacles. Some seem insurmountable and we can't think of any earthly way around them. We don't know what to do, but there is a God who does. He is willing to show us the way if only we trust Him completely. I've found that to be true in my life. I've experienced it many times when a problem before me didn't seem to have an answer. I would rack my brain for ideas and answers, but nothing I could think of worked. Then, in a "flash of brilliance," an answer would come, one that usually required me to get out of my comfort zone or take a completely different approach. I had a choice: follow the flash of brilliance or keep trying to come up with an answer my way. Because I knew the flash of brilliance had been given to me, I almost always followed it with stunningly good results, earning me a good name and favor with others. Those times when I refused to follow the flash of brilliance? Let's just say things didn't turn out nearly as well.

He who writes love and faithfulness on his heart and demonstrates it by his actions gains a good name. More importantly, he will gain favor in the sight of the LORD. That favor shows up in tangible ways for the man who trusts in the LORD; the LORD will make his paths straight. These are remarkable benefits for those who choose to implement these first two commands.

Personal Application

This chapter starts out with a simple equation:

Don't forget my teaching + Keep my commands in your heart = Prolonged life + Prosperity.

Before we skip past this equation, we would do well to ponder its implications for us.

Isn't it interesting the first variable is stated as "Don't forget" rather than "Remember"? Do you see the sizeable difference between the two? When we are asked to remember, it's usually about a faded memory, one so faded we often need clues to break through our fuzzy memories. But "Don't forget" implies we have learned something so well it is seared into our memory; we would have to actively work at forgetting it. Can you feel the urgency Solomon is placing on his son, and us, to sear these teachings into our minds?

Then Solomon tells his son to "keep my commands *in your heart.*" Wow! It isn't good enough to not forget Solomon's teaching and commands; the son has to have them lodged deep in his soul. You know the difference. A common example might be stopping at a red traffic light when no other traffic is in sight. You stopped and kept the command, but in your heart, you may have thought about going through the red light (or other things, like the wisdom of those who set the light cycling times). Did you keep the command? Sure. But did you deep down in your heart? No.

The heart question is a key point in the first two commands. Love and faithfulness are to be written on the tablet of our heart. Trusting in God is to be done with all of our heart. Think about it: If love and faithfulness is written on your heart, you will live your life with love and faithfulness. The only way you couldn't is to purposefully erase or turn your back on them. Trust isn't written on your heart; rather it requires you to trust *with all your heart*. Why is that important? Because if you have any doubt in your mind when asked to do something, you will hesitate or make your own decision. That is more like "trust but verify," which is not trust. While okay in most human relationships, Solomon is talking about something much greater—our relationship with God. Without 100-percent trust in Him, you may choose a rocky, rough, and windy path rather than the path God promises to make straight.

One more thought on this section. The sentence on trusting isn't the first command Solomon gives, but it is usually the one people quote. That's understandable; we want our troubles to be taken care of as soon as possible. But don't miss where Solomon starts with his commands.

The first step is to do those things that win favor and a good name with God and man. If we win favor with God, isn't He going to be more willing to help us in times of trouble? If we have a good name in the sight of man, won't those people be more willing to help us when troubles come our way?

Although these are commands, the choice is always yours. Are you willing to do what it takes to embrace love and faithfulness so closely it will never leave you? Are you willing to trust God with all your heart and lean on His understanding?

Chapter 11

Healthy Body, Full Barns, Overflowing Vats, and Loving Rebukes Proverbs 3:7-12

Do not be wise in your own eyes; fear the LORD and shun evil. This will bring health to your body and nourishment to your bones. Honor the LORD with your wealth, with the first fruits of all your crops; then your barns will be filled to overflowing, and your vats will brim over with new wine. My son, do not despise the LORD's discipline and do not resent his rebuke, because the LORD disciplines those he loves, as a father the son he delights in.

Background/Circumstances

In this chapter, Solomon gives his son several commands. In the last article, we reviewed the first two:

1. **Let love and faithfulness never leave you.**
2. **Trust in the LORD with all your heart.**

With those two foundational commands in place, Solomon gives three other commands. Note each of them builds off the first two, especially trusting in the LORD.

3. **Don't be wise in your own eyes.**
4. **Honor the LORD with your wealth.**

5. Do not despise the LORD's discipline.

Don't be wise in your own eyes. It's helpful to remember Solomon is talking to his son, the one most likely to become the next king. Growing up in a time of peace and amazing luxury, his son may become prideful and believe he has as much or more wisdom than his father. Solomon sees the danger and provides the antidote: 1) Develop a loving reverence for God—fear the LORD—and 2) shun evil. If the son implements this command, he will enjoy 1) health to the body and 2) nourishment to the bones. When the son implements this command, he will enjoy physical and mental wellbeing.

Honor the LORD with your wealth. Israelites, under their law, were required to bring the first sheaf of grain harvested from their fields, the finest olive oil, and the finest new wine to the priests. In turn, the priests used them to perform a ceremony thanking God, honoring Him for the harvest. Although the full tithe—10 percent of the harvest—remained a requirement, Solomon emphasizes these first gifts as they represent a physical acknowledgment of the LORD's provision. He wants his son always to remember the bounty his son sees and enjoys comes from God's blessing. When his son honors the LORD through these first fruits, God's blessings on the nation will be so great the nation will never have enough barns to store all the grain or vats to hold all the new wine from the annual harvest! The son's material needs will be more than satisfied.

Do not despise the LORD's discipline. Solomon has assured his son that his physical and mental wellbeing, as well as his material needs, will be fulfilled by following the two previous commands. What else could the son want? Solomon answers the question: His son will want to know he is loved. The way he will know? As a loving father disciplines and instructs the son he delights in, so the LORD will demonstrate His love and concern for Solomon's son through careful discipline and rebuke.

While each command deserves your consideration, pay particular attention to one feature included in commands 2 through 5. Did you notice the term "LORD" is used in each of them? If you remember from the last chapter, LORD is the personal and covenant name of God. It emphasizes His role as the nation's redeemer and His covenant relationship with it. By emphasizing the LORD in these commands, Solomon makes it clear his son needs to develop a personal relationship with this Supreme Being to succeed. Knowing about the LORD is not going to be good enough; he has to *know* the LORD on a personal basis. In addition, the son must understand the covenant relationship between the LORD and the nation.

Business Application

As we experience business successes and victories, it becomes easier to think we are special and rules don't apply to us. But it is a trap! Too many have believed this way and engaged in behavior leading to their ruin. One that comes immediately to mind is Richard Nixon. In his first term as president of the United States, Mr. Nixon achieved many international and domestic breakthroughs resulting in his winning the 1972 presidential election in a landslide. But his success magnified some of his personal flaws, leading him to think the rules didn't apply to him. Because the rules didn't apply to him, he approved unlawful activity—a break-in of Democratic headquarters at the Watergate complex in Washington, D.C. Although he denied it for two years, as the truth came out Mr. Nixon was forced to resign in disgrace. To this day, he remains one of the great enigmas of American politics: The person who reopened relations with China and engaged in detente with Russia was also the person who, in the 1950s, went after members of the Communist party and sought to destroy his political enemies with "dirty tricks."

If you have been in the workforce for much time at all, you probably know of a situation where a successful person in your company or profession, maybe at the top of their game, suddenly and unexpectedly left the company or profession without any explanation. Not always, but often, it will be over an egregious violation of the company's rules, a profession's code of conduct, or the law. It's a common tale: A talented person who achieves great success starts making poor choices, ruins his life, and damages those around him. Each tale is sad; every one of them could have been prevented if only they had followed Solomon's advice.

And what is that advice? It is to remember to be humble. Take a closer look at the traps that beckon the successful and how to step around them:

- **You can slip into the trap of thinking you have special knowledge and wisdom no one else has.** Because you are "special," you think the rules don't apply to you so you start crossing lines to get things done—described as evil here. It's easy to let success go to your head and think you have the answers in fields not yours to tend. I've seen that kind of arrogance grow in a leader, and the results were never good. Eventually, the leader went too far and his superior would rein him in, usually with a notice of dismissal. There is no need for such a thing to happen to you. While you may be successful and know a lot, it is good to remember you don't know everything and there are others who have wisdom exceeding yours. When you are humble, you'll be more apt to seek out truth wherever it may reside in your company or with your associates. As you seek truth, your wisdom will help you find it and shun evil.
- **It is easy to forget about those people who helped you.** We all want to think we have achieved success through our own devices. But that isn't the truth. We have all been helped by others. Who helped you along the way? Do you really and truly appreciate their devotion and sacrifice? Have you thanked them

in a public and sincere way? Honoring those who have or are helping you—employees, suppliers, etc.—is a good thing. True appreciation goes a long way toward a happy and productive team, one willing to move mountains for greater corporate success.

- **You can ignore wise advice or other warning signs**. You have probably seen this in action. One of my examples relates to an executive team meeting discussion immediately after the Board of Trustees chairman talked to us about a report he wanted prepared. After the board chairman left the meeting, the executive team discussed his direction. We only had a few hours to get the report back to him, so we had to make the right assignments right away. Most of the group heard the chairman's comments one way and agreed he wanted us to go a certain direction. My understanding of the chairman's direction was 180 degrees opposite from their understanding. In a departure from my normally calm demeanor, I forcefully disagreed with their understanding and tried to convince the other executives they had misunderstood the board chairman. Instead of stopping and considering why I was objecting so forcefully, the group dismissed my comments, made work assignments, and went about preparing the requested report.

  When the CEO delivered the report that evening, the board chairman ripped him up one side and down the other; the report was 180 degrees from what the chairman had requested. In the next day's executive team meeting, the CEO reviewed the "new" direction, the one I had advocated for the day before. You can be sure the subsequent report aligned 100 percent with the board chairman's direction!

In its extreme form, a leader will surround himself with "yes" men and get rid of those who keep pointing out problems. It's a foolish path to take. Employees who want the best for you and your company will point out weaknesses or problems so you and your team can correct them before they drag down you or the company.

So, as you climb the path of success or enjoy the pinnacle, remember to practice these three steps to humility:

- Love truth and don't stray from it; otherwise, you'll think you are wiser than you really are.
- Take time to honor and sincerely thank those who have contributed to your success.
- Pay attention to those who love you enough to tell you hard things; they are looking out for you.

Personal Application

After challenging us to embrace love and faithfulness and trusting in God wholeheartedly, Solomon points out three areas where we often have trouble: 1) judging how wise we are, 2) honoring God with our wealth, and 3) accepting discipline and rebukes.

- **Judging how wise we are.** As you might expect, we all have a hard time judging exactly how wise we are. I'm sure you've heard of the surveys where 80 percent of those surveyed consider themselves above average. It's a mathematical impossibility but it gives us an indication a lot of people think too highly of themselves. I've done that. I'll observe someone, start to make judgments about them and, whether I intend to or not, start comparing myself to them. (Hint: I'm almost always better.) As I talk with them, I find out many of my judgments were wrong. I don't know nearly as much as I think I do. In fact, I have a lot to learn from them!

  How about you? Do you compare yourself to others and find

you are better—wiser—than everyone else? If so, it's time to do a reality check. Thinking like that takes you down the path to becoming a prideful person, a person who is wise in their own eyes. It's a dangerous place to be. Such a person tends to ignore truth and play with evil.

Prideful people often endure great falls. I'm sure you can think of a respected, highly moral leader who, thinking he was "special," started engaging in immoral behavior that led to a great fall and his ruined reputation. What he started to dabble in and thought he could control ended up controlling him. Too many lives have been ruined this way. Don't be one of them.

- **Honoring God with our wealth.** Two ideas are contained in this sentence. First, God loves to honor those who honor Him. With the entire resources of the universe at His hand, God can demonstrate this is any number of ways. In Solomon's day, successful crops were important, and great harvests year after year would certainly show others Israel's God was worth honoring. Some would like to see this as a formula, such as "I gave to God, now He *has to* reciprocate and shower me with material blessings." That thinking misses the second idea: What does it mean to really honor God?

  Let me suggest, at a minimum, honoring the LORD involves implementing the three commands Solomon has given before this one. Because you will see the good God has done in your life, your thankfulness will lead you to honor God for who He is, *expecting nothing in return.*

  Think about this, if you decided to "honor" someone but expected that person to give you more in return, did you really honor that person? Of course not. It's a game you are playing for your gain. You know what you are doing, and so does the person you honored. If you really want to honor someone, you are specific about their achievements and give them something of value to commemorate those achievements. The same holds true in honoring God. In this passage, it was God's abundant provision in the annual harvest being honored.

As in Solomon's day, don't we have incredible blessings come our way? If you are having trouble seeing them, take a closer look because they are there. When you see them, take some time to be thankful and thank God for sending them your way.

- **Accepting discipline and rebukes.** Do you look forward to discipline? How about a sharp rebuke? I don't, and I don't think anyone else does. But the distinction here is to not *despise* or *resent* them. Why? There are two reasons:
    - **The LORD gives them because he loves you and only wants what is best for you.** Rather than let you wander off on a poor path, a loving person will reach out to protect you. The correction may have momentary discomfort and pain, but the intent is to save you from greater discomfort and pain. Those who don't love you behave quite differently. Their actions are intended to hurt you and increase your pain. Rather than listen to them, you should accept the discipline and rebukes given in love, learn from them, and hasten to get back to where you should be.
    - **A person who despises discipline is a Fool.** (See the section on Chapter 1, Verse 7 for that discussion.) Not only will the Fool reject discipline, but he also will plunge deeper into his foolish ways and suffer the consequences.

I hope you have noticed the first part of Chapter 3 is talking about a very personal interaction with a Supreme Being ("the LORD"). All five commands have been about that relationship and the benefits from wholeheartedly entering into it. If you haven't done so before, now would be a good time to pause and consider these commands. Making them your own could change your life for the good. As we'll see in the next section, there are even more blessings in store for those who embrace and implement these commands.

Chapter 12

Wisdom's Incomparable Value
Proverbs 3:13-20

Blessed is the man who finds wisdom, the man who gains understanding, for she is more profitable than silver and yields better returns than gold. She is more precious than rubies; nothing you desire can compare with her. Long life is in her right hand; in her left hand are riches and honor. Her ways are pleasant ways, and all her paths are peace. She is a tree of life to those who embrace her; those who lay hold of her will be blessed. By wisdom the LORD laid the earth's foundations, by understanding he set the heavens in place; by his knowledge the deeps were divided, and the clouds let drop the dew.

Background/Circumstances

In the first part of Chapter 3, Solomon reviewed five commands the son should follow if he wants to become wise. Each command also came with a blessing. If the son will follow the commands, the blessings will come. The five commands and blessings are:

- **Command:** Let love and faithfulness never leave you. **Blessing:** Win favor and a good name in the sight of God and man.
- **Command:** Trust in the LORD with all your heart. **Blessing:** He will make your paths straight.
- **Command:** Do not be wise in your own eyes. **Blessing:** Health to the body and nourishment to his bones.

- **Command:** Honor the LORD with your wealth. **Blessing:** Barns will be filled to overflowing and vats brim over with new wine.
- **Command:** Do not despise the LORD's discipline. **Blessing:** You will know He loves and delights in you.

After giving these commands, Solomon moves from specific blessings gained from each command to the larger blessings coming to one who finds wisdom and understanding. If the son had any doubts earlier about the value of wisdom and understanding, Solomon gives a comparison of their value to those things Solomon had in abundance—silver, gold, and rubies. Because of his situation, wealthy and wise Solomon can best judge what is most valuable and why. He first addresses worldly wealth and flatly states wisdom, understanding, and knowledge are worth much more than what one can gain from silver and gold. Wisdom, understanding, and knowledge are more precious than gems. In fact, whatever the son desires in his heart of hearts pales in comparison to them. Then Solomon lists those things that will accrue to those who have wisdom, understanding, and knowledge:

- **Long life.** One's life will be prolonged by many years.
- **Riches and honor.** Prosperity comes to the one who uses wisdom, understanding, and knowledge. Because love and faithfulness permeate his life, he will win favor with God and man and be honored.
- **Pleasant ways.** Life will proceed in a pleasant way because wisdom, understanding, and knowledge will keep him from leaning on his own understanding and pursuing evil ways.
- **Peace.** One will have peace of mind and an absence of significant conflict.
- **Tree of life.** One who has his roots well established in wisdom, understanding, and knowledge has a source of strength feeding every aspect of his life. He can become all he was meant to be.

- **Blessed.** In addition to all of these things, his life will be blessed.

When weighed on the scales of value, Solomon can say with confidence wisdom far outweighs worldly wealth in value. Nothing compares to the value of wisdom.

Emphasizing his point further, Solomon talks about what the LORD did with wisdom, understanding, and knowledge during Creation. He:

Laid the Earth's foundation – Created an Earth that supported life and operated within certain rules.

Set the heavens in place – Created the sun, moon, and stars and put them where they needed to be.

Divided the deep and let clouds drop the dew – Broke open the springs in the ocean and made clouds to rain.

It's a dramatic point. The LORD used wisdom, understanding, and knowledge to create the world his son lives in. The son knows Solomon possesses wisdom, understanding, and knowledge and used them in establishing a safe and secure Israel nation, exactly what God intended. Likewise, if the son will obtain and use wisdom, understanding, and knowledge, he, too, can accomplish great things!

Business Application

Some believe it is wrong for people to have wealth. You won't find that sentiment here. In fact, Solomon says there is profit to silver, good returns to be made through gold, and gems are precious.

While working to increase your business, income, and net worth is fine, Solomon points out the huge difference it makes when you use wisdom and understanding. In addition to riches, you can have a longer life, receive honor, avoid unnecessary conflict, have a more peaceful life, become all you are meant to be, and experience a thoroughly blessed life.

Using wisdom and understanding sounds simple, but if you aren't grounded in them, application can become very fuzzy. For instance, take the issue of work-life balance. My generation of baby boomers leaned more toward work. For us, work came first and life occurred during those times when we weren't working or doing our duty. In its extreme, work became all important; family and everything else played second fiddle. Recent generations lean more toward life. For them, work has to occur when it doesn't interfere with life. Living life is more important than anything else, and their motivation to work is secondary.

It's safe to say neither generation has the right answer; as we have learned, there isn't one correct answer. People and seasons of life widely vary within our workforces and they constantly change. Marriage, babies, injuries, divorce, loss of a loved one, and other personal events often mean an adjustment to work-life balance. Changes at work can have their impact, too. Consider how the advent of online buying, remote work, and the gig economy continue to evolve and force changes in business models. To their credit, many business leaders recognized early in the game they needed to change their business models in order to better match a changing work environment to their workforce's changing personal needs. From what we've seen thus far, those businesses have a better chance of surviving and prospering.

The key in addressing your work issues comes down to how well you use your wisdom and understanding to address them. Start by working on understanding the issue. What is really going on here? What problem(s) do you need to solve? What resources can you bring to bear on a resolution? After you understand the issue(s), you can apply wisdom. How do you resolve the problem so it's fixed for the short term and long term? Do you need to sequence actions so you can tell if they are working? How will you know when you have really solved the problem? There are lots of questions to ask to get at the real problem(s) and solutions.

One thing to think about is whether you should import solutions that have worked for others to solve their problem(s). My best advice is to be careful for at least two reasons:

- **Things are not always as they seem.** It's only natural when a company launches a new program to talk about how wonderfully things are going. After all, time and effort have gone into putting the new program in place and the sponsors need to claim victory. Maybe I'm jaded. I've seen "total victory" declared, although several significant problems still needed to be resolved. Those were never mentioned in the press release. I've found the same to be true with accomplishments others have touted. While the headlines said the solution was great and all problems were solved, the reality was much different; several problems still existed and much was yet to be done. Before adopting someone else's solution, make sure you know the facts about their solution.
- **What worked for them may not work for you.** Many variables contribute to a company's success. Before adopting another company's solution, you need to understand how closely your situation matches their situation. Although the situations may closely match, do your due diligence. Seek out and understand the differences. Minor differences can usually be resolved with minimal changes. However, if the differences are material, you either have to modify the solution to fit your situation or make major changes in your company's operations so the solution will work for you. Both options create risks you need to evaluate so you can decide whether to apply the other company's solution or pass on it.

This dilemma shows up in sports all the time. George Brett, a third baseman for the Kansas City Royals from 1973 to 1993, had great success—3,154 hits and a lifetime batting average of .305—using a unique batting stance he and the Royals' batting coach Charley Lau developed to help improve his batting skills. Seeing George Brett's success, others considered emulating his stance. Few, if any, exactly emulated George Brett's stance and had the same level of success. What worked to solve George Brett's batting problems didn't work for others. The same may hold true should you try to overlay another company's successful program on your company.

One other thought. As a "higher-up" in an organization, it's tempting to think you know your organization's problems and their solutions. Certainly, cases exist where you do and the solution turns out well. But there will be times when you don't know the problem or the solution. In that situation, use wisdom and seek others who can help you. When you seek others' wisdom, you need to be purposeful about it. To be most successful, you must be completely open to others' feedback, process it without bias, use it to develop solutions, and communicate to those who helped you how you did or why you didn't use their input. Failing in one or more of these areas can create more problems.

- **It's easy to create an atmosphere in which employees won't provide honest feedback.** Consider this exchange between a boss and his employee.
    - **Boss:** "I'd like your input on a problem that we're having."
    - **Employee:** I wonder if he really wants my input or if he wants me to go along with what he wants. I'll ask a question to find out. "What's the problem?"
    - **Boss:** – "The problem is we are falling behind meeting our production goal."
    - **Employee:** He thinks, "Gee, we've told him before we

need more parts on hand to keep the machines running all the time. I wonder what he is thinking." He says, "Boss, what do you think the problem is?"

  - **Boss:** He thinks, "I see this work group standing around from time to time shooting the breeze. They just need to work harder and we would meet our goals." He replies, "I know you have done a lot to help us work smarter, but I think we need to concentrate on working harder for a while."

    At this point, the boss, who has come up with a bad solution because he jumped to a conclusion, has lost the employee's willingness to help in the future.

- **How often do we get information from our staff and ignore it or miss what someone is trying to tell us because we are applying our own filter to it?** Some examples:
  - Boss thinks: "Jill didn't say anything so she must be okay with where we are heading." Jill thinks: "I'm pretty sure I know what the problem is, but I didn't want to speak up and be embarrassed before my peers."
  - Roger tells the boss, "We don't have enough time to get to that right now." What he meant was "We have all this other work on our plate. Is this the priority?"
- **Some do well in gathering the right information but, because it doesn't suit their purposes or what they think the situation is, choose not to use it.** Numerous examples have been recorded where military leaders received intelligence reports they chose to ignore. Ignoring those reports allowed the enemy to proceed with their plans unimpeded, leading to disastrous results and catastrophic losses to the military leader's forces.
- **Employees detest providing good, honest feedback and never hearing how the bosses used it.** You can do everything else well and fail in this area. When an employee reaches out

> to help you, he wants to know how you used his help. From his perspective, he feels like he gave you a perfect solution to your problem. While this perfect solution may work for this employee, it may cause complications in many other areas of the company so you keep things the way they are. You may think your work is done, but it isn't. You need to pull the helpful employee aside and talk to him about his suggestion. By taking the time to discuss the outcome with him, you are showing great respect for him and his ideas. He'll continue to make suggestions. Ignore him and he will be less likely to be helpful the next time you want valuable feedback.

In business, there seems to be more problems than you can "shake a stick at." Rather than waving a stick, or carrot, at them, you should apply wisdom and understanding when working on them.

Personal Application

Thus far, as I've read and reread Solomon's letter to his son, I've often wondered how much of his advice is tailored to his son. Is he addressing specific areas where he knows his son has a weakness, or is he basing his advice on his own exploration of wisdom and understanding?

Why is this important? If Solomon is addressing his son's weaknesses, we may see Solomon's advice as interesting but probably not applying to us. If that were the case, then this book would hardly be worth including in holy scripture. But it is included because of the great wisdom Solomon is providing to all who will read and strive to understand it.

We see it in this section. When you read the list of benefits to be gained, aren't those the things you would like to have in your life? Wouldn't you raise your hand and say yes if someone asked if you wanted a longer life, riches, honor, pleasant pathways, peace, reaching your potential, and being blessed? Solomon says it is within reach if we only will take hold of and practice the commands in this chapter. And that's the rub, isn't it?

- **It's hard to have love and faithfulness never leave you.** We want to make them conditional rather than unconditional. We want to put them on and take them off like a necklace when God's plan is for them to be written on our hearts.
- **It's hard to trust in the LORD with all our heart.** We want to lean on our understanding and take credit for the good things we receive. We want to think we know best even though we can't see what lies before us.
- **It's hard to realize we aren't as wise as we think we are.** We want to think we know the score—what's right and what's wrong. We fail to realize how easily we can be led astray.
- **It's hard to honor the LORD with our wealth.** We want to keep all we've earned and believe it was gained through our efforts. Somehow we think we will get to take it with us after we die.
- **It's hard to accept the discipline and rebuke we deserve.** We want to see it as punishment from an enemy rather than discipline and instruction from a loving father.

Once again, Solomon gives his son, and you, a stark choice. You can live a normal life based on how most people understand things or you can live an incredible, fulfilling life based on the wisdom and understanding Solomon tells us about. I hope you'll choose to start, or continue, the path to this wisdom and understanding. The results are well worth the journey!

Chapter 13

Keep Sound Judgment and Discernment in Sight Proverbs 3:21-26

My son, preserve sound judgment and discernment, do not let them out of your sight; they will be life for you, an ornament to grace your neck. Then you will go on your way in safety, and your foot will not stumble; when you lie down, you will not be afraid; when you lie down, your sleep will be sweet. Have no fear of sudden disaster or of the ruin that overtakes the wicked, for the LORD will be your confidence and will keep your foot from being snared.

Background/Circumstances

After finishing his interlude to discuss the larger benefits of finding wisdom and gaining understanding, Solomon adds a sixth command—preserve sound judgment and discernment.

An assumption needs to be pointed out. By following the previous five commands and the prior teachings and instructions, Solomon believes his son will have obtained wisdom and understanding plus sound judgment and discernment. With sound judgment, he will be able to sort through the verbal and nonverbal information heading his way and come to a perfect understanding of every situation. Having this understanding allows him to use discernment to take the appropriate action or say the right thing. He will be at the cusp of becoming the wise person needed to succeed Solomon as king.

Because of all the benefits that Solomon has explained, he assumes his son will accept his teachings, instructions, and commands and become wise. But Solomon realizes obtaining and retaining are two different things. Hence, the warning to "preserve" sound judgment and discernment. According to Merriam-Webster, to "preserve" means to "keep safe from injury, harm or destruction (protect)" and "keep alive, intact, or free from decay (maintain)." It's clear that preserving sound judgment and discernment requires action. Solomon's recommended action is "to never let them out of his sight."

Never letting them out of his sight sounds like a simple action, but it requires a disciplined life—making every decision through the filter of sound judgment and discernment. Just like obtaining wisdom was hard work, preserving it is going to be just as hard.

Solomon may have been thinking about when he lost sight of sound judgment and discernment. In that day, to ensure peace with another country, the king would marry a princess from that country. Although it was strictly forbidden by Hebrew law, Solomon decided to go the political route and marry, starting with Pharaoh's daughter. Once he broke the law by marrying Pharaoh's daughter, Solomon justified his marrying other foreign women from countries where Hebrew law forbade taking a spouse. Eventually, he ended up with seven hundred wives and three hundred concubines. These women he married led to Solomon's downfall; they led him away from worshipping the LORD only. Knowing his downfall started when he failed to preserve sound judgment and discernment and began marrying foreign women, Solomon earnestly tells his son to hold on to wisdom.

By preserving sound judgment and discernment, the son will reap new benefits. In addition to those he would get from following the first five commandments, adhering to this commandment would:

- **Be life for him.** He always will use sound judgment and discernment in all he does. Whether it is affairs of state or family matters, he always will judge aright and do/say the right thing.

- **Act like an ornament to grace his neck.** People in all walks of life will see those qualities in him. He will become known and looked up to as a person of sound judgment and discernment.
- **Let him go on his way in safety.** As he goes about his business, he can do so without any fear for his safety. His conduct has earned respect and a great amount of goodwill.
- **Keep his foot from stumbling.** As he goes about his daily life, he will see clearly those things that could cause a moral lapse. With his sound judgment and discernment, he can avoid getting into those situations.
- **Allow him to lie down and not be afraid.** Because he has used sound judgment and done/said the right things, he will have no need to worry he has created an enemy who will be out to get him. He can lie down in peace with no cause for fear.
- **Let him lie down and enjoy sleep.** He will be able to lie down, go to sleep, stay asleep, and wake up refreshed. No nightmares, just sweet and pleasant dreams.
- **Let him have no fear of sudden disaster.** Having exercised sound judgment and made right decisions, he will have thought ahead, evaluated contingencies, and developed a plan for dealing with them. While things may come up that require his attention, he will have no worries about sudden disasters.
- **Let him have no fear of the ruin that overtakes the wicked.** He will have kept to the good path rather than striking out on paths of illegal or immoral activities. Ruin awaits those who follow those paths and, because he hasn't followed them, he has no cause to fear the outcome awaiting the wicked.
- **Keep his foot from being snared.** Although he has used his sound judgment and discernment to make good decisions, some people will try to trap him. Having embraced all of Solomon's commands, in the midst of snares, he can have confidence in God's guidance and direction.

Business Application

Wouldn't it be great to have people with sound judgment and discernment in all key areas of your business? Based on what we've read above, a company with an abundance of people demonstrating sound judgment and discernment would be an amazing place:

- All actions are viewed with sound judgment and discernment.
- Opportunities are identified and evaluated. Decisions work in the short term and long term.
- Your company and your people enjoy a great reputation within your industry and community.
- Employee and company wellbeing are joined at the hip with teams working toward a common purpose.
- Because employees care, no one remembers the last time an internal mistake harmed the company or an employee.
- Fear is absent from the workplace.
- People rest easy at night, enjoy life, and truly can rest and relax.
- Because your company knows market needs, runs efficiently, and delivers quality products and services, you never are caught off guard.
- You comply with all legal requirements and go out of your way to exceed them.
- Your best-of-class ethical code sets clear expectations. You promptly counsel and correct anyone who fails to meet them.

Alas, very few companies are like the one I just described. As I filter my work experience through this light, it is easy for me to come up with situations—way too many—where a lack of sound judgment and discernment, by myself or others, created problems or made existing problems worse.

In the mid '90s, healthcare costs were skyrocketing and our executive team decided to increase the amount employees would need to pay toward medical insurance premiums. Although relatively new to the city, I was selected to meet with employees and present the changes. While I provided accurate financial information that made sense to me, my presentation failed to address and answer the employees' pressing questions. As a result, the longer I talked the employees became more and more upset. The initial employee question felt like a high and tight fastball—a knockdown pitch in baseball—and the meeting went downhill from there.

Finally, my benefit supervisor entered the discussion. Her discerning words and actions dissipated the anger in the room significantly and allowed us to enter into a more fruitful discussion. I got to hear the employees' real concerns; they listened to the financial situation. As we talked, we realized the city needed to change how it handled annual medical insurance premium changes. We appointed an interdepartmental team and tasked them with learning about medical insurance and understanding the factors driving healthcare cost increases. With both sides operating with the same knowledge base, we could share our respective viewpoints well before decisions had to be made. In succeeding years, this team recommended medical insurance coverage changes and reached consensus on medical insurance premium allocations between the city and its employees. With their new knowledge, team members served as liaisons to their fellow employees, providing a conduit for information to go back and forth between management and employees.

If you want to have an amazing company, you must consider and act upon the following:

- **Take a good hard look at yourself when asking the question "Do I consistently use sound judgment and discernment?"** Answer the question as honestly as you can. As a check, ask those with whom you deal with on a regular basis if they feel you use sound judgment and discernment. If there is any hesitancy on your, or the others', part to answer this question, you can be assured you need to take a deeper dive.

- **Does your company stress the importance of sound judgment and discernment?** Rather than allowing people to go off half-cocked or embrace the latest trend, do you have measures in place to ensure enough information is gathered and appropriately considered? Are you disciplined enough to wait until you have enough good information to make a reasoned and judicious decision?
- **In your hiring process, how important is it to find out if a candidate for a key position has sound judgment and discernment?** Do you design specific interview questions for the candidate and his references to find out? At some point, placing enough people with these principles in your key positions will bring about significant positive change.
- **Are there key employees who constantly display a lack of sound judgment and discernment?** If so, then you need to bring them up to speed or help them find another company in which they could succeed.

Are you willing to make the commitment to have an amazing company? If so, keep your sight on preserving sound judgment and discernment for yourself, your employees, and your company. Even with all of the other things you have to do, never take your eye off of it.

Personal Application

When you think about it, isn't it sad so many choose to focus on something besides sound judgment and discernment? The worst part is we often know we are putting sound judgment and discernment aside. Here are just a few examples:

- **Money is tight in the household but unnecessary, expensive or impulsive things keep getting purchased.** Although both spouses know money is tight, they keep buying and can't seem to help themselves. As a result, the family falls deeper into financial debt and misery.
- **A spouse has "feelings" for someone other than their spouse, manages to meet this someone in a place where they can be alone, and they end up in bed together**. The spouse knows this isn't a good thing to do but does it anyway. Feelings turn into action and a series of familial destructive actions unfold. Almost everyone in both families is hurt. Relationships with mutual friends may never be the same.
- **A friend tells someone else about a confidential and embarrassing event their close friend experienced.** The friend gets with someone else and, because he isn't supposed to tell the secret, starts giving enough hints about the event the other person eventually "drags it out of him." When the close friend finds out the event was shared with others, the relationship between the two friends will be damaged, if not completely destroyed.
- **A big test is scheduled for Friday, but the fun things available to do until then diverts one's attention.** Rather than allocate enough time during the week to study for the big test, a student chooses to do something much more fun. Friday morning comes and, because this student spent a few hectic late-night, last-minute hours studying, the student is completely unprepared and fails this important test.

This list could be a lot longer, but you get the idea. Most of us, most of the time, know what we need to do *and we do it*. Let's give ourselves a little pat on the back and realize we do exercise sound judgment and discernment most of the time. When we do, our lives are better for it. We all seem to have this understanding: Sound decisions produce good results. Then why do we, at one time or another, make dumb decisions or head off in nonsensical directions likely to have bad results? Why do we fail to use our sound judgment?

Like those in the examples above, we fail because we have, however momentarily, taken our eyes off the ball. In sports, that lapse leads to strikeouts, turnovers, poorly struck balls, and other mistakes. Sometimes the impact on the game is known immediately—a bases-loaded strikeout that ends the game. Sometimes the impact isn't known until later—a missed field goal in the first quarter contributes to a loss by one point. Sometimes the impact is frantic efforts for the rest of the game to overcome a distracted goalie giving up two early soccer goals.

I'm not saying it is easy. In sports, so many things are going on at one time. The other team, the fans, and weather conditions are just a few things that can distract you. It's easy to take your eyes off the ball. Like a punt returner trying to concentrate on the football coming his way, you can hear the footsteps and heavy breathing of tacklers (big, strong distractions!) streaking your way, sneak a peek at them, and muff the catch. While most of the time you will exercise good judgment and discernment and do those things you need to do, there will be times when the distractions grab your attention and shift your focus to something else that isn't best for you. A wise person quickly refocuses their attention to what they should be doing and will be fine. However, those who let their minds and thoughts linger very long on forbidden fruit start to desire it. That desire, if unchecked, eventually leads to wickedness and the loss of all the benefits that come with obtaining and *preserving* wisdom.

Solomon gives a lot of focus to the benefits to be obtained by preserving sound judgment and discernment, but don't miss the outcome for those who fail to do so. Sudden destruction and ruin are coming their way. Because they have turned away from sound judgment and discernment, they will not see the storm clouds and destruction heading their way. Having taken no precautions, their destruction will be complete—total ruin. Solomon's message is clear: "Why let this happen to you when there is such a better outcome available? Preserve wisdom!"

What does preserving sound judgment and discernment look like? In the next section, Solomon gives us five only-too-real life examples for us to chew on.

Chapter 14

Losing Sound Judgment and Discernment
Proverbs 3:27-35

Do not withhold good from those who deserve it, when it is in your power to act. Do not say to your neighbor, "Come back later; I'll give it tomorrow"—when you now have it with you. Do not plot harm against your neighbor, who lives trustfully near you. Do not accuse a man for no reason—when he has done you no harm. Do not envy a violent man or choose any of his ways, for the LORD detests a perverse man but takes the upright into his confidence. The LORD's curse is on the house of the wicked, but he blesses the home of the righteous. He mocks proud Mockers but gives grace to the humble. The wise inherit honor, but fools he holds up to shame.

Background/Circumstances

In the prior section, Solomon emphasizes how important it is for his son, once he has acquired wisdom, to keep it by preserving sound judgment and discernment in his life. If he will exercise these things at all times, the son will experience an amazing life.

From there, Solomon gives five examples where emotion rather than sound judgment and discernment may determine his son's actions. In this section, Solomon describes the downward spiral his son will take if he fails to keep sound judgment and discernment in his sight. Each step down this spiral will move his son further from wisdom and closer to becoming a wicked man. All five examples begin with a "Do not" clause. Let's take a look at them:

- **Do not withhold.** You know someone in your circle of acquaintances who deserves to be helped and you have the ability to provide help. You are under no requirement to help him but you could if you wanted to. Rather than assist him, you decide to forgo the apparently easy effort to help. After all, someday you may need what you could give.
- **Do not say.** A neighbor has come to ask you for something you borrowed or owe him. He needs it right then, and although you have what he needs readily available, you put him off by saying he should come by your house tomorrow to get it. Yes, you'll fulfill your obligation, but something inside you wants to keep it for yourself.
- **Do not plot.** The next example takes a more sinister turn. In the first two examples, Solomon warned about refusing to help those in need or returning things to his neighbor. Now, the warning is about starting to plot harm against your good friends and neighbors who trust you. You are starting to engage in treachery and treason.
- **Do not accuse.** The next step is even lower; you are willing to make accusations you know are false. You want to destroy this person's reputation, although he never has done anything remotely close to hurting you. You have become someone who likes to hurt others.
- **Do not envy.** Finally, you come to the place where you envy those who engage in violence. You see others get what they want through violent means and you start to picture yourself getting what you want using the same means. Even though you know the LORD detests such a person, the draw is too much and you become violent.

By going through these steps, Solomon shows how poor judgment in a seemingly trivial situation—failing to help when you could—can lead to increasingly poor decisions, which eventually can take you from having been an upright person to now being a perverse person—the Fool.

Solomon wants his son to see the difference in outcomes awaiting someone who preserves sound judgment and discernment versus someone who lets them out of his sight. And the different outcomes are stark:

- **The one who takes his eyes off sound judgment and discernment becomes wicked, a Mocker, and a true Fool.** As a result, he has earned several things: 1) the LORD's curse, 2) God's mocking of him, and 3) shame. I think it is safe to say having the LORD's curse means things are not going to go well for the wicked person. His mocking of events isn't going to go well either; God will mock him right back—and have the final word in the exchange. Finally, as he completes the downward spiral, he becomes like the Fool and acts in shameful ways. His shame is fully exposed and placed on public display.
- **The one who preserves sound judgment and discernment becomes righteous, humble, and wise.** As a result, he likewise has earned several things: 1) the LORD's blessing on his home, 2) grace from God, and 3) honor. I think it is safe to say having the LORD's blessing on your life would be completely amazing. God will show his favor toward you in all you do; things will turn out much better than you might have expected. Finally, you will have lived a life worth honoring.

Although he doesn't say it explicitly, it is easy to see which path Solomon is recommending—preserve sound judgment and discernment.

Business Application

Have you done a Root Cause Analysis? If you're not familiar with it, let me explain. After something with potentially major negative implications occurs, a team reviews all work processes backwards from when the problem became evident until a process breakdown—the cause—is found. Although the cause has been identified (e.g., a part doesn't meet specifications), the analysis continues until the root cause (e.g., the specification given to the vendor was wrong) is determined. Often, the causes turn out to be things that would have been a simple fix if they had been addressed at the time (like installing a process to double check specifications before sending them to the vendor). Usually, someone failed to use sound judgment and discernment.

So many business problems, or blessings, come down to whether we and our employees choose to use sound judgment all of the time. Sound judgment usually yields good things. Poor judgment usually yields bad things. Knowing this connection, why don't we spend more time stressing the importance of and teaching sound judgment and discernment? Knowing trained people will lose sight of them from time to time, shouldn't we have systems in place to alert us to early distress signals? Those early distress signals would allow us to apply sound judgment to fix things before they spiral out of control.

When you think about the interactions you have with customers, employees, management, and an assortment of others, to succeed you have to consistently use sound judgment and discernment. That's a good thing, and you should take some time to pat yourself on the back for all your good decisions. But even though things are going well and you'd like to focus on what's going well, strong leaders pay attention to areas needing improvement. While a minor annoyance now, if not addressed in short order, it's only too easy for a minor annoyance to turn into a bigger problem. Truly, a stitch in time does save nine.

Let me give you an example. When I arrived at one of my CFO stops, I was confronted with a major conflict between my purchasing group and one of the operating departments. Instcad of the two department directors helping each other, they seemed to be working overtime to aggravate each other. It was impacting our service delivery. I couldn't let it continue. After talking to a few people, I learned the original conflict between the two department directors had started decades earlier. Even though many in the organization knew about this conflict, no one had addressed it. It had grown from a minor incident that should have been easily resolved years earlier to one in which employees were aligning themselves with one of the department directors and acting accordingly. This internal feud had impacted the company and our service to our customers for years. Although the matter was resolved fairly quickly, the two department directors' failure to exercise sound judgment and discernment was costly to the company, their peers, employees, and our customers.

If you find yourself constantly putting out fires, you need to take some time to find out why these fires keep happening. In the midst of the firefighting, you may think you can't take the time to find out the root causes and fix them. But if you want to do the work you were really hired to do, the work that adds value for your company, you have to find the time to take away the fuel for these fires. Sure, fighting fires is exciting. But let's be honest; fires cause loss. Rather than using your sound judgment and discernment as a last resort to minimize loss, wouldn't it be better to use them from the beginning to seek gains and prevent loss?

Personal Application

Solomon ended the previous section by saying preserving sound judgment and discernment will keep your foot from being snared. With his next breath, he says to not withhold good from those who deserve it when it is in your power to act. Rather than being two separate topics, this is a continuation of the previous topic and gives the first example of letting sound judgment and discernment out of your sight. If someone withholds from others, it becomes much easier to move on to the next step and then the next step and so on, until that person ends up on the last step in the land of the perverse. Seeing how this works, we should take a closer look so we won't put our foot in the snare.

There are several assumptions we need to address.

- **We may know a deserving person who could use some help.** What does it mean to be "deserving"? We likely would think of someone who has tried hard to provide for his family, working extra shifts or going to school at night to increase his advancement potential. Or maybe he suffered a sudden setback, illness, or tragedy in his life. Whatever it is, he is doing all he can to cope and get back onto the good path, but he is coming up short in some way.
- **We know this person well enough to know what good would be helpful to them.** While we usually think giving money is the good this person needs, and it may well be, the good could include things like groceries, babysitting, house cleaning, yard maintenance, car maintenance, or any number of other things.
- **We have, or can provide, the needed good.** Because we have the power to do it, providing the good doesn't seem to impact us very much.

A person with sound judgment will go ahead and provide the good he can. He wants to encourage the deserving person to stay on the good path he has taken. He also understands someday the shoe may be on the other foot and he may need help from others. Finally, he knows that the LORD looks favorably on those who show love and faithfulness and trust in God's leading to provide for others. He looks at the situation and provides what he can to the deserving person.

The thought process for the person without discernment and sound judgment is completely different. You can almost hear the questions he will ask: "Is this person really deserving?" "Does he really need something?" "What will happen to me if I provide this good to him?" "What happens if he needs more?" Although it is apparent he could and should help, he looks for a way to "withhold" what he easily could give for another's benefit. By doing so, Solomon says he has placed his foot into a snare, one that might not be obvious for a while but a snare nonetheless. For having turned away from this opportunity to help someone, he has taken a first step away from love, faithfulness, and trust. More steps in that direction and he eventually will be described as wicked, a Mocker, and a Fool.

But a word of caution: We have to use our discernment and sound judgment to know if someone is deserving and in discerning the needed good. This knowledge may be easy to obtain, especially if you know the person well or if you have trustworthy friends who know the person and situation well. But the further removed from someone's situation you are, the more difficult it becomes to know if a person is deserving and what their true need is. In too many situations, people have given one type of good when the person really needed another type of good—resulting in waste and unmet need—or given things to people who don't deserve to be helped.

One classic example is the friend or relative who keeps asking for and getting money from you and others. While there may be a need, if he created the need by wasteful spending, is giving him more money the answer? Not really. If you keep giving him money, the cycle will keep going and no one will be better off. Instead, wouldn't it be better to find out the real need and provide it? For example, if the need is helping him achieve financial discipline and wisdom and you have the ability to provide it yourself or through others, then by all means deliver it. You will have used discernment and sound judgment to meet the real need; everyone will be better off.

Solomon could have provided more examples but he stopped at five to show us the progression—from withholding, to holding, to plotting, to accusing, to harming through violence—and how a person can move from being wise to being evil. Here are some examples of choices you make where sound judgment and discernment are crucial:

- Your choice of friends and the time you spend with them.
- The type of work you do, your clients, and for whom you work.
- Staying single or marrying and, if marrying, the person you wed.
- Where you choose to worship.
- The kind of lifestyle you lead.

By using sound judgment and discernment in each of these areas, you will have entered into the courts of the righteous, humble, and wise enjoying blessings on your house, God's grace, and honor.

If you don't know someone like this, you really are missing out. For these folks care about others and willingly share their blessings. The quickest way to find someone like this is to start attending an active Bible-believing church. While a wide spectrum of people may be attending the church, you'll likely run into several people exhibiting a form of grace, wisdom, and peace different from anything you have experienced. Hang out with them as much as you can and you'll find they have a lot of wisdom to share. If you accept their wisdom, and Solomon's, you will be taking positive steps toward becoming the upright person the LORD loves.

Proverbs

Chapter Four

Chapter 15

Listen to the Voice of Experience
Proverbs 4:1-9

Listen, my sons, to a father's instruction; pay attention and gain understanding. I give you sound learning, so do not forsake my teaching. When I was a boy in my father's house, still tender, and an only child of my mother, he taught me and said, "Lay hold of my words with all your heart; keep my commands and you will live. Get wisdom, get understanding; do not forget my words or swerve from them. Do not forsake wisdom, and she will protect you; love her, and she will watch over you. Wisdom is supreme; therefore get wisdom. Though it cost all you have, get understanding. Esteem her, and she will exalt you; embrace her, and she will honor you. She will set a garland of grace on your head and present you with a crown of splendor."

Background/Circumstances

For the fourth time in Proverbs, Solomon tells his son—"sons" in this section—to listen and pay attention to the instruction, sound learning, and teaching he has given. If he does, he will gain understanding, a very valuable commodity. In case his words about wisdom and understanding aren't good enough, Solomon tells his sons to listen to what their grandfather David—in those times *the* hero of the Israeli nation—said about wisdom and understanding. Solomon clearly remembers David's words about wisdom and understanding and passes them on to his son.

Although kingly duties required a good amount of time, David must have set aside time to teach Solomon. By the time Solomon reached a teachable age, David would have been in his late 50s or early 60s. David's life was an eventful one. He experienced lots of mountain-top and valley experiences, especially as Israel's king. While he strayed from God's law—some of the straying and results were absolutely horrible—he was quick to acknowledge his sins before the LORD and repent. (See Psalm 51 for an example.) Because of his ongoing pursuit of a personal relationship with the LORD, throughout the Bible David is known to be a "man after God's own heart." Accordingly, David's teachings, instructions, and songs point to a closer relationship with the LORD he knew and loved. Anyone else who was receptive to David's words could use them to draw closer to the LORD.

Solomon was receptive. David talked to Solomon when he was young and malleable. "Tender," the term used, is a beautiful way to describe those few years in a young person's life when they are most open to being influenced by a parent. In addition, as his mother's only living child, she deeply would have loved Solomon. This is especially true when you consider the events leading up to Solomon's birth.

Looking out from the roof of his palace one day, David notices Bathsheba bathing on her nearby roof, a somewhat transparent invitation for David to send for her. David sends for Bathsheba and brings her into his bedroom. Soon, she sends word to David that she is pregnant. Trying to hide what was illegal, and could result in David's and Bathsheba's deaths, David calls Bathsheba's husband, Uriah—one of David's great friends—back from the war he has been fighting for several months and encourages him to go to bed with his wife. Because the men fighting the war are not able to be with their wives, Uriah refuses to sleep in a nice bed with his wife and sleeps with the men outside on a mat. Hearing of this, David decides to get Uriah drunk so he'll go home and sleep with his wife. Although drunk, Uriah refuses to enjoy the comforts of home while the army is fighting elsewhere. David sends

Uriah back to the war along with a note to the commander. The note directs the commander to place Uriah where the fighting is most intense and then to order the withdrawal of his comrades so that Uriah will be killed by the opposing forces. The commander follows David's instructions and notifies David of Uriah's death.

David thinks he has gotten away with his dangerous tryst, but God knows and confronts David through the prophet Nathan. As part of God's judgment on David, Nathan tells David the son he has fathered through Bathsheba will die. David realizes his great sin, repents of it, and starts praying and fasting, hoping God will change His mind and let David's son live. Although David prays and fasts for seven days, on the seventh day the infant dies. In spite of their sin, God is gracious to David and Bathsheba—who marry after Uriah's death—and gives them another son, Solomon. Because of this history, David likely had special feelings for Solomon.

While we don't know how often David taught Solomon, we do know David's teachings on wisdom and understanding came during Solomon's tender years. We know those teachings affected Solomon because they show up in two ways:

1. **The comparison of David's teachings to Solomon's teachings in the first three chapters of Proverbs.** They are so similar Solomon can use David's teachings to support his own. The shared points are:
    - **Listen, pay attention, don't forget, and hold to my teachings.**
    - **Follow my teachings with all your heart and live.**
    - **Get wisdom and understanding; hold on to it with all you have.**
    - **Understand the incredible value of wisdom and understanding; nothing else compares to them.**
    - **Love wisdom and enjoy the protection it provides to you.**

- **Esteem and embrace wisdom and you will be exalted, honored, enjoy God's favor, and enjoy splendor.**

2. **When God tells Solomon to ask for anything he wants, Solomon asks for wisdom, a discerning heart, and knowledge so he can rule the nation well.** He could have asked for many other things such as wealth, riches, honor, death of his enemies, or a long life. Instead, he remembers the advice David gave him several years before: Wisdom is more valuable than anything else; give up everything you have to get it. So he asks for wisdom.

During his lifetime, David learned wisdom and understanding were supreme. When Solomon was ready to listen and learn, David took the time to teach Solomon the same thing: Do all you can to gain wisdom and understanding; they are supreme. After gaining wisdom and understanding, Solomon saw their value exceeded anything else he had or might want to have. Because Solomon understood wisdom's and understanding's exceedingly great value, he tells his son it will be worth whatever it costs to acquire wisdom and understanding. If his son will esteem and embrace wisdom, he will be exalted and honored before the nation.

Business Application

It should be obvious. You, your employees, and others would benefit greatly if you sought wisdom, a discerning heart, and knowledge.

Knowledge ensures you know what you need to know. But using only knowledge in your decision-making process leaves a lot to be desired. Based on my own experience, I can verify making decisions using only knowledge as the determining factor leads to sterile what's-best-for-the-company decisions. While those decisions may be good for the company's bottom line, it can be tragic for your employees.

Applying knowledge and a discerning heart uncovers previously unconsidered options and eliminates heartless options. As you consider the remaining options, you can weigh their impacts and rate the rightness or wrongness of each one. Having completed that work, you can apply your wisdom and select the best one.

Too many times, leaders fail to apply wisdom, a discerning heart, and knowledge in making their decisions. You can see the result of those failures in the daily headlines—product recalls, large fines, ongoing legal troubles, poor decisions, and poor employee relations. Incidents like these happen when we lock ourselves into one viewpoint and refuse to listen to others' viewpoints.

This happened to me. The city manager wanted me to gain experience with labor negotiations, so he assigned me to the team entering into negotiations with the firefighters. We started meeting a year before the contract renewal deadline. Not much happened in the first ten months: We met, chatted for an hour, and set a date for the next meeting. With the deadline approaching, our team placed our first offer on the table and the fireworks started! We went from genial to contentious in a few seconds. The next meeting was just as contentious, and it looked like we were heading toward impasse and arbitration.

Rather than declaring impasse, our team caucused. In order to understand the cost implications of the firefighters' proposal versus the city's proposal, I asked our Human Resources leader if she had prepared a cost-comparison worksheet I could review. To my amazement, the estimated three-year costs of the two proposals were essentially the same. The main difference was allocation of costs: Human Resources wanted it one way while the firefighters wanted it another way. After deciding allocation of costs didn't matter to the city, our team went back to the negotiating table and came to a tentative agreement with the firefighters within minutes.

Reflecting back on that experience, I see how each side was set on winning the negotiation by having its proposal accepted. As a result, neither side spent much time exploring the other's proposal; rather, each side was locked into convincing the other side its proposal was best. Exhibiting those mindsets, it's no wonder we kept talking past each other during the negotiation sessions. At the last minute, we relented and turned our eyes toward understanding the firefighters' proposal and viewpoint. Only then did we understand the reasoning behind the firefighters' preferred compensation mix. Once we understood their reasoning, we agreed with them and completed negotiations. We could have saved ourselves and the firefighters a lot of anxiety, acrimony, and time if both groups had taken a wiser approach at the beginning.

That's one example from my career. Trust me, there are several more. I learned a great deal from going through that experience. What about you? Do you keep having disruptive issues that could have been avoided if more wisdom, discernment, and knowledge had been applied? If so, you may have one of the following problems:

- **You took your eye off the ball and failed to use wisdom, discernment, and knowledge.** It happens to all of us. When it does, you have to realize the problem: You allowed your attention to be diverted elsewhere. To correct it, you have to refocus your attention back where it should be.
- **Wisdom, discernment, and knowledge are secondary in importance to you.** You esteem, value, love, and embrace other things more than you do wisdom, discernment, and knowledge. Unless you place wisdom, discernment, and understanding as your top priorities, your life will be plagued by compromise and shortcuts.

You can identify root causes of problems by doing your own analysis or using an experienced and wise group to help you with the assessment. As you do the analytical work, develop conclusions, implement corrective actions, and check on the results, make sure you integrate wisdom, discernment, and knowledge in every phase. Not only will you arrive at the best results, but you also will have the opportunity to do a complete reset within your company by highlighting the value you place on wisdom, discernment, and knowledge.

Personal Application

Isn't it interesting Solomon veers from relating his global thoughts on wisdom to insert a personal testimonial from David, his father and his son's grandfather? Why now? I can think of a few possibilities:

- Solomon wants to add a personal touch, relating his own experience with his father. David took time to talk to Solomon about the importance of wisdom; Solomon is doing the same for his son. David talked to Solomon when he was young and still tender. Solomon may be emulating his father, giving his son advice while he is still young and tender.
- Solomon never forgot the impact David's words had on him and the unbelievable blessings—wisdom, riches, and honor—he received by following them. Because he wants his son to experience the same blessings, Solomon passes on the exact same advice David gave him.
- Sometimes a grandchild will listen more attentively to a grandparent. Solomon is using David's words to add credence to the advice he is giving his son.

Of course, it could have been all three of these (wise people are like that). So what can we take away from this? I think there are several things. Wise parents will:

- **Talk to their children about the important things of life (wisdom, discernment, knowledge, etc.) while they are young and tender.** This implies parents have developed wisdom, discernment, and knowledge themselves and are determined to present it to their children. Being intentional is much better than letting this parental responsibility slide. Wise parents know they have to begin this instruction while the children are young and tender. At some point, the child will no longer be young and tender and the best opportunity for teaching will have passed.

- **Use positive language.** Look at the number of positive statements Solomon makes in this section—"listen," "pay attention," "gain understanding." It continues through "lay hold," "keep," and "get." Even the "do not" phrases are positive invitations to hold on to Solomon's teachings. The last two—"esteem" and "embrace"—create a new image; wisdom, like a person, can be esteemed and embraced.
- **Use examples of the times they received and used wise counsel.** While lessons can be learned from others, a story involving people you know adds color, makes it memorable, and creates a living example of wise living. The best stories are repeated time and again, continuing to drive home the point with each telling.
- **Incorporate the grandparents into the development of the grandchildren.** Parents are with their children a lot and get tied up in bedtime, meals, baths, and a myriad of other daily details. A family's life can be very rushed. But grandparent and grandchild time together is much different. Daily details may intrude, but their time together is much more relaxed. During their time together, a grandchild will bring up a topic that gives the grandparent(s) an opportunity to teach a young and tender child and impart wisdom.

Most grandparents provide helpful guidance and the children's parents can trust them to do so. An exception requires parents to exercise wisdom. Perhaps an open discussion with the grandparents will solve the matter. If that doesn't work, one of the parents may have to be present anytime the grandparent is around the grandchildren. If all else fails, you may have to limit severely or discontinue grandparent-and-grandchild interaction. Tough talk, but the parents' primary responsibility is to their young and tender children.

Talking to your children about important issues isn't a "one-and-done" proposition. You need to continue discussions throughout their childhood and teen years and into adulthood. Keep discussions positive and a child is more likely to listen to you. Keeping discussions positive is a challenge; kids will frustrate you and make you mad. While the temptation is to lash out at them, wisdom and understanding argue for a different course—you may be in one of your child's young and tender teachable moments.

While it is good for you to talk to your children about wisdom and understanding, your life must align with your teaching. Kids are the very best at comparing your words to your actions and letting you know when they don't match up. Solomon would have known about the wrong David did. He also would have known about David's love for God, how quickly David recognized his sin against God, David's total repentance, and how David strove to reestablish his personal relationship with God. When Solomon compared David's actions to his words, David's heart for God stood out.

As it was then, so it is now. Your kids, and grandkids, will be listening to your words and observing your actions to see if they match. Of course, you will make mistakes; we all do. The question is whether you will have a heart like David's. If you do, you will acknowledge your mistakes, make things right, and use them as teaching opportunities. Chances are, your kids will never forget those lessons.

As a parent, you have so much to offer to your children. Because you have had to do it, you can help them navigate life. You can point them to wisdom and understanding and help them acquire it. You can equip them to be right, just, and fair so they can gain the blessings from being upright and blameless. Do all those things and your children and grandchildren will honor you for the rest of their lives.

Chapter 16

Choose and Follow Wise Advisors
Proverbs 4:10-19

Listen, my son, accept what I say, and the years of your life will be many. I guide you in the way of wisdom and lead you along straight paths. When you walk, your steps will not be hampered; when you run, you will not stumble. Hold on to instruction, do not let it go; guard it well, for it is your life. Do not set foot on the path of the wicked or walk in the way of evil men. Avoid it, do not travel on it; turn from it and go on your way. For they cannot sleep till they do evil; they are robbed of slumber till they make someone fall. They eat the bread of wickedness and drink the wine of violence. The path of the righteous is like the first gleam of day. But the way of the wicked is like deep darkness; they do not know what makes them stumble.

Background/Circumstances

Once again, Solomon talks about the benefits his son will receive if he listens to and accepts Solomon's words, guidance, leadership, and instruction. But it's not all on Solomon. His son has to walk and run on the right path—never veer off it—and hold on to and guard Solomon's instructions. When he does those things, these benefits occur:

- **The years of his life will be many.** In that day, a long life was considered to be proof of God's favor. Not only will his son be blessed, but others also will know he is blessed because of his long life.

- **His path will be a straight one with no obstacles to hamper him.** Because Solomon's son is using wisdom, he will choose the good path and obstacles on the road won't stop him.
- **He can run and not stumble.** This path is so smooth his son will be able to run as fast as he can. Because this path is straight, his son will be able to see and avoid potholes or bumps that could cause him to lose his balance.
- **Wise living will be his life.** Solomon's son will like and enjoy the benefits of following wisdom. By holding on to and guarding wisdom, his son will continue on the good path.

Solomon reminds his son of the two ways he could get off track: 1) start down a wicked path or 2) walk in the way of evil men. As it is described here, setting foot on a path is an intentional act, a choice made to turn from one path and enter another. It's interesting to note it is the "way" of evil men rather than the "ways" of evil men. No matter the methods used, which could be many, there really is only one way for evil men—to do evil. The obsession is so strong, they can't sleep until they have done something to somebody, up to and including violence. No wonder Solomon tells his son to avoid this path. Instead, his son's intentional choice should be to turn away from the evil path and speed ahead on the good path.

Finally, Solomon gives a beautiful word picture describing the different outcomes for the righteous compared to the wicked. For the righteous, this path is a beginning, dim like dawn, but as time goes along and the sun rises, everything about life becomes completely clear. It's a different picture for the wicked; the darkness they live in is so dark—absent even the tiniest light—that they can't identify what causes them to stumble.

Business Application

This section raises a few questions related to wise counsel. Let's take a look at them.

1. **How do you know the counsel you are receiving is wise?** During my career, I received advice from bosses, peers, employees, attorneys, consultants, vendors, government officials, and a host of others. A good deal of the advice related to the technical aspects of my job. Because accounting and other technical standards were in place, it was relatively easy for me to determine whether a technical advisor was giving good advice. Other advisors provided soft skills instruction (e.g., communicating effectively with others) I needed to be a successful supervisor. Much of their advice was based on well-documented work adapted to our specific industry. Again, standards were in place and I could determine whether their advice was good advice.

   But one type of advice—words to the wise—was completely different. How so? Usually, the advice came in a one-on-one setting, such as a closed-door formal meeting, a luncheon, or a pull-aside in the hall. I could tell right away this talk was going to be different; the counselor's mood was serious. What he had to say was important. In every case, the counselor had some wisdom he wanted to share with me. I'm sure you've experienced similar meetings and counseling, too.

The rub is how to evaluate this words-to-the-wise counseling. What makes some counseling wise and other counseling just garbage? This passage provides the standards you can use to evaluate counseling you receive. Wise counsel will:

- **Guide you in the way of wisdom.** To meet this standard, counseling needs to move you toward sound judgment, discernment, knowledge, and the other attributes of wisdom. Rather than give you an answer, the best counselors guide you along so you better understand how to use sound judgment and discernment. These counselors will help you deal with the short-term matter, but they are concerned more with developing your wisdom.
- **Lead you along straight paths.** These counselors help you see obstacles in your way. They help you understand and minimize them. Obstacles can take on many forms. While often about aspects of work to be done, wise counselors help us address the obstacles created by our attitudes and actions, whether intentional or unintentional. That counseling is hard to give and harder to take. But if following that counseling makes things better for you, it is wise counsel.
- **Allow you to go forward unhampered and keep you from stumbling.** Wise counseling helps you understand what is holding you back and frees you from burdens you've been carrying. With understanding, you'll see and address potential problems well in advance. With a lighter load, you'll be able to maneuver more easily.

Poor counsel will fail in one or more of these areas. Poor counsel may recommend actions or thinking that soils your character. Poor counsel may take you down a path that seems okay, but obstacles start showing up fairly soon. This poor counsel may result in more burdens being placed on you, making it harder for you to do your job. Poor counsel may limit your foresight, with new developments continually surprising you. If the advice you get leads you down any of these paths, reject it and seek wise counsel.

2. **What do you *do* with wise counseling?** This can be much harder than *getting* wise counsel. While you may seek wise counsel, some wise counsel shows up unsought and unannounced. It may be unwanted, too. Rejecting unsought wisdom may be your first reaction, but you should consider it—someone cared enough to give it to you. Once you've determined their advice is wise counsel, take these actions:

- **Listen to and accept the advice.** In the moment, listening to good advice can be difficult because it points out one or more of your flaws. Although rarely an enjoyable experience, if you can set aside your feelings and listen, you will see your advisor is offering you something of great value. If listening to wise advice is hard, accepting wise advice is harder. Accepting wise advice means you have agreed you have to make a change. Although making the necessary adjustments may be difficult and trying, you'll be better off for making the changes. Compare that to those who refuse to accept wise advice. In rejecting wise advice, they often double down on their behavior, becoming more and more hardened in their ways.
- **Let those with wisdom help you along the way.** If the counselor cares enough to take you aside to tell you something, he likely is willing to mentor you and help you make needed corrections.
- **Hold on to wise advice and keep up your guard against losing it.** A wise advisor will pass along a great deal of his wisdom, including how to make sound judgments and use discernment. Having absorbed his wisdom, you may think you can stop your wisdom work. But, beware! Wisdom can be lost if you fail to:
    - **Grasp wisdom tightly and hold on to it.** Do you remember coming back to school after summer break and being surprised you had forgotten so much from the prior year? With a short review, you likely remembered what you

had learned. Over the summer, you paid attention to other things and let some of your knowledge slip out of your hands. Letting go of wisdom is very similar. Unless you are intentional about preserving wisdom, you will begin to lose it.

- **Guard wisdom.** A variety of enticers will assail your sound judgment and discernment. They will attack your character, what you believe, and how you act. Knowing those attacks are coming, you must keep your guard up against them. Letting your guard down lets the enticers tear away at your sound judgment and discernment until your defenses are breached and defeat is at hand.

What a great and valuable gift wise counsel is. Besides giving wisdom and understanding, it provides great benefits like straight paths, unhindered steps, and no stumbling. In contrast, unwise counsel is worthless. It leads you into a deep darkness where you'll stumble around without knowing why. Between the two types of counsel, wouldn't you rather choose wise counsel?

Personal Application

Isn't it amazing how many movie scripts could be based on the lessons in this section? Here are a few themes you might recognize:

- A good-hearted lad follows his father's or grandfather's good advice, overcomes adversity, and emerges from a gloomy existence to one full of promise.
- A good-hearted lad goes along doing right, is led astray by a friend, and sees the error of his ways before it's too late. He rejects his friend's advice and steps back into the good life he had before.

- A lad gets in with the wrong crowd, learns their evil ways, and resolves to outdo them all. As a result, he becomes more and more evil and hurts or kills people with little or no reason. Eventually, he finds himself in a situation that he can't get out of and perishes.

While I expect few, if any, writers have read and used this section of Proverbs as the genesis of their overall storylines, their narratives align well: Those who follow good advice get good outcomes while those who follow bad advice get bad outcomes. Nevertheless, the writers' stories usually include characters contemplating advice they've been given and wondering "Is this wise advice?" Sometimes it's obvious to the reader whether the advice is wise. Most of the time, the reader won't find out until later in the story whether the advice was wise or unwise.

That's the way it is in life. Most advice doesn't come with a tag that says "Wise" or "Unwise." For example, take diet advice. You can find multitudes of dietary advice, what to eat, how much to eat, when to eat it, what combinations are best, and so on. Some of the advice is based on years of research and is pretty good to follow. Some advice is based on one person's experience. That advice might help some people, but many won't find it helpful at all. Some advice is so bad, if you follow it for long, you may be putting your long-term health at risk.

Choosing a diet is one important decision for you to make, but there are many others. Although you have many decisions to make in your life, Solomon implores you to carefully consider the one decision that will affect the entire trajectory of your life: Will you listen to and follow through on wise counsel?

Hearing good advice isn't enough; you have to hear it, accept it, cling to it, and guard it. Does that expectation seem too big? I think not. You likely have a story about a piece of good advice you received that changed how you thought and acted from then to now. Let me give you an example from my life.

My father ran a meat counter in a small Kansas grocery store in the late 1960s. One day, an infrequent customer came in to buy a string-tied roast. After some friendly banter back and forth between my dad and the customer, including the old thumb-on-the-scale gag, the customer paid his bill, took his roast, and walked out of the meat counter area. In a moment I'll never forget, my dad turned to me and, in language I won't repeat here, told me that skin color doesn't determine whether a person is good or not. Having grown up in a rural setting void of people of color, that one sentence, as well as the teachings of Martin Luther King Jr., helped crystalize my thinking about people and racial differences. I found my dad's piece of wisdom so valuable that I accepted it, clung to it, and guarded it well ever since.

My dad's advice was worth holding on to because it fit the definition of good advice: It leads you on straight paths, lets you walk unhampered, and keeps you from stumbling. In my work world, and my personal life, knowing and evaluating people individually rather than by skin color—or other immaterial things—has been a blessing in my life. In many instances, I gained a better, though not complete, understanding of where others were coming from.

For example, I still reflect, with amazement, on a conversation I heard between two peers, who were only a year older than I. One had graduated from the city's all-white high school while the other had graduated from the city's all-black high school, both in the early 1970s. During the conversation, they compared their experiences growing up. One had complete freedom of movement; the other knew, from a young age, if he stayed on the bus past a certain street, there was a high chance he would be beaten. While I will never understand what it was like to live in the segregated South, after that conversation I understood more than I had before and gained new wisdom.

How well are your "wisdom" antennae working? Have you honed your ability to determine what is wise counsel? If you need any help, Solomon gives great guidelines: Wise counsel leads to straighter paths, an unhampered journey, and no stumbling. Eventually, wise counsel leads to a longer life. And, in a beautiful word picture, wise counsel brings in the first rays of hope, which leads to overwhelming brightness—something like having the dirt in your life washed away until you are completely clean.

That's the way with wise counsel; it leads you to your best life. So pay close attention to the wise counsel you receive. You will be well served to accept it, follow it, and never let it go. Then the movie of your life will be filled with wisdom, devotion to that wisdom, and a truly blessed life—a life full of sunny, beautiful days.

Chapter 17

Above All Else, Guard Your Heart
Proverbs 4:20-27

My son, pay attention to what I say; listen closely to my words. Do not let them out of your sight, keep them within your heart; for they are life to those who find them and health to a man's whole body. Above all else, guard your heart, for it is the wellspring of life. Put away perversity from your mouth; keep corrupt talk far from your lips. Let your eyes look straight ahead, fix your gaze directly before you. Make level paths for your feet and take only ways that are firm. Do not swerve to the right or the left; keep your foot from evil.

Background/Circumstances

In the prior section, Solomon said accepting, practicing and holding on to wisdom will keep his son from stumbling, while those who reject wisdom stumble around but don't know why. In this section, Solomon reviews six actions to avoid as doing them will cause one to stumble:

- **Letting wise words slip out of your sight.** People tend to become distracted by or latch on to the idea of the moment. In order to avoid forgetting about wisdom, Solomon tells his son to make these words more than a bunch of wise sayings; he should accept and make them the force that drives his life. Momentary lapses will disappear.

- **Failing to guard our heart.** Once wisdom is in his heart, Solomon's son can stumble by not guarding it. If his son isn't careful, he can let other conflicting ideas lodge in his heart. The resulting internal conflict will affect his life and health. Placing a strong guard to keep conflicting ideas from ever getting in is the best defense.
- **Allowing perversity and corrupt talk to come from your lips.** Talk reflects what is in your heart. By controlling how you speak, you also control what is in your heart. If the speech is wrong, so is the thought. Moving toward corrupt and perverse talk will reveal unwise ideas are taking root and affecting Solomon's son.
- **Looking somewhere else besides where wisdom leads you.** Once the corrupt and perverse thoughts become strong enough, his son will be tempted to let his eyes wander toward seemingly more attractive things. Solomon is pointing out the grass isn't greener on the wayward side so his son should keep his eyes on living a wise life rather than pining for other things.
- **Making trouble for ourselves.** If Solomon's son goes the wrong way, he will start seeing self-made obstacles looming before him where there were no obstacles before. If he engages in questionable activities, he is going to create problems for himself—a smooth path will become a rougher and harder path to travel. Solomon tells his son not to go there, because he would be setting himself up for a fall.
- **Taking the first step toward wrong.** The fall will come when Solomon's son takes the first step toward the evil he has been considering. His son needs strong guardrails in place to keep him from swerving to the right or the left—the son, and we, can get off the path either way.

Note the progression: Letting wisdom out of your sight leads to lowering the guard around your heart, perverse and corrupt talk, heading toward things better left alone, and trouble.

Business Application

Unethical and illegal behaviors can be difficult to catch in real time. But according to Solomon, unethical and illegal behaviors have a starting point and a series of tells that occur before a person commits unethical and illegal acts.

In order to protect yourself, your business, your employees, and others, you need to think about and implement ways to discern what's going on with your key personnel. Because you are busy working through your normal business problems, it's easy to miss these signs of impending trouble. After trouble comes and you are doing your review of what went wrong, you will wonder how you could have missed the subtle signs indicating trouble was brewing. You'll kick yourself for not paying enough attention.

To keep yourself from having to kick yourself repeatedly, let's take a closer look at trouble indicators and what you can do to catch issues before real trouble happens. I like to use extremes to prove a point. So, to examine how this works, in the following example we'll use a most trusted employee, the one who has been with the company a long time and understands better than anyone else the corporate culture.

Candance has never been a problem, but lately, there have been a few instances when she was distracted and failed to live up to her previously impeccable performance. It wasn't something you noticed; rather, she came and told you where she had messed up. She recited the applicable rules and indicated where she failed. Because the problem was identified, reported, and corrected—with no work on your part—and you had lots of other things to do, you let it drop.

But you may want to think again. Sudden fluctuations in Candance's performance could be an early indication she is starting to take her eye off the ball. When sudden performance fluctuations begin, you need to ask Candance a few questions. How did this happen? When and how did you discover it? What have you changed to make sure it won't happen again? You need to discover whether Candance was: 1) conscientious and erred or 2) uncharacteristically careless. If you determine Candance was uncharacteristically careless, you may want to start looking for the next sign.

The next sign will be reflected in subtle changes in Candance's life. Little, if anything, has changed in her work performance, but she is acting differently than she did not too long ago. This change can show itself in any number of ways: not as enthusiastic as before, quieter than normal, subdued, taking positions that are slightly different than before, and so on. It's as if there is an alien living in her that is starting to affect her behavior. In a way, there is. Because of a work grievance, real or perceived, Candance begins questioning whether the company is looking out for her. While Candance still holds on to corporate culture and all that it entails, she has let opposing words, thoughts, and ideas into her heart. The internal conflict she is beginning to experience is reflected by these behavior changes. Candance is now of two minds.

While these behavior changes have been somewhat subtle, now Candance starts talking about things in a different way. Her language may inch toward becoming coarse, crude, and uncomfortable. The person you knew before has added an edge to some of her comments. She may start joking, suggesting things that she never would have suggested before. In an extreme case, where before Candance's language would have been rated "suitable for children," the rating has changed for the worst, trending toward "adult only" conversation. A change in language like this is something not to be ignored. Such a change may indicate some dramatic change is taking place within Candance and new words, thoughts, and ideas are winning. From here, the next three steps can happen in rapid order.

Candance, rather than thinking of what she can do to advance the company's goals, begins thinking about what she needs to do to advance her own career or take advantage of the company. Rather than placing these self-advancement thoughts in their proper place below achieving company goals, Candance begins to dwell on self-advancement more and more. While it is unlikely Candance will tip her hand at this stage, her work may be affected as she spends more time actively considering what she wants and how to get it. She may seem distracted at times. If you interrupt her thoughts, you might get an embarrassed, overreaction explanation for her inattentiveness. If you walk away thinking, "I wonder what that was all about," you're on the right track.

What's next? Candance moves from contemplation to preparation. Depending on what she intends to do, this step may involve obtaining information from key personnel, gaining access to areas normally off limits to her, seeking out and enlisting other employees who may want to help her, and recommending or making procedural changes needed to ensure her plan succeeds. With all these preparations, Candance is starting to tread on dangerous territory and, if discovered, she may have a difficult time explaining away all of the circumstantial evidence against her. Then again, knowing Candance, she will have a good explanation for everything, explanations you are likely to accept from such a trusted employee.

Finally, Candance is faced with the final step: putting her plan into action. At this juncture, Candance may have second thoughts. She knows once she puts her plan into motion there is no turning back. A little voice may be whispering in her ear telling her to turn away from what she has planned. However, with all her preparations completed, Candance is more likely to take a "damn the torpedoes and go full speed ahead" attitude and launch her attack. Once she starts, she won't stop. She will have gone over to the dark side.

Though fictional, this example tracks closely to real situations I've faced. In several cases, internal control sensors indicated a potential problem and we closed it before anyone exploited that weakness. In two of those cases, internal controls failed but watchful employees detected wrongdoing. We stepped in and stopped the wrongdoing with minimal losses. In one instance, a trusted employee covered his tracks well for a long time and took more than a million dollars before we caught him. Though I've described embezzlements, a partial list of unethical and illegal behaviors includes thief of company property, personal use of company property, bribery, back-door deals, falsification of records, hiding safety issues, and making untrue statements.

You can trace every one of these unethical and illegal behaviors back to an employee who failed to preserve wisdom, who let doing what is right, just, and fair out of his sight. Because you never know if or when an employee is going toward the dark side, you need to notice when any of these six indicators begin flashing and thoroughly explore the possibility foul play is going on.

Personal Application

Does this slide from "paragon of virtue" to "doer of dastardly deeds" look familiar to you? It should. Several prominent people have fallen from being classified as a great saint to a great sinner. We usually think their dastardly deeds took place "in a moment of weakness." In reality, the moment of weakness was preceded by all of the steps Solomon gives us. The sixth step—the decision to do wrong in the moment of weakness—would never have taken place if the prominent person had stopped at any one of the prior five steps. Because they didn't heed the warning signs right in front of them, the story of their fall is a sad one.

You can probably think of friends or family who have taken a similar journey from high esteem to disgrace. We look at those situations and wonder how what happened ever happened. They have probably wondered the same thing.

The same holds true for us. When we've experienced a similar fall, we usually wonder how it happened. Some choose to make excuses and blame others; it wasn't their fault. But those who are honest with themselves will see they stopped paying attention to what they knew was right. Although Solomon is going to provide several situations in which his son must preserve his wisdom, I'll use stealing as an example now.

I doubt a previously pure person, in the spur of the moment, decides to grab a woman's purse and run away. The trip from purity to stealing isn't instantaneous; rather, it starts with a thought about stealing. If the thought is dismissed, that is the end of it. However, if it is allowed to linger, our pure person may start to think, "There is a little larceny in all of us," and accept it's okay to think about stealing from others. The person will start talking about stealing with some buddies and begin noticing things he would like to steal. From there, plans outlining how to go about stealing are made. Then the theft happens. It's a predictable pattern here and in other areas.

Knowing all of this, what can you do to protect yourself? The first, and best way, is to kick evil thoughts from your mind and your heart. When an evil thought comes around—and they do come around—don't dwell on it or give it an excuse to linger; impolitely throw it out! Put up a "no admittance" sign and enforce it! Once you allow an evil thought to get a foothold in your heart, the next steps become easier to take and resisting them becomes harder.

While not an evil thought, my thinking when it comes to replacing one of our vehicles can serve as an example of how this works. Although my spouse and I have had an agreement to buy new vehicles and hold on to them for at least fifteen years, I usually have a thought about getting a new car several years before our agreed-upon date. If I let it stick around, soon I'm talking about the deficiencies of the current vehicle and the need for replacing it. If my wife doesn't stop me there, I start thinking about what kind of vehicle I want next and start noticing those models when I see them. I'll start looking at vehicles available for sale and may talk to a salesperson, who feeds my desire for a new vehicle. Unless my wife stops me here—she has a few times—or the new-car fever breaks, I'll be at the car dealer within a few days trading in my still-good vehicle for a new one.

Replacing a vehicle may seem like a silly example, but the process described is exactly the one we use to get into all sorts of mischief. Substitute an evil desire of any sort for "vehicle" and the example isn't so silly anymore. For instance, we have a passing thought like "This isn't the spouse for me anymore," and if we dwell on it, we can find ourselves headed down a very similar path. Unchecked, bad things happen. It's how things occur in real life.

The second defense is to have a trustworthy person who serves as a checkpoint for you. It may be your spouse, a family member, or a close friend. Whoever that person is, he needs to be someone who is wise, listens well, and is willing to intervene to keep you from heading toward evil things. That trustworthy person is a jewel you should respect and keep. If you are really blessed, you'll have more than one such jewel in your circle of family and friends.

Although others may advise you, in the end it comes down to you and your willingness to follow Solomon's commands. Will you pay attention to wisdom, guard your heart, put away perversity, look straight ahead at worthwhile things, remove moral hindrances, and stay on the good path neither swerving left or right?

As we go through the next two chapters, it will become apparent why Solomon spent the first four chapters encouraging you to gain wisdom and understanding. You'll need all of that wisdom and understanding to withstand the temptations and folly coming your way.

Proverbs

Chapter Five

Chapter 18

Protection from an Almost Irresistible Enticer
Proverbs 5:1-6

My son, pay attention to my wisdom, listen well to my words of insight, that you may maintain discretion and your lips may preserve knowledge. For the lips of an adulteress drip honey, and her speech is smoother than oil; but in the end she is bitter as gall, sharp as a double-edged sword. Her feet go down to death; her steps lead straight to the grave. She gives no thought to the way of life; her paths are crooked, but she knows it not.

Background/Circumstances

In the previous section, Solomon went through the six steps one takes going from purity to evil. In this chapter, he uses the topic of adultery as an example of how one goes down that pathway.

As you may recall, the first two steps are not: 1) keeping your eyes on wisdom with your head and heart and 2) guarding your heart to keep evil thoughts from entering into your heart. The adulteress uses her speech to entice her victims to take their eyes off wisdom and let evil thoughts enter their hearts. Because she is a smooth talker and her pitch presents a sweet picture of how great things will be, the adulteress' speech is extremely seductive. You almost can hear her say, "Take a look at me! Wouldn't it be great to spend some time together?" It's a hard pitch to ignore, so Solomon alerts his son to this seductive woman and her ways.

Along with his warning, Solomon describes the real outcome from getting involved with the adulteress. Instead of getting honey, his son will end up with gall—a bitter herb—in his mouth. Instead of smooth oil, his son will get a sharp, double-edged sword—a lethal weapon—stuck into him resulting in his death. Rather than a sweet, smooth life portrayed by the adulteress, the son's life will be a bitter one that is destined for death.

Solomon knew adultery was a great evil. In addition to violating the marriage covenant one had made with their spouse, adultery was a direct violation of two of God's ten commands in Exodus, Chapter 20:

- **You shall not commit adultery.**
- **You shall not covet your neighbor's wife.**

As he wrote this, Solomon may have been thinking about David's adultery with Bathsheba, Solomon's mother. Although the law required David and Bathsheba to be stoned, God expressly forgave David and let him live. However, that didn't mean David escaped punishment; he didn't. Besides the death of the first child he fathered with Bathsheba, God told David two things would happen to him: 1) The sword would never depart from David's house and 2) someone in David's house would rise against him and lie with David's wives in a public place. And it was so. David had conflict throughout the rest of his time as king, and his son Absalom led a coup against David and made a public demonstration of sleeping with David's concubines. David's forces defeated Absalom, but David's rule was never the same.

Solomon would have been old enough to experience Absalom's attempted coup, hear about Absalom's treatment of the concubines, and observe the negative effect on David's leadership. Is it any wonder Solomon wants to warn his son about the adulteress?

I find it interesting that three of the five types of people are reflected in this section. Solomon is the Wise person, who is trying to guide the Young, his son, away from the folly of the Fool, the adulteress. We know his son is part of the Young because Solomon said his son needed to maintain discretion and preserve knowledge—two things Solomon told us the Young lack in the first few verses of Proverbs. We know the adulteress is like the Fool because she rejects knowledge—her paths are crooked—and she despises wisdom and discipline—gives no thought to the way of life. Unsaid, but strongly implied, is this thought: If the adulteress doesn't give much thought to the consequences she'll receive because of her lifestyle, she won't give any thought to what will happen to her victim.

Business Application

Bosses have a lot of responsibility to new employees, especially those new to the workforce. While they likely have the basic knowledge needed to do their job, for them to become the employee you want them to be, you need to ensure they learn technical and soft skills. As they advance and their work becomes more complex, you need to have a plan in place for them to develop the specialized knowledge and high-level management skills they will need to be successful. Like Solomon, you want your new employees to listen to your words of insight so they learn discretion and preserve knowledge.

How does learning take place in your company? Is it taught or caught? I think back to my first job out of college, auditing at a large public accounting firm. As a college graduate in accounting, I was expected to have a good understanding of accounting. However, my knowledge about specific accounting, legal requirements, and terminology related to the industries of the companies I would audit—banking, real estate trusts, nonprofits, trucking, and automobile dealers—was lacking. Knowing new hires would have little knowledge about auditing these companies, the firm had developed industry-specific auditing instructions for each auditing area. Those instructions gave us a step-by-step audit plan we could follow to ensure we properly audited the company and could say the company's financial statements were materially correct.

As you might expect, the auditing instructions were much more detailed for those areas most susceptible to misstatement. While those audit work programs were valuable, the company knew I needed onsite guidance, too. Accordingly, the firm assigned an experienced auditor who, besides doing his work, was there to answer my questions and immediately review my completed work.

Although the system was set up to teach me what I needed to know, it often missed the mark. Audit supervisors had their own audit work to perform within the audit hours allowed, leading to a heads-down-and-work environment. While my audit supervisors had good technical skills, many lacked the soft skills needed in a mentoring environment. Those factors and some faults of my own created an environment where I felt like I had to learn on my own, catching what I could. Maybe that environment works for others, but it didn't work well for me. As a result, my auditing career was fairly brief.

Over the years, I've worked with some great bosses. While I could go on and on about what made them great, for this discussion I'll focus on how they prepared me for a new task they wanted me to do. Like the audit programs I had, these bosses would provide some specifics about the work they wanted me to do. But they didn't stop there. The best bosses took fifteen to thirty minutes to talk to me about the situation and share background information I needed to know, their desired outcome, and potential landmines. Having that information upfront made a big difference for me. I could step into the situation with a head start on the right direction to take. More importantly, I was much more aware of potential problem areas and could bypass dangerous pathways or gird myself appropriately for those problems I couldn't bypass. Because I was better prepared for the project ahead of me, my "win" percentage was high and included several big, big wins for the company.

I've often wondered how my first job out of college would have gone differently if my supervisor had taken thirty minutes at the beginning of an audit to fill me in about the industry, the company, and anticipated audit problems. I would have had a better understanding of my role and my work. My employer would have benefitted from the improved quantity and quality of my work. The company's accounting personnel would have appreciated fewer interruptions and a new auditor who knew the basics about their industry. Everyone would have gained something from a thirty-minute overview.

Back to your business and bringing new employees into your company. You certainly can have an environment where you throw people into their work and hope they catch on. Some may do well in that environment and excel. However, others will develop serious, though initially unnoticed, flaws. An example of this is the basketball player who has dominated through high school and college, but when he gets to the pros, a weakness—such as poor free-throw shooting—becomes evident. Other teams will take advantage of that weakness and foul him rather than let him score an easy basket. Other teams will keep on fouling him until his free-throw shooting improves.

If you follow basketball, you know correcting a well-established flaw like free-throw shooting takes a lot of extra work. Even though a player puts in extra work, the player many fail to improve because the flaw is so ingrained. Others may improve for a while before slipping back to bad free-throw shooting habits. The poor free-throw shooting problem could have been avoided if someone had taught him the right free-throw shooting mechanics at the beginning.

Teaching proper free-throw shooting technique to a young basketball player usually makes them a better free-throw shooter for the rest of his career. In the same way, taking some time to guide a new employee into the work world almost always gives better results. Besides the typical technical and physical danger topics, you can instruct them on discretion, understanding, and wisdom, guiding them around pitfalls. Although it takes some effort and time on your part, in the end, everyone wins.

Personal Application

As much as we don't like to admit it, we can fall for a good story. The more innocent examples are practical jokes. The prankster comes up with a believable story to lead you along, handles any doubts you might have along the way, and catches you completely unaware at the last turn of events. The joke is on you. While you might be a little embarrassed you didn't catch on sooner—or even be temporarily mad at the prankster—everyone has a good laugh because no real harm was done and life goes on as it did before.

But that isn't the situation being described in this section. Rather, a deceiver, in this case the adulteress, is working to lure her victim into an addictive behavior that will destroy them both. The story she tells must be a good one—it is described as sweet and smooth. No doubt her story is enticing, mesmerizing, and seductive, intentionally designed to draw the son into the adulteress' web, one in which he will die.

Before we become too critical of the son and dismiss his lack of discipline, we should give thought to those things "too good to be true" for which we have fallen. We all have done this in one form or another. In the least harmless form, the inexpensive product we were enticed to buy failed to perform as promised, maybe breaking on first use. In its most harmful form, a person takes the bait and steps into a life of destructive habits. Although there are other examples, let's use the example of drugs.

When I was in high school, illegal drugs were becoming more available and popularized. Musicians, entertainers, and others of the "in-crowd" were talking about them—sometimes in code, sometimes not—and encouraging others to join in. Some of my friends dabbled in drugs for a while and got out before anything bad happened to them.

But others were hooked from the start; their lives changed for the worst. How to get drugs became the driving force in their lives, supplanting normal teenage activities associated with school, church, or friends. At that point, most came to their senses and sought help to escape the trap they had entered. The remaining few continued their downward spiral and ruined what their lives could have been.

Most of us have lived through some of these choices and come out the other side much wiser. We immediately can spot the too-good-to-be-true stories and skip around the seductive opportunities they offer. But what about our children? Like the son in Proverbs, they are young, inexperienced, and lacking discretion. They won't be able to tell when something sounds too good to be true and may be lured in.

That is where you come in. Because you have the experience and know to what your children might be susceptible, you are in a perfect position to provide wisdom and insights about life. When the children are very young, your wisdom could be "Don't accept rides from strangers" or "Keep your hands away from the fire." As they mature, parental wisdom and insights have to mature, too; otherwise, young adults will stop listening to you and turn to others—let's hope wise ones—who will talk about their mature problems. Like Solomon did with his son, you need to talk to your soon-to-be-adult about the allure of adultery and the associated consequences.

One interesting thing to me is Solomon doesn't discount how attractive this temptation is going to look to his son. He flat out tells his son it's going to look and sound great. Just as clearly, he tells his son about the ugly truth behind the curtain of false promises: Taking this path will lead to bitterness, pain, and death.

Solomon's model is a good one. You can use it to discuss topics with your young adults. It goes like this:

- I have something to talk to you about.
- You will have a choice to make in this area.

- Of the choices available, beware of the seductive ones that require you to compromise in some way.
- Taking the seductive choice will have these bad consequences.
- Stick to the things you have been taught and use wisdom to guide you.

Of course, the example Solomon gives is one of many topics to discuss with your young adults. If you compile a list, it might look daunting. Start thinking about the age at which to discuss each topic and you'll quickly understand why parenting takes courage, determination, and heavenly wisdom!

Let's be honest, in spite of your commitment to be a good parent, you are going to make mistakes. It's too easy to miss a topic needing to be discussed, or the right time for the discussion. If you put too much pressure on yourself to cover every single topic at the perfect time, you will tie yourself in knots and become a less-effective parent.

Solomon is setting an example for us in his letter to his son. Rather than come up with a long list of topics and writing a book for each one, Solomon picks out the major issues for which his son needs guidance. As he talks about them, Solomon continually points his son back to the most important issues of all—attaining wisdom and understanding, developing godly character, and making wise choices. Solomon wants his son to become a mature, righteous man.

You should desire the same for your children, grandchildren, students, and other youngsters. It's a wonderful thing to advise, guide, and watch young ones become mature and righteous men and women, individuals growing in wisdom and understanding, making great decisions, and passing on wisdom to the next generation. It's the kind of legacy you want to leave. Future generations will bless you!

Chapter 19

Don't Be Foolish and Give Your Best Away
Proverbs 5:7-14

Now then, my sons, listen to me; do not turn aside from what I say. Keep to a path far from her, do not go near the door of her house, lest you give your best strength to others and your years to one who is cruel, and your toil enrich another man's house. At the end of your life you will groan, when your flesh and body are spent. You will say, "How I hated discipline! How my heart spurned correction! I would not obey my teachers or listen to my instructors. I have come to the brink of utter ruin in the midst of the whole assembly."

Background/Circumstances

In the prior section, Solomon talked about the adulteress' seductive speech, how enticing it would be, and how the real result—disaster—was much different than the promises in her speech. He continues that discussion, telling his son(s) about the danger of playing with sin.

How is he playing with sin? Instead of staying far away from the adulteress, his son chooses to take a path going into her neighborhood. He thinks to himself, "If I keep a comfortable distance from the adulteress' house, what is the harm?" Because nothing bad happens as he walks through the neighborhood, the son's curiosity is piqued and he decides to take a path going much closer to her house. Again, nothing bad happens and he starts to wonder whether he should go right past her house. Solomon warns his son—going near the adulteress' house is the path to disaster. No, he hasn't gone into her house yet, but he is working his way through the steps leading to the evil actions Solomon described at the end of Chapter 4.

In his warning, Solomon describes the nature of the disasters awaiting his son should he flirt with passing by the adulteress' house. He will:

- **Give his best strength to others.** By going to her, his son will be wasting time and energy he could have spent on a more productive endeavor. He will divert his life from one of righteous living to one of increasing evil.
- **Be under the thumb of a cruel person.** Remember, the penalty for adultery was death by stoning. If the husband, or another person, becomes aware of this son's actions, the husband would have leverage over Solomon's son and could make his life a living hell.
- **Have strangers feast on his wealth.** With the leverage the cruel husband has over Solomon's son, he may demand the son forfeit his wealth rather than his life. It is also possible the adulteress will demand more and more material goods from him. Either way, the wealth the son had will go to others.
- **Work hard to enrich another man.** When his wealth becomes depleted, Solomon's son will be reduced to toiling for and enriching the cruel person's wealth. The son will be left with scraps and it appears he never will get relief.

Finally, at the end of his life, Solomon's son will spend a lot of time thinking about how wrong he was to reject wisdom, instruction, and discipline. He can see and feel the results of his folly. He will groan from the physical aches and pains he has brought onto himself. He will see he has come to the brink of utter ruin in all areas of his life—physical, financial, and social. The final humiliation? Everyone around him knows he behaved very foolishly and is suffering the consequences that come to the Fool.

Business Application

Taking advantage of unusual opportunities added spice to my career. As finance director for a Kansas city in the early '90s, I was responsible for placing the city's cash into various investments. At the time, interest rates were low, and State law restricted the city's investment options to a limited number of safe investments and maximum maturities of four years. We did all of the standard things to invest well and had a successful program in place.

One day, during our regular discussion about investing, the city's investment broker brought to my attention a potential investment in bank certificates of deposits, or CDs, that could benefit us. Typically, CDs have a three- to six-month interest penalty for early withdrawal. However, these CDs offered by smaller Kansas banks had no penalty for early withdrawal. In addition, they were paying higher rates than we could get with other investments. Because CDs were insured up to $100,000 by the FDIC, the broker recommended we invest in these CDs to earn more interest income until interest rates on other investments increased. When interest rates on our normal investments exceeded the interest rate on the CDs, we would redeem the CDs and reinvest our money into our normal investments.

It sounded good to me. After a few more discussions about how this idea would work, I authorized the purchase of twenty-seven CDs at $94,000 each. This assured the CDs value of principal plus earned interest never exceeded the FDIC insured amount. The idea worked exactly as envisioned. The city earned the higher rate of interest on the CDs for approximately two years. When interest rates for our normal investments rose higher than those we were receiving on the CDs, we redeemed the CDs and reinvested in other securities.

While these investments turned out to be a great opportunity benefitting our taxpayers, we rejected several other investment opportunities. The best example is the out-of-state broker/dealer who would call and talk about the great investment deals he could offer us. It didn't take very long in the conversation to understand the broker/dealer didn't know: 1) the investment restrictions placed on Kansas cities or 2) his proposed investment violated the law. Those phone calls didn't last very long; I had no appetite to violate State law!

In the business world, opportunities abound. That's a good thing as you can use your intellect and drive to evaluate and pursue the ones that appeal to you. Like the spectrum of allowed investments under State law, many opportunities clearly fall within the bounds of being okay. Those opportunities can vary from relatively safe ones with minimal risk to those that have considerable risk and require tremendous skill and effort to accomplish. Whether they are easy or hard to implement, they all are permissible and qualify as following the good path of legal and ethical business.

However, other opportunities edge into or embrace illegal or unethical realms. These options often are very attractive and seem lucrative. Unless you apply wisdom and understanding from the beginning, you may start flirting with the idea of taking the opportunity. You'll let it get lodged into your mind. From a distance, you'll look at it from different angles, thinking about how it might work. You may start talking about the opportunity with others, especially those who would be prone to encourage you to take the risk. As you edge closer and closer to accepting the opportunity, the easier it becomes for you to ignore the alarm bells ringing in your head. Suddenly, you find yourself at the door of accepting this illegal or unethical opportunity and reaching for the doorknob. What a dangerous place to be in!

A wise person does two things to keep from traversing in dangerous places:

- **A wise person knows to turn away from these kinds of opportunities from the very beginning.** No matter how attractive the opportunity looks, if there is any hint of something illegal or unethical, the wise person just says "no" and walks away.
- **A wise person keeps wise counselors around him and uses them.** Knowing he can miss things from time to time, a wise person will ensure he has other wise and discerning people around him who can and will appraise opportunities impartially. When the wise man is being unwise, his counselors will take him aside and impress upon him the dangers ahead.

If you are the boss, let me encourage you to find good counselors like these and use them.

If you aren't the boss and the boss becomes infatuated with a terrible business opportunity, this can be a touchy task. In situations where I've had this task, I looked for a time when I could pull the boss aside and talk to him in private, broaching the topic with as much tact as I could muster. While a touchy task, if you care about the company, it is a task you need to do. Otherwise, bad choices will be made that can endanger the company and result in, to name a few, loss of great employees, takeovers, reduced profits, and legal action or fines.

When those outcomes start to happen, the wailing starts. "How did we get here?" "Why didn't we see this coming?" "Why didn't someone speak up?" By then, it's too late. Despite everyone's efforts to change the outcome, because of the decisions made long before, the outcome is a foregone conclusion. In extreme examples, everyone will get to see your dirty laundry and you'll become a symbol of that particular evil. A good example might be Enron. Although Enron did many good things, in many people's minds Enron and fraud always will be synonymous.

It's worth repeating. The steps to get to that point start off innocently enough. Going about your business, you spot an enticing, but bad, opportunity and set your gaze on it. Ignoring the little warnings ringing in your head, you spend more time thinking and talking about it. Somehow what you are supposed to do starts to lose its luster as you put more effort into this new idea. As you turn off those pesky internal alarm bells, you move closer and closer to ditching your standards. Finally, no matter what the cost may be, you step away from wisdom's protection and jump headlong into folly. It's the Fool's errand, and those who take it will suffer.

Don't let that be you! Don't listen to those who try to entice you to their evil ways. Make sure you have a wise group of counselors in place and use them. Your collective wisdom will keep you from going down that attractive but disastrous path. With these opportunities, it's better to miss out than mess up.

Personal Application

It's a common tale. A good guy (or gal) is doing all the right things and has a wonderful job, family, and friends. All who know him speak about how wonderful he is and wish they could be more like him. Then, to everyone's surprise and bewilderment and especially his family's disbelief, he tosses aside what he has so he can be with someone else. As the pieces of the puzzle come together and the timeline is put together, it becomes apparent the affair started when the guy took more than a passing notice of the other woman.

She is different and exciting. Soon, she starts to consume his thoughts. He reciprocates her little signals with signals of his own. Before long, they are running into each other a lot, enjoying each other's company with a tinge of naughtiness adding to the excitement of being together. At last, they meet in a more private location, one making intimacy not only possible but also likely. With the final leap into folly complete, he goes about destroying his prior life so he can have his new one. But, as he deals with the fallout of his decisions and takes a clear-headed look at what he has done, the new life doesn't look so good. In fact, he is becoming more and more miserable. His family is gone, as are his friends who can't stomach what he has done. His reputation is shot and people no longer respect him.

As Solomon does in these verses, we tend to focus on sexual sin because it is so foolish and such a betrayal. Foolish because one is taking a huge risk with outcomes likely to be bad. A betrayal because a solemn promise made before God and witnesses is broken willingly. In Solomon's letter, the son's flirtation with the adulteress serves as an excellent example demonstrating the steps one takes from acting wisely to becoming foolish (see the article on the last part of Chapter 4).

But it's not the only example. If you think about your life, you probably can come up with an example of where you slipped from wise to unwise thinking or behaviors. If you can't come up with one, here are a few real-life examples for you to consider:

- Losing your best friend by sharing with others an intimate and embarrassing secret she told you in strictest confidence.
- Turning an ally into an enemy by stealing the credit for their project's success.
- Deepening your financial crisis by spending more and more when you can't afford what you already have.
- Drowning your sorrows in an alcoholic binge.

If those don't ring a bell for you, just look at today's headlines. You'll likely find one or more stories about the "good" person who descended into "bad" behavior. This rogues' gallery includes just about any type of person you can think of: public official, employee, business owner, pastor, husband, wife, family member, friend, average Joe, etc. Bad behavior ranges from mildly bad—if there is such a thing—to shockingly bad—you can provide your own list of these. You read those headlines, shake your head in disgust, and wonder how it ever happened to them.

Their exploits should be cautionary tales for you. You, too, have weaknesses, ones that if left unchecked could take you down a similar path. Then the sensational story would be about you, all on full display for everyone to see.

Knowing all of this, wouldn't it be better for you to walk the straight and narrow path all of the time? It would. But as we saw in the previous article, the promised rewards just off the path may look beautiful and taste sweet. The one promising the rewards may paint a picture showing how wonderful this new path will be and how everything will be great.

But everything will not be great. The adulteress will always leave out or hide the eventual, severe outcomes from turning to her ways of evil—entrapment, ruin, and complete embarrassment. Accordingly, you have to beware of those who try to lead you off the pathway of wisdom and understanding. Most assuredly, their intent is to harm you.

How much better it is to walk in the ways Solomon advised, experiencing a good and fulfilling life! So, resolve today to learn from Solomon. Be wise, follow good counsel, turn away from anything leading toward evil, and watch your step.

Chapter 20

Understand the Value of What You Have
Proverbs 5:15-20

Drink water from your own cistern, running water from your own well. Should your springs overflow in the streets, your streams of water in the public squares? Let them be yours alone, never to be shared with strangers. May your fountain be blessed, and may you rejoice in the wife of your youth. A loving doe, a graceful deer—may her breasts satisfy you always, may you ever be captivated by her love. Why be captivated, my son, by an adulteress? Why embrace the bosom of another man's wife?

Background/Circumstances

In the prior sections, Solomon highlighted the negative outcomes that result from submitting to the adulteress. Now he reminds the son of the following:

- **You have something of great worth already (your wife).** In that time, having your own source of water, especially a well producing running water, and a place in which to store it—the cistern—was of tremendous value. Unlike communal sources that provided inconvenient access for herds or household use and had to be shared, a private water source would make life much easier, minimizing the time spent hauling water. Having the cistern provided protection should drought come upon the land. Even better, running water would be fresh water, likely cool and refreshing to all those who had access to it. If his son gives some thought to all these things, he will understand his wife is just as valuable!

- **Why ruin a great thing?** This private water source is valuable because it is his son's. If his son begins sharing it with others, the private source will become a communal source, available even to strangers. He will have given away this valuable resource for no purpose. If the son cavorts with other women, especially an adulteress, he recklessly reduces the value of his marriage. Adding insult to injury, his wife may decide "what's good for the goose is good for the gander" and strike out to find other men who value her. His adultery may well encourage his wife to seek love somewhere else, turning her into an adulteress.
- **Take a good look at what you have and rejoice in it.** The son's wife is amazing! She is as valuable as the fountain of water belonging to him. She knows the son, and he knows her; she has been around the son since he was young. Their shared experiences create a special relationship the son can't have with anyone else. His wife is loving and graceful. Those two characteristics in one person can be very hard to find, especially when the wife is that way toward her husband. The love the wife and Solomon's son share covers all facets of married life, physical, mental, and emotional.
- **There is no comparison between this relationship with your wife and an adulteress.** A wise man sees and understands his loving relationship to his spouse is superior to anything else. It is a thing of beauty, especially when compared to the lust-filled and empty relationship with an adulteress. One would be out of his mind to make that trade.

Solomon tells his son sexual temptation will beckon. When it calls, the son should take a close look at how good he has it. Whatever he thinks he might gain from hooking up with the adulteress, it doesn't compare with the woman and relationship he has now.

Business Application

I know, you're wondering where I am going to find a business application in this section. Of course, there is one—it's how enticing things captivate us to the point where we lose sight of the value of those things we have.

It makes me think back to a situation when we were seeking to fill a key executive position. Several of us on the selection team were extremely impressed by the experience and knowledge of a candidate outside of the agency. The in-person interview was equally impressive. I remember thinking, "We need to have this person on our staff!" Still, I and others on the interview team had some reservations about whether the candidate would fit in with the culture we were establishing. We tasked our Human Relations department to conduct a thorough reference check. They did with all references coming back with flying colors. We made an offer, and the candidate accepted. In a short time, he was on board. But the reality was different than the promise. Within a very short time, it became apparent we had made a mistake in hiring him; his skills and our needs were a mismatch.

Looking back now, it is easy to see how our hiring process was flawed. The interviews were relatively brief for such a key position and focused mainly on technical issues. The answers to those interview questions gave us a good read on technical skills. They were terrific! Where we made our mistake was in assessing the candidate's soft skills and preferred culture. Our interviews contained only one or two general questions in those areas and we left the interviews without a clear understanding of his abilities in those areas. As a result, we hired someone who didn't fit that well into our organization. We had become captivated by the candidate and it threw off our entire assessment. Our poor judgment created a turbulent period for all involved.

After that situation was resolved, we stepped back and made a better value judgment. We found we had a person on staff, who had chosen not to apply for the job, who fit what we needed in the position better than any of the candidates we had interviewed. She took the job and performed admirably. What was interesting about the interviewing process was how those involved had misjudged value.

Those of us doing the interviews had looked at resumes (value judgment No. 1), conducted interviews (value judgment No. 2), and sought reference checks (value judgment No. 3). Even with all of that work, we managed to misjudge who would be the best candidate for the job. If we had stepped back at the beginning and taken a better look at possible internal candidates, we would have made sure the staff person applied for the job.

That is Solomon's point: You get used to working with those around you. You get locked into thinking about their skills and abilities one way and miss seeing their potential and long-term value. You can get so fixated on the new and shiny you misjudge the value of those who work for you now.

What's also interesting to me is how the staff person considered her value. Although possessing what was needed to fill the position well, she discounted her own value and skipped applying for the job. While it may seem unlikely to you, you need to recognize there are employees who fail to appreciate their own abilities and decide on their own not to seek promotions. They have doubts about themselves and their ability to perform well at the next level. Whether they undervalue themselves or overvalue the job requirements, they and the organization miss out on the value they could have brought to the job.

So, we come back to being "captivated." As I think about how we use the word, we usually think of those who accomplished great things because they were incredibly focused on a wonderful invention (e.g., the lightbulb), great idea (e.g., supply chain logistics), or community good (e.g., Habitat for Humanity). Indeed, where would we be now if someone hadn't been captivated by the idea of flying machines, computers, medical treatments, and a host of other things? If you want to be successful in what you do, you almost always have to be captivated by your work.

For instance, after I moved into a new house, I had a problem with my irrigation system I couldn't solve. The man I hired to fix my irrigation system tried one solution, then another, then another. In the end, it took him a combination of four changes to get the irrigation system working again. What impressed me the most wasn't his ability to get the system to work; it was his passion about irrigation systems and taking care of my yard. Besides fixing my irrigation system problem, he gave me advice on how long each of the seven cycles should run. That advice cut my water usage by more than 50 percent, and my yard and landscape areas looked much better. But he didn't stop there. He noticed I was mowing the yard one setting too low and recommended I move the lawnmower setting higher. When I found out he also provided fertilizing and weed management services, I signed up for those services, too.

But if you don't appreciate what you have, you can turn your attention elsewhere and be captivated by the wrong thing, spend increasing amounts of time chasing it, and suffer the consequences. In Solomon's example, his son may have been making moves toward the adulteress (wrong subject) rather than his wife (good subject). This isn't about decisions that looked promising but turned out to be bad ones (Ford Edsel in the 1950s); rather, it speaks to those situations where business leaders jump the rails and willfully engage in evil behavior. What kind of evil behavior? Fraud, false advertising, price gouging, kickbacks, bait-and-switch schemes, bribes, theft, contract breaches, tainted advice, deceitful products, window dressing, and the list goes on. These formerly respected leaders become entranced by the likely "gain" and literally sell their souls to go there. As we know from the prior two articles, those who listen to or flirt with the idea of getting close to the adulteress are headed toward disaster and ruin.

So as business leaders, it's worth your while to think about your associates and employees, customers, vendors, and all the others who assist you. Think about them until you understand their worth and what they bring to the table. Think about them until you see their potential, for themselves as well as for the company. Regularly think about them that way and you won't be enticed and captivated by the temptress' siren song.

Personal Application

Is the grass really greener on the other side? Instead of quickly dismissing that question, let's take a closer look at it.

The residential neighborhood I live in is one where most homeowners take care of their homes and yards fairly well. Many of my neighbors buy fertilizer, hopefully the right kind for the time of year, and apply it as best they can. These neighbors also work at controlling the weeds in their yards. Weed control requires applying the correct products at the correct times. Busy schedules, weather events, and lack of product all contribute to their difficulties in applying the correct products at the correct times. When they miss the needed weed control, weeds begin to crop up in their yards. Most of the neighbors have working irrigation systems and irrigate their yards. Because my neighbors pay attention to their yards, most of the yards in our neighborhood look good most of the time.

But if a neighbor isn't paying close attention to fertilizing, irrigating, and performing weed control at the right times, his yard starts to deteriorate. Weeds begin to sprout and take over sections of his yard, or the yard becomes light green from lack of food or brown from lack of water.

Several owners in the neighborhood, including me, hire professionals to help. The professional takes care of fertilizing and weed control, with products not available to homeowners, and helps set the irrigation schedules for each section of the yard for each season. With the consistent, professional care provided, our yards look good year-'round. Although I enjoy how well my yard looks, the truth is most of the time my yard looks about the same as those who do their own fertilizing and weed control.

What is important to note is all these owners I've described value their yard. So they spend time considering what needs to be done to keep the yard looking good. While the products and timing may vary, each owner cares enough about what they have to take steps to keep their yards green, healthy, and weed-free. That's one of the points in this section of Proverbs: Those who see and understand the value of what they have will work to keep it valuable.

Although this applies to many areas of life, it may be best illustrated in the home. If you value your relationship with your spouse, you will take actions to enrich that relationship and make it even more valuable. Using the yard analogy, you'll do everything you can to water and feed your relationship while taking care that weeds never enter, or if they do, are quickly dealt with. And, when needed, you'll keep the relationship fresh and beautiful by addressing matters that threaten to make your relationship uneven or unkempt. It's not a hard formula to ensure a successful relationship with your spouse, but like a yard, you can't let things slide and then wonder why the relationship with your spouse has gotten ragged, dull, or dry. If you will stop and consider how valuable your spouse is, you'll be motivated to do the things you need to do to keep your relationship fresh.

Whether it's your spouse, children, family, friends, or others, when you see and appreciate their value and take the time to show your appreciation, your life can't help but become more enriched and exciting. At that point, you won't care if the grass on the other side is greener or not because you'll be focused on how green the grass is on your side of the fence.

And that is exactly Solomon's point. If his son will look at the value and beauty of his relationship with his wife and invest in it, he never would consider the advances of the adulteress. What she offers is counterfeit—a green yard comprised of weeds. At first glance, what the adulteress proposes might look attractive, but there is no real value to it in the long run. Given the choice, why would he ever choose what the adulteress offers?

Of course, marriage isn't the only area where you face the question of whether the grass is always greener on the other side. When you consider changing jobs, churches, locations, and friends, you can find yourself thinking the grass may be greener with the new job, new church, new location, or new friends. When you find yourself captivated by those thoughts, you should check in with your wise counselors and make sure you are valuing aright. The new things may glitter, but that doesn't mean they are gold.

But right now, Solomon is addressing how to keep your marriage strong and stay away from infidelity. The key turns out to be one of assessing value correctly. Those who value their spouse will put all of their love and energy into that relationship from the beginning. But in case you have forgotten about your spouse's value, Solomon tells you to step back and consider all of the good things your spouse brings to the relationship. When you correctly assess your spouse's value, you'll realize the grass is very green on your side of the fence!

Having said that, it's time for you to give some thought to your own relationship. What would it look like if you really rejoiced in, and was captivated by, your spouse?

Rather than skimming over that last question, I hope you seriously will ponder it for a while. The answers you receive, if acted upon, will bring you amazing blessings, ones only available when a man and a woman rejoice in, and are captivated by, each other.

Chapter 21

Lack of Discipline, a Great Folly
Proverbs 5:21-23

For a man's ways are in full view of the LORD, and h amines all his paths. The evil deeds of a wicked man en him: the cords of his sin hold him fast. He will die for l discipline, led astray by his own great folly.

Background/Circumstances

Having given lots of advice in the course of five chapte makes three significant, and connected, statements:

- **This personal God, the LORD, sees everythin** what is in your heart ("a man's ways") as well as w chosen to do and why ("paths").
- **A wicked man is his own worst enemy.** Every performs restricts him more and more. Eventually so bound by sin he can't get away from it.
- **The wicked man despises discipline and beco Fool.** He plunges headlong into all kinds of folly his life.

In many ways, this is a transition paragraph to Chapte Solomon will talk about several examples of great folly. (few chapters.) This paragraph also serves to answer the "wh

ı the prior verses: Why be captivated by an adulteress? Why embrace ıe bosom of another man's wife? In addition, Solomon summarizes ıe eventual outcome for the wicked man. Finally, Solomon says, no ıatter how careful and secretive a man might be, there is one, the ,ORD, who sees everything that goes on and examines it to determine ʼhether a man is righteous or evil.

Besides warning God is watching, this passage serves as a clear cau-.on about following the path of the Fool. Solomon shows the wicked ıan is as foolish as they come. He tries to get ahead with his evil :hemes and only makes things worse for himself. Rather than listen ɔ wisdom and discipline, he casts them aside to do what he wants to o. As he runs toward evil and away from righteousness, he earns his ternal place with the wicked, a place of destruction and ruin. You al-ıost can hear Solomon saying, "Why go down that path?"

usiness Application

Vhat happens in your organization when someone asks a question like Why go down that path?"

Throughout my career, I observed several different types of re-ɔonses. Most fell into the category of dismissing the question in one ʼay or another. Especially dramatic was the direct attack on the person sking the question from a higher-ranking person during an executive :adership meeting. Whether done in a coolly controlled manner or in fire-breathing dressing-down, the result was the same: a crushing re-uke for one person and a clear signal to everyone else to toe the line. Vhile that solved the immediate "problem" within the meeting, it ıiled to address the questioner's concern: Was the group about to make poor decision and hurt the company?

Military campaigns provide some of the best examples of this kind f folly. A commander can convince himself his masterful plan is going ɔ succeed, and he ridicules anyone who tries to point out the weakness

of the plan. Intelligence reports giving enemy strength or movements counter to the commander's thinking are dismissed out of hand. Although the examples are almost endless, we'll look at the 1944 World War II operation Market Garden, which was memorialized in the movie *A Bridge Too Far.*

Gen. Bernard Montgomery's audacious plan called for American, British, and Polish paratroopers to capture and hold five bridges on the Northern Front, which would allow the Allied army in a quick thrust to advance sixty-five miles to the German border. If successful, he and others in military headquarters felt the war could be shortened. Because of that dream of success, Gen. Montgomery and others used their authority to dismiss: 1) concerns being raised about the resistance the army might encounter and 2) the difficulty of going sixty-five miles into enemy territory in a narrow push dependent on using one road. Although Allied forces tried to make it work, the fatal flaws in the plan resulted in overall failure and a setback in the war effort. Finger-pointing and blaming started as soon as the first major setback happened and reached a crescendo as soon as the total failure of the attack became apparent.

Dismissing or ignoring issues doesn't work, especially if the survival of you or your army are in the balance. So why do organizations, leaders, and employees still ignore or dismiss issues? While some do it for evil reasons, in too many cases it's for lack of discipline or being led astray by our own folly.

For an example, let's look at one that I lived through. In 2012, I went to work for a nationally respected transit agency in Utah. At that time, work was being completed on a 2006 voter-approved rail expansion. During the planning phases, the agency wanted to learn from the best and endorsed international travel by key personnel to see and learn from successful international transit agencies running similar rail systems. There isn't any doubt those trips resulted in a better ending product.

However, as often happens, the agency's standards for international travel relaxed and more agency personnel began traveling internationally even though stateside education options were available. As the community became aware of the extent of the agency's international travel, including newspaper articles about the outgoing CEO spending more than $600,000 on travel during his last two years, several community leaders told the agency it needed to limit international travel. In spite of the changing community attitude and increasing anger toward the agency, international travel continued. During the next three years, international travel became one of several flashpoints roiling relationships between community leaders and the agency. Although the governing body eventually took action to bar international travel unless it approved the travel in a public meeting, the damage to the agency's local reputation had been done. The State legislature stepped in and completely changed the governance model for the agency, which assured there would be a completely new governing body and executive director.

Now, I'm not saying international travel was the reason for the drastic change in governance; you can look at a 2014 legislative audit or news articles from that time to gain an understanding of the major factors. Rather, international travel illustrated how the agency had lost touch with local leaders and the public. Those in government know that keeping in alignment with the public—not getting too far ahead or too far behind—requires discipline to gather information continually, understand its implications, and adjust accordingly. Most do it very well—a quick shout-out and thank-you for all of you dedicated government officials!

However, the transit agency got off track because its leadership entered into a certain folly: a belief they knew how to run the agency better than anyone else. To a great extent, their belief was true. The agency had an incredible collection of dedicated and experienced talent in almost every area. Many were industry experts, who were sought out for their knowledge and advice. But at some point, the idea that the agency's leaders were the experts and didn't need to listen to community leaders took hold. Telling became more prevalent than listening. Community leaders' and detractors' ideas were ridiculed or dismissed rather than considered. As more and more people had their ideas ridiculed or dismissed, especially those people who had power or connections at the State level, State-mandated changes became inevitable—a day of reckoning, if you will.

As certain as the sun rising every day, a day of reckoning awaits any organization lacking discipline. That lack of discipline will lead its leaders to pursue great follies. In order to avoid pursuing great follies, you must ensure mechanisms are in place that put a premium on people speaking up when they sense the company is venturing off course. Better to catch and correct early; that pain and effort is nothing in comparison to the agony caused from an undisciplined person engaging in great folly.

Personal Application

What does it mean when Solomon states your ways are in "full view" and all your paths are being "examined"? Let's think about those words before moving on.

- **Full view.** As I'm writing this, my computer screen is in my view and well-focused. In my peripheral vision, I can see, not as clearly, the dining room table and hutch behind the computer screen, as well as parts of the house to my left and right and above and below the computer screen. But that is only a partial view of my home. To see the rest of my house, I have to turn around, walk to other rooms on the first floor, and climb the stairs to walk through the rooms upstairs. More work is involved if I want to see everything else in the house. Every drawer in every room has to be opened and contents brought out into the open for me to see them. Every closet, the garage, and even the attic have to be inspected to view all the things in my house. After all that work and even though I've seen everything, in the current moment, my view of the house and the things in it is still just a partial picture.

We see and understand our own ways through a partial view. As an example, consider my baking cookies at Christmastime. For several years, I baked hundreds of cookies—seven or eight kinds—to be placed on platters we gave to neighbors and friends. While I would like to say my only motivation was to prepare and give a gift to others, that wouldn't be true.

My pure motive—giving—was always tinged by other aims. You may laugh at some of them, but they were very real. For instance, I wanted to be seen as generous, so I made sure the platters were large enough to hold a generous number of cookies. I also wanted to be seen as the perfect cookie baker, so only perfect cookies made it on the platters. By baking several types of cookies—including several drop cookies, which take longer than bar cookies—I wanted others to see how much time it took to prepare the platter. Finally, a group at our church held an annual fundraiser selling decorated homemade cookies around the same time I was preparing the platters. I could support the group by purchasing some of their fancy cookies *and* add them to the top of my platters for a more festive look. So while my primary motivation was a pure one, other motives not as pure were going on at the same time.

Although all of the motives existed, even now as I discuss them, my focus is limited to one motive at a time. But God sees all our ways at one time. He has the complete picture; nothing is hidden or obstructed.

- **Examined.** Have you ever taken time to look at a flower closely? At first, you see the general outline of the petals and the color. But if you continue to gaze intently at it, you'll start to notice how the petals are shaped and variations in its colors. Looking at the center, you'll start to notice its individual parts—stigma, style, anther, filament—as well as its colors, shapes, and design. Turning the flower over, you can examine the base and its connection to the stem, and whether the stem is smooth or fuzzy, thin or thick, or short or long. You can sniff the flower to catch its aroma and touch its various parts to understand how each one feels.

  After five minutes of this kind of examination, you'll know and understand the flower so much more than you would from a glance. Imagine how much more you would know if you spent five minutes or more every day watching the entire lifecycle of the flower: seed planting, sprouting, growing to its full height, flowering, and finally germination and seed dispersal. If you really wanted to know the flower, you would plant its seeds in a variety of soils, locations, and weather conditions and examine the resulting flowers as they go through their lifecycles. Eventually, you would understand the conditions in which the flower thrives, struggles, or perishes.

The "examined" here is similar in its intensity. Everything is in full view so the examination can be thorough, taking the time needed to look at every aspect of a person's path and the choices made.

The thought of our ways being in full view and our paths examined isn't what we normally experience. If I'm careful enough with my speech and actions, people won't know what I really think about the situation or them. If I'm really careful, I can bring about the downfall of someone else without them ever being aware that I was behind it all. If I'm practiced and careful enough, I can make almost everyone think

I'm a good guy while I do my best to hide the not-so-good parts of my life. Knowing that is our natural tendency, Solomon makes it clear we can't hide anything we do, or our motives, from God. In fact, it is all laid out before Him and He examines it.

That thought alone should give you pause. No matter how hard you try, you can't hide your actions, thinking, or motives from God. Your whole life is open to His examination. He sees and knows about everything you think and do. How should that fact affect how you live? According to Solomon, it means you should: 1) seek to live a life of discipline and 2) reject folly.

A life of discipline sets you on the path of the righteous, because it takes discipline to learn to be right, just, and fair while gaining wisdom, knowledge, and understanding. As Solomon has pointed out time and again, the righteous path leads to a good life with fabulous outcomes. Those who are disciplined enough to follow this path are blessed.

But living a disciplined life isn't enough; you also have to reject folly. That may sound like a simple enough rule to follow, but consider the folly around you and how many people get sucked into doing foolish things. Headlines abound about those who spent their lives carefully gaining financial freedom only to lose it via some huckster's scheme or who let their passion for another person take them into illegal, deadly actions. Just as a lack of discipline can take you down a wicked path, engaging in folly pulls the disciplined person off the good path onto the wicked path. As you live your life, you are going to need to be able to recognize folly and reject it.

Because folly can disguise itself, in Chapter 6 Solomon is going to show you several types of folly. It's quite a list. But be prepared; he may bring up a folly in which you engage. If so, remember Solomon wants to point out to his son, and you, the dangers of these follies. He wants you to reject them, engage in the ways of the righteous, and receive the bountiful blessings the LORD gives to the righteous.

Proverbs

Chapter Six

Chapter 22

The Folly of Making Promises You Can't Keep
Proverbs 6:1-5

> *My son, if you have put up security for your neighbor, if you have struck hands in pledge for another, if you have been trapped by what you said, ensnared by the words of your mouth, then do this, my son, to free yourself, since you have fallen into your neighbor's hands: Go and humble yourself; press your pleas with your neighbor! Allow no sleep to your eyes, no slumber to your eyelids. Free yourself, like a gazelle from the hand of the hunter, like a bird from the snare of the fowler.*

Background/Circumstances

Solomon ended Chapter 5 warning his son about the dangers of being "led astray by his own great folly." In this chapter, Solomon gives specific examples of great folly. He starts with the concept of putting up security for a neighbor or making a pledge for another.

Putting up security and making a pledge are voluntary agreements whereby one person agrees to be responsible for someone else's debt or obligation. If the original debtor can't or won't pay when the debt is due or fulfill his obligation at the appointed time, then the creditor will turn to the one who guaranteed the debtor's obligations for satisfaction. While putting up security for a neighbor and shaking hands on a pledge may seem like good things to do to help out the neighbor or friend, Solomon plainly tells his son not to do it.

It's easy to see why. In those days, when a debt came due, the entire amount was due. If the borrower couldn't pay, then the lender could throw the borrower into prison until he paid the entire amount. The lender could take everything the family had and leave the rest of the family destitute, gleaning fields and begging. If the obligation still wasn't fulfilled, the lender could demand the cosigner pay off the debt or obligation. If the cosigner couldn't pay, he was subject to imprisonment with his family becoming destitute, gleaning fields and begging.

While the borrower knows the obligations he has and whether he will be able to fulfill them, the cosigner may have little information about the borrower's financial situation. Because the borrower is a neighbor or friend, the cosigner trusts he will fulfill his obligations. The cosigner keeps his focus on his own financial affairs and family, doing what he needs to do to provide food, shelter, and a home. Unfortunately, his neighbor or friend is unlikely to let the cosigner know he is unable to meet his obligations. As a result, the cosigner will be totally unprepared on the day the lender comes to his house, reminds him of his pledge to take care of the neighbor's debt, and demands full payment.

The comparisons Solomon uses are vivid and startling. Putting up security or making a pledge for another is like knowingly walking into a trap. The trap is in plain sight. It's obvious the trap will ensnare the cosigner in a way that won't allow him to escape. Although the cosigner sees other paths without traps, he plays the Fool and walks right into the ensnarement. As the trap closes in on him, the surprised cosigner is shocked to find he is now caught, ensnared, and helpless.

If his son is foolish enough to fall into this trap, Solomon goes over the escape options available to him. Neither option is pleasant.

- **His son can go to the lender, humble himself before him, and seek relief.** The picture is one of a cosigner groveling before the lender and declaring how much of a fool he was, likely in front of an audience. It's hard enough to do one-on-one—how unpleasant to be shown a fool in front of a whole company of friends and neighbors. Life will never be the same.

- **His son can do whatever he can to get out of the fix he is in.** Like an animal trying to find a way out of a trap, the cosigner must struggle and struggle to work his way out of the trap he is in. Although his options are limited, he needs to try every one of them. Although every attempt fails, he must keep trying them again and again until he is totally exhausted. Perhaps a miracle will take place and one of the attempts will lead to his freedom. The more likely outcome is he will remain trapped and life will never be the same.

Although there isn't much hope either of these options will work, Solomon says his son shouldn't ever rest; truly, because his situation is so desperate, he will need to work day and night to try to get out of the trap. Unless he can find a way out, he is heading off to prison until he can pay off a debt that originally was not his to pay.

Business Application

The watchword in this passage: Be careful when making promises, especially when you will be on the hook for another's nonperformance.

While many focus on the part of the passage dealing with cosigning situations, make sure you notice what it says about those situations where you, or someone in your organization, makes a promise you will have to fulfill or suffer the consequences.

Businesses make promises like that all the time. Common examples are price guarantees ("We'll meet any advertised price for the product we're selling."), warranties ("unlimited warranty for three years and a limited warranty for seven years"), or quality ("If not satisfied, return this product within thirty days for a full refund."). The promises are usually well reasoned, intended to assure the customer he can buy with confidence while not breaking the company bank to fulfill them. The longer the time period covered or the more liability assumed by a proposed promise, the more cautious you need to be in calculating the true cost.

Because I'm very familiar with employee pension plans, I'll use them as an example. No doubt you've seen headlines about poorly funded pension plans or plans that simply went away. It's really no secret what happened. For those failing plans, political or business leaders—overseeing public pensions or private pensions, respectively—made promises to provide long-term benefits their entity couldn't afford. In the public pension world, some of the behavior was short-sighted:

- Politicians made promises to public employee groups to gain or keep their support and votes, knowing the cost of those promises would fall to future administrations.
- In good financial times, when pension plans looked better funded because of high returns, the governing board sweetened retirement benefits or reduced/eliminated annual funding.
- In bad financial times, rather than cut other services, governing boards reduced/eliminated pension funding.

Changes in governmental accounting have made it harder, though not impossible, to engage in such short-sighted behavior. Bond rating agencies, actuaries, and the Governmental Accounting Standards Board all took actions resulting in more transparency. New financial reporting standards added current and historical information about pension benefit changes and their costs, funding status, and the unpaid liability for pension benefits already earned but unfunded.

Similar changes took place in private industry more than a decade earlier with dramatic impacts. Several large companies curtailed their pension systems, often reducing or eliminating promised retirement pension payments. As the business environment became more and more competitive and employees switched jobs more often, it became harder and harder for private businesses to justify pension plans geared toward providing a lifetime pension to a thirty-year employee. Instead, many companies replaced the lifetime pension with a less costly 401(k) option. This change limited the company's pension costs and shifted more retirement funding and risk to their employees. It's a much different promise, but one they can keep.

For a more specific example, let me talk about challenges at the transit agency where I worked. The agency developed and used a thirty-year financial forecasting model for several years. That model allowed the agency to understand the long-term impacts associated with adding large capital projects and new bus and rail service. As the new CFO, I spent some time reviewing and understanding this model. It didn't take long to observe ending cash balances were forecasted to decline for the next nine years until they reached a level just above the agency's minimum cash balance requirement. From there, the model forecasted cash balances would stabilize and start to increase.

The forecast looked good until I learned more. Several years before, the agency had signed an agreement to pay 50 percent of a $1 million study. Somehow that obligation hadn't made it into the financial forecasting model. Because we were dealing with much larger numbers in the model, adding in a $500,000 obligation reduced forecasted ending cash balances, but those balances still exceeded the minimum cash balance requirement every year.

Then I found out about a signed agreement for the agency to pay up to $50 million to relocate its airport rail line when the airport expanded. That $50 million obligation wasn't in the model either. Finding two misses in the financial forecast model, I knew I had to do more work to find out exactly what promises had been made but weren't included in the model.

It turned out there were several large capital promises absent from the financial forecast model. When I had them all—at least I hoped I had them all—and incorporated them into the long-term forecasting model, it became apparent the agency had to make several sizable downward adjustments to planned capital and operating costs if it was going to maintain required fund balances in the near term. More changes were needed to do the same in the long term. Fortunately for me, no one shot the messenger. Working with the governing body and executive team, we developed a more feasible long-term plan to provide the most service possible, meet promises made, and maintain financial stability.

It wasn't easy. From the financial perspective, all of those unrecorded promises were almost too much to overcome. Higher-than-expected sales tax revenues and the ability to refinance debt at lower rates helped us absorb most of these expenses. Even then, we had to renegotiate some of the agreements to amounts the agency could afford. From the political perspective, these unexpected financial issues added to the growing image that the agency was out of control and needed to be reined in (which the State legislature eventually did).

So the word to the wise is to be careful when making a promise. Promises made easily can be difficult, if not impossible, to fulfill. Words you speak, or write on paper, can entrap you just as surely as a snare. If it's foolish to make a promise you can't keep, imagine how foolish it is to cosign for someone who may have made a promise they can't, or won't, keep. By doing so, you are taking on a risk that may well bring you to the point of ruin either: 1) requiring you to work to the breaking point to recover or 2) forcing you to throw yourself at the mercy of the creditor demanding satisfaction. It's best to never, ever put yourself in that situation!

Personal Application

Cosigning on a loan creates a situation fraught with danger.

By cosigning on a loan, you place your own full faith and credit behind the person taking out the loan. If he doesn't pay, you are on the hook to make the payments. Some people may have the financial wherewithal to absorb a sudden demand for payment, but most people don't have those resources. Instead, a sudden, required payment creates financial havoc and pushes them over a financial cliff. Don't expect the person you cosigned for to come to your rescue. He abandoned you when he failed to pay. You are on your own, and you alone get to figure it out. There is so much risk here, only the foolish would ever cosign for someone.

Let's take a closer look. Why does the bank want someone else, usually someone with ample financial resources, to serve as a cosigner? It's because the bank has judged the primary borrower is a higher risk than it is willing to accept. The bank will accept the risk only if someone else is willing to guarantee the loan. Now you may say the borrower I'm cosigning for—a child or close family member—would never leave you holding the bag. Hopefully not, but be aware anytime you cosign for another, the potential is there. And when potential becomes reality, your relationship with the borrower you cosigned for more than likely will be damaged, possibly forever. Even in the best of relationships, while the deed may be forgiven, it will not be forgotten. Trust, once broken, is never quite the same.

Making a promise you can't keep is just as bad.

Have you ever made a promise you wished you hadn't made? I've been in conversations where I've promised to be someplace at a certain time and, a few minutes later, realized I already had a commitment for that day and time. As soon as I could, I asked the person to whom I made the promise to let me out of it. Usually, the person graciously agreed, especially if I offered to substitute a different day and time. However, when we discussed the different day and time, the other person often asked me to check my calendar twice just to be sure I was making a promise I could keep. They might have asked in a joking manner, but the message was clear: "Can I really trust you?"

That example is a mild one, but notice I followed Solomon's admonition to a T. I went to the person to whom I made the promise, humbled myself—admitted my mistake—and sought to be freed from my promise. I can imagine in the ordinary course of life you have done much the same thing as I did. You made a promise, realized you couldn't keep it, and contacted the other person to adjust. In many of our relationships, those adjustments are easy and natural. We are willing to give the other person a bit of grace, because we know we need it too when we flub up.

But this section is talking about something different than these daily, somewhat inconsequential promises we make. How do we know that? Look at how urgent it becomes to get out from underneath the ill-advised promise. Having made it, the one who promised is in as much danger as a gazelle in the hand of the hunter—caught and ready to be slaughtered—or a bird in a snare—captured and ready to be imprisoned or eaten for dinner. If you don't understand those illustrations, you should find a video of a wild animal that has been trapped and watch its strenuous efforts to escape. The wild animal understands the danger it is in and its desperation shows; it will do anything and everything to get away.

So, Solomon warns his son and us about making promises that will trap or ensnare us. I wish I could say my past didn't include promises I couldn't keep, but it does. As a result, I've had to eat humble pie more than once to get out of ill-advised promises I made. Because of those broken promises, I've lost friends, damaged relationships, and suffered financial setbacks.

It doesn't have to be that way with you. To escape this folly, Solomon gives two pieces of advice:

1. **Never cosign for another or make promises you can't keep.** Those will come back to haunt you.
2. **If you have cosigned or made a promise you can't keep, do whatever it takes to get out of the situation.** The sooner, the better!

Chapter 23

The Folly of Being a Sluggard
Proverbs 6:6-11

Go to the ant, you sluggard; consider its ways and be wise! It has no commander, no overseer or ruler, yet it stores its provisions in summer and gathers its food at harvest. How long will you lie there, you sluggard? When will you get up from your sleep? A little sleep, a little slumber, a little folding of the hands to rest—and poverty will come on you like a bandit and scarcity like an armed man.

Background/Circumstances

As you will recall, Solomon ended Chapter 5 talking about those who are led astray by great folly. In the first part of Chapter 6, he talked about the first example of great folly—the person who makes unwise promises, like cosigning for another, or promises he can't keep. Now, Solomon turns to the second example of great folly—the sluggard.

This is the first of thirteen Proverbs sections dealing with the sluggard. How great a problem sluggardly behavior must have been for it to be addressed so many times! In this section, we learn several things about the sluggard. Let's go over them. The sluggard:

- **Isn't anywhere close to being wise.** In a comparison intended to shock, especially because it is true, an ant is deemed to be wiser than the sluggard. Solomon could have used many other comparisons but chose the tiny ant. It shows just how preposterous the sluggard's actions, or more properly inactions, really are.

- **Isn't curious or interested in learning.** Most people, especially as children, have spent some time watching ants. It doesn't take long to see ants bringing food back to their anthill or heading out to find more food. Apparently, our sluggard didn't consider ants the least bit interesting or he just watched them and never contemplated or understood what they were doing.
- **Lacks self-motivation.** Unlike the ant, which doesn't need a commander, overseer, or ruler to rouse it to action, the sluggard has to have someone in authority who can oversee him and tell him what to do. Without that person trying to get him to do something—and it will be a struggle—the sluggard will stay in bed and sleep or take the opportunity to rest whenever he can.
- **Prefers comfort now.** Rather than do the things he knows he needs to do, the sluggard wants to stay in his warm bed. When he should be working, he sits and rests. He literally loves sleep and resting and willingly puts aside what he should be doing so he can do what he loves most.
- **Is unaware disaster lies ahead.** Apparently, the sluggard doesn't think very far ahead. If he did, he would know his laziness now means hunger and poverty later. His pantries may be full now, but one day he will go to the pantry and there won't be any food. The sudden realization will be like that of a person going about their business when a robber jumps out of his hiding place and takes all the person has, leaving him penniless.

It truly is great folly to be as unwise and lazy as the sluggard. Somehow, even though an adult now, he has remained much like a child, only concerned for today, needing someone around to tell him what to do and keep him on task. If he fails to learn from the ant, he will perish.

Business Application

Sluggards. I hope you have never had to work with one. I have, and they frustrated me to no end. Many of the ones I've worked with have been talented, but their laziness and poor work habits held them back. They exhibited many of the same traits described in this section of Proverbs.

- **Attendance** – I never knew when these workers would show up to work. For some, it was directly related to sleep; these folks just couldn't get up in the morning. For others, it was lack of foresight; they had to take care of something that morning and wouldn't adjust their wake-up time to accommodate the extra trip or two. Others would rush in on time but spend the first thirty to forty-five minutes eating their breakfast at their desk, putting on makeup, or running an electric razor over their face. Whatever the reasons, these employees had a hard time starting work on time.
- **Focus** – Several workers spent quite a bit of time chatting with their coworkers. The worst offenders could be hard to find during the day. Rather than being in their office, they moved from office to office talking with their friends. A short business conversation could evolve into an hour discussion on a topic of joint personal interest. Lunch hour with friends or business associates easily could expand and chop away at time available for work. Others would spend hours each day on their phone or the internet conducting personal business.
- **Direction** – Within this group was a subset of workers who would do only what you told them to do. It was as if they lived a self-chosen life of "Mother, may I?" Even in a work environment where initiative was encouraged and appreciated, these employees wouldn't make decisions on their own.

Sluggards are hard to deal with because they often will do just enough to keep their jobs. Other employees never would count on a sluggard to help them on one of their crucial, time-sensitive projects. However, because sluggards tend to be likable and popular, other employees like to have them around. Because sluggards do just enough to keep their jobs, upward movement escapes them, and they miss out on opportunities and advancements that could have been theirs. At some point, sluggards may realize they have been doing the same job for years and work advancements have passed them by. Rather than rethinking their folly, don't be surprised if they decide that you, as their boss, are responsible for their fate. Things can take an ugly turn from there.

As with all personnel issues, it's best to handle them as quickly as possible. Sluggards are no exemption.

Enough of thinking about this section from a boss' perspective. The real lesson of the section is intended to be applied to you, the reader. The obvious lesson is don't be lazy in the sense of putting things off. If you have a project to tackle at work, then get to it! There are any number of excuses—and they are excuses—one can come up with to let things lag.

- The first excuse given is not having anyone around to tell you what to do. That explanation might be expected from a young and inexperienced person, but as an adult in the working world, your boss has an expectation you know what you are supposed to do or can figure out what you can do to help things along. One summer, I worked as the fry cook and person in charge at my father's drive-in restaurant from 9 A.M. to 4 P.M. every weekday. As you might expect, the noontime rush kept us very busy fulfilling customer orders. Then the afternoon doldrums would hit, and the pace slowed down. As Dad had instructed, we used the afternoon hours to clean up from the rush period and make the place presentable. My crew went beyond that. Without being told to do so, we implemented a late-afternoon stocking process to make sure the next shift would have everything it might need for the evening rush. It didn't take much extra work on our part. We left our shift knowing the place was ready for the evening's business. But based on how the place looked when I arrived every morning, the night crew left things as they were at quitting time.

Two groups, two different results. The only difference was one group didn't need a leader to tell them what to do. In which group do you fit? Hopefully, you are the kind of person who can look ahead, evaluate, and initiate needed actions on your own. People like that are valuable to an organization. They take care of small problems before they become big problems or see and undertake revenue/efficiency opportunities that enhance the bottom line. A wise person takes care of the business when the boss isn't around.

- Sleeping and resting, when you should be working, is the second excuse. In an agrarian world, when there is only so much sunlight in which to work, sleeping or resting during the day meant the work didn't get done. At the very least, work started to pile up and something, maybe planting a whole field, couldn't be accomplished in the planting season. Or by sleeping the day away, the farmer might miss harvesting his field before a strong storm ruined it. In both cases, the farmer's current laziness led to serious problems later.

In today's world, this laziness shows up in other ways. An example that comes to mind relates to staff presentations to their governing body. As you might expect, governing body agendas are planned well in advance, giving the staff notice of when their topic will be considered and the deadlines for submitting their agenda materials. The agenda materials usually include all information needed for the governing body and other interested parties to understand the agenda item and consider the staff's recommendation. Routine items are clustered into a consent agenda, which the governing body votes on without discussion. All other agenda items come before the governing body separately. For each of those items, the staff is expected to make a professional presentation, covering background, key points, and their recommendation.

I wish I could tell you agenda preparation went like clockwork, but it rarely did. Usually, the problem came about because a staff member waited until the night before, or even the morning of, the submittal deadline to start preparing his agenda information and presentations. It was like he had awakened to the reality the board meeting materials were due that day. Then, it became a mad rush and an emergency to meet the deadline. Because he operated that way, it was rare for him to have all required agenda materials submitted on time. His submittals could drag over a few days, completely upsetting the CEO's and governing body's review process. Because the agenda item was usually time sensitive, the item had to be included on that agenda.

While the CEO and governing board staff moved mountains to get the agenda materials ready and published in time for board and public review, the staff member's lack of preparation usually showed up during the presentation to the board in several ways:

- **Rather than knowing the answer to an expected question, the presenter faked his way through an answer.** It was painful to watch. It worked when the governing body let it go. But rest assured, the governing body understood he wasn't prepared and made mental notes to check his work more closely the next time.
- **He would give an incorrect answer or veer off topic.** When that happened, if possible another staff person would jump in to tactfully provide the correct answer, bring the discussion

back on track, and stay alert for any other misstatements. When quick intervention wasn't possible, a knowledgeable board member corrected the presenter. Usually, a board member intervened by asking a gentle question. This gave the presenter the opportunity to restate his answer correctly or easily return to the topic at hand. In some instances, in order to play to his constituency, a board member would seek to embarrass the presenter.

- **He would give a misleading answer.** In some instances, the presenter would fudge the truth, making things seem better than they were by leaving out critical information. Whenever the board sensed that was happening, several board members shifted to attack mode. What should have been a relatively easy agenda item suddenly turned into an inquisition. Board members' questions became increasingly pointed and confrontational. Ill prepared from the start, the presenter floundered trying to answer these new questions. To prevent complete embarrassment, the CEO would break in and ask the board to delay consideration of the matter until the next meeting. While not the ultimate disaster in a formal board meeting, having to pull an item from consideration is near the top.

Whichever turn the presentation took, it was apparent to all one or more people had acted like the sluggard—failing to do the required work when it needed to be done. An isolated "sluggard" event might raise a few eyebrows, but if they continue to happen, an impression might begin to form—staff might be "asleep at the wheel" or resting on their laurels. If that impression becomes a belief, it is only a matter of time before changes come to the agency, usually starting at the top.

In whatever form it might take, being a sluggard is a great folly. Because the sluggard doesn't handle today's matters well, he is going to have big, big problems later. The outcome of sluggardly behavior is as predictable as the sun always rising in the East and setting in the West. Knowing the preordained outcome from sluggardly behavior, and still being a sluggard, is indeed great folly.

Personal Application

Every time I read this section of Proverbs, I wonder what situation brought Solomon around to observing ants. It's all speculation, but I like to think he was lazing away one day and happened to notice ants going about their business. Looking at the anthill and the string of ants going in and out, the activity intrigued him and he wondered what was going on. He noticed the ants coming back to the anthill were carrying food while those going out were returning to the food source to gather more food. He must have wondered why the ants brought the food back to the anthill rather than eating it where they found it. Then it dawned on him; the ants were finding and storing food when it was plentiful in preparation for the season when food wouldn't be as available. How brilliant! But who was in charge? Surely there was a commander, a large or distinctive-looking ant in charge. He didn't see one. He concluded all the ants knew they needed to gather food for the winter, so they just did it.

As Solomon pondered what he observed, I like to think he suddenly was convicted. Here he was, the epitome of wisdom lazing the day away while the ants, which no one would have thought wise, were in fact wiser than he. And I like to think he appreciated the irony of the moment and enjoyed a good belly laugh. Then, with renewed vigor, Solomon leapt up and headed back to the pile of work waiting for him.

Later, as Solomon thought about the steady activity of the ants, he began to think about his assistants who were as industrious as the ants. These industrious assistants took care of a good portion of the kingdom's business with little oversight from Solomon. But Solomon's thoughts wandered to people who were completely unlike these assistants, those who chose to sleep or rest when work needed to be done. As he thought of those who were lazy, Solomon realized the outcome of their laziness would be hunger and ruin in the coming winter. It is quite possible Solomon had a lazy acquaintance in mind, someone who came to ruin because of this sluggardly behavior. Not wanting anyone else to have the same disastrous end as his lazy acquaintance, you can almost hear Solomon yell out, "HOW FOOLISH IS THE SLUGGARD!"

What about you? Do you entertain this great folly of being a sluggard? Because Solomon points to a lack of provisions and food, poverty, and scarcity as the outcomes, you first have to look at how well you are managing your finances.

- **Spending all you have now is tremendous folly.** Rainy days, or retirement, come around, and the wise person prepares for them. If you haven't learned that lesson, now is the time to learn it. Good financial counselors can help you get started and stay on track.
- **Taking action to ensure your financial future is your responsibility.** Does your work have periods where your income is greater than other periods? Then set the extra money aside for the slow periods or for longer-term financial needs. Do you know your expenses are higher at the end of the year? Then set aside money each month to handle those later expenses. Do you want to retire at a certain age at a certain standard of living? Then determine how much you need to set aside each year between now and then and make those changes. But let's not make finances the only focus here; this applies to every other facet of your life, too. If you know something needs to be done, don't wait; jump in and get it done.
- **Taking your eye off the prize will result in failure.** If you want to meet your financial, spiritual, or other goals, you have

> to stay focused on what needs to be done. It is so easy to let today's distractions take your focus off your long-term best interests. In Solomon's day, it was sleeping and resting during daylight hours. Rather than making hay while the sun shines, the sluggard slept. In today's world, distractions like entertainment and adventures have their place. However, they become great folly when you choose them over what you know you need to do.

The final result of this folly is awful. Because the sluggard is so focused on today, he is going to be surprised when his world comes crashing down. Everything suddenly will be gone and the sluggard will be destitute. A life that held so much promise can be ruined by this great folly.

The message is clear: Don't act like the sluggard. Instead, be wise—look ahead, take action, and provide for the future. You, and all those around you, will be blessed!

Chapter 24

The Folly of Stirring Up Dissension
Proverbs 6:12-15

A scoundrel and villain, who goes about with a corrupt mouth, who winks with his eye, signals with his feet and motions with his fingers, who plots evil with deceit in his heart—he always stirs up dissension. Therefore, disaster will overtake him in an instant; he will suddenly be destroyed—without remedy.

Background/Circumstances

Thus far in Chapter 6, Solomon has addressed two kinds of great folly: 1) making promises like cosigning for another person's loan and flippant, but enforceable, promises, and 2) being a sluggard. Now he turns to a third example of great folly—one who stirs up dissension.

Solomon describes a person who stirs up dissension as a "scoundrel and a villain." The New Oxford American Dictionary defines a "scoundrel" as "a dishonest or unscrupulous person." Dishonest and unscrupulous behavior is what we see in this person's actions; he uses his mouth, eyes, feet, and fingers—any means he can—to stir things up.

Dealing with his advisors, foreign dignitaries, and others, Solomon had many opportunities to observe and understand how others communicated with their associates without saying a word. It must have amused Solomon as he watched others making their odd motions to each other. He also heard others, through their comments, seeking to disrupt, create confusion, or divide. Solomon observed those who were trying to create dissension instead of seeking the greater good. Because this was a prosperous time in the nation, Solomon must have thought, "Why are these people trying so hard to muck things up?"

After giving it consideration, Solomon concluded those trying to create dissension were really villains. Why? Because their motives weren't good ones; their motives were evil. Worse still, these people had been plotting and scheming their evil actions. Worst of all, their deceit came from their heart. Were they scoundrels? Definitely! But they were more than that. Because of their deliberate and evil approach, they were villains—bad actors out to do harm. These villains specialized in creating discord and dissension, the breaking up of what had previously been harmonious. Striving to break up a good thing made no sense to Solomon; it was indeed a great folly.

As with other evil, no matter how well it is disguised, the scoundrel and villain will be identified. When that happens, his demise will be swift and complete, without any remedy. Perhaps Solomon was thinking about what happened between him and his brother in the early days of Solomon's kingship. Although the brother said he accepted Solomon as king, it didn't stop him from asking Solomon's mother if he could marry the young woman who had kept David warm in his last days. While asking to marry David's bed warmer doesn't seem like a big deal to us today, in Solomon's time it was a backdoor way of contesting the kingship. When Solomon's mother makes the request, Solomon realizes his brother is seeking to create dissension and take the kingship away. Solomon has him put to death that very day. His destruction was swift, complete, and without remedy.

Business Application

As I consider these verses, it makes me think back to the different people with whom I've worked. It was my great fortune to have worked with so many who were positive influences for me. Their questions and comments, some of which were hard to take, were all intended for my good. The hardest comments to accept were usually the most productive, because they zeroed in on a flaw that, if left unchanged, would hold me and my career back. These positive influencers wanted to clarify my thoughts, correct a bad habit, or contribute to my development. Because they cared so much for me, I thoroughly enjoyed working with them. Together we improved our skills and each other. Our employers benefitted from our innovations and productivity while we created a great environment for our other employees. Working with those folks was dynamic and invigorating!

But others, rather than working toward positive achievements, specialized in throwing monkey wrenches into things. Their comments were couched in respectful language and delivered with sincerity, but they really were seeking to cause confusion, conflict, and dissension among the group. Some of the worst offenders were those who would wait for a meeting to ask a divisive question. They could have asked and received an answer earlier. Instead, they purposefully waited for the meeting. Although they would ask the question in an "I'm looking out for the company" manner, their real reasons were to make themselves look good, grind a particular project to a halt, or embarrass someone else. The disruptive nature of the question commanded the group's attention. After spending way too much time dealing with something that should have been handled outside of the meeting, someone in the group would get us back on track.

Be aware, these people will claim they are trying to make things better, but their actions tell a different story. Conflicts and unnecessary interruptions seem to follow them around. Rather than seeking harmony, they create dissension.

You likely will run into this villain in your business dealings. If at all possible, try to deal this villain out of any major decision processes; if he can, he will make life miserable for you and the company. Identifying this disruptive person can be difficult. He will say and do the right things. He will put on a good act. To identify him, you have to look at results. Someone who is on the team brings up things to improve the company and create better internal relationships. While there may be momentary interruptions, the end result is always better. That's not true for this villain. Rather than seeking a better result, his intent is to cause dissension.

While a villain may show up in all levels within an organization, it is really bad when he is allowed to reside within the upper echelons of the company. Rather than a unified team pulling together, the team will struggle mightily with a scoundrel and villain on board. Because the scoundrel is deceitful and covers his tracks well, no one may realize what the true problem is for a long time. But if all is right in the world, the scallywag will be discovered and thrown off the team.

Take a minute and think about your business. Is there someone on your staff who leaves a trail of conflict, dissension, and problems behind them? You know, the person with whom no one really wants to work, but because he is a "key" employee, they have to work with him? Whenever I've challenged others with those questions, I've given them a few seconds and then asked, "Who did you think of?" Without exception, every person came up with an employee who created more conflict and dissension than he/she contributed to the work product. As the names came forward, we knew we needed to address those situations. Our discussions revealed some of these employees didn't have any evil intent. Rather, they just needed some coaching to change their behavior. However, the truly disruptive employees were invited, or forced, to leave the company.

Did you come up with a name or two of people in your company who leave a trail of conflict and dissension? If so, you need to weigh the situation now and move as fast as you can to resolve it one way or the other. Letting it continue only gives this scoundrel and villain more opportunities to continue his evil ways.

Personal Application

Have you noticed some people just love to stir up dissension? Although many of them will say their intentions are good, it might be worth looking behind the curtain more closely. According to Solomon, it is much more likely their intentions are evil.

A person can innocently say or do something that turns placid waters into rough waters. When that person becomes aware of what he's done, and how it has impacted others, his contrition is obvious; he humbly goes to the injured parties and clears up everything. Sometimes the injured party will go directly to that person to check things out. When confronted with whatever he said or did, the offending person is mortified and immediately seeks to make things right with whomever he has injured. Someone who didn't intend evil acts this way.

But let's be honest. Most people creating dissension have less-than-pure motives. We know because we have been in situations where we created dissension out of impure motives. Think back to your childhood. Did you ever say or do something to get back at another person? As I think back over those times, I distinctly remember being disappointed when a close friend chose to spend more time with someone else. The desire to strike back by saying something to defame my close friend welled up within me quickly. Suddenly, the hurtful words were out of my mouth, and I could see pain on my close friend's face. My sharp comments to my close friend put a wedge between us that we were never able to overcome.

It was exactly the kind of reaction you might expect from a young person. As we saw in the first few verses of Proverbs, the Young and the Simple lack prudence, knowledge, and discernment. Without those in place, it's easy for a youngster to act with evil intent in his heart and fall far short of being right, just, and fair. Such are the foolish ways of youth.

But as we transition into adulthood, we are expected to put away childish things and acquire prudence, knowledge, discernment, and wisdom. With those in hand, it's almost inconceivable a person would deliberately go about interjecting dissension and havoc into a peaceful situation. The only explanation is a desire to do evil to others. That folly is obvious. While the scoundrel lights the fire of dissension and pours fuel on it, he also is putting into place the dry wood that will catch fire and destroy him and his world. It really is a foolish thing to do.

Which brings up the question of why anyone in their right mind would go about speaking and acting in a way to destroy others when they, too, will be consumed by the fire they set. Deceit is the answer. Just as this person is using deceit to spread lies and innuendos, he also has managed to deceive himself. He has convinced himself he is so smart, or righteous, that none of the mud he throws at others will get on him.

Gossip is one of the examples we can use to highlight this section. Gossip, by its very nature, has a certain evilness about it. The gossiper knows, or thinks he knows, something about another person. Rather than keeping it to himself, he intentionally gives that information out to a third person, perhaps with a little added twist or even a smug indication of disapproval—verbal or otherwise. This third person is only too happy to gain this information—how sad!—which serves as positive feedback and emboldens the gossiper even more. So much so, the gossiper lives to gather dirt on others and pass it along, all the while deceiving himself about the damage he is doing.

But that isn't how it is playing with others. Others quickly understand they should never tell the gossiper anything about their lives—business or personal. While they may engage in some conversations with the gossiper, they know the gossiper has no scruples and is just as likely to pass on untruthful, or secret, information about them. Eventually, others will shy away from the gossiper and stop talking to him altogether. This doesn't stop the gossiper; he just finds new "friends" for his evil game.

I've known several gossipers. They have all been "sweet" people who share their "concerns" about others. When I was younger, I was deceived easily by the gossiper. After all, she was concerned about others, and the concern was presented in an interesting way. As I grew older, I started to see how destructive gossip was; there was actually evil intent associated with the gossip. None of the gossip was meant to build others up. Rather, the gossip was intended to tear others down.

So, I've learned to identify gossipers much more quickly. If at all possible, I try to stay away from them. If I can't, I stick to neutral discussion topics and never tell them anything they might be able to use as gossip. While I've gotten better at identifying gossipers, there are times when I can't tell for sure. In those situations, I will give that person a seemingly juicy tidbit just to see if they will share it with others in our social group. If someone else in our social group brings it up with me, I know I have identified a gossiper and treat her accordingly.

But gossiping isn't the only thing in play in this section. How often have you been in a group when someone makes a comment and others in the group share a knowing glance, maybe even a wink at each other, or give some indication of disapproval by how they move around? If you pay attention, you'll see those motions happen a lot. The subtle, or exaggerated, eye roll. The disapproving finger or toe tapping. The body shift away from the person. The fake smile letting others know how you feel. You might hear the "nice" comment others know has a more sinister meaning behind it. One example might relate to a person's new hat. You might say, "That's an amazing hat you're wearing." That hat-wearer takes it as a compliment while all of your friends know you are really saying, "That is an amazingly *awful* hat you're wearing." It's deceitful and evil to do that.

Getting even more personal, how often have you said something in your marriage, or within your family, that created dissension? Whether purposeful or not, creating dissension within your family is great folly. Instead of building on their hopes and dreams to create something beautiful, too many spouses pull out the verbal knives when something doesn't go exactly as he or she wanted it to go. In the beginning, the verbal knives are used for little jabs intended to sting a bit, not causing lasting damage and intended to bring about reconciliation. But using verbal knives that way is a dangerous game. It's too easy to cut someone far deeper than you intended, or in your anger, to intentionally cut someone very deeply. Both instances leave a long-lasting scar. If the spouses fail to put away the verbal knives in time, the marriage, which once was full of dreams and promises, becomes a mangled mess and crashes and burns. It's a tragedy every time. What could have been beautiful ended up on the garbage heap of broken marriages.

What about you? Are you being a scoundrel and villain in what you say and do? Let's hope not! It's a behavior foolish enough to be included in the list of great follies. Rather than engage in that folly, choose to be a wise person, one who does what is right and just and fair for all those around you.

Chapter 25

Seven Detestable Behaviors, More Great Folly! Proverbs 6:16-19

There are six things the LORD hates, seven that are detestable to him: haughty eyes, a lying tongue, hands that shed innocent blood, a heart that devises wicked schemes, feet that are quick to rush into evil, a false witness who pours out lies and a man who stirs up dissension among brothers.

Background/Circumstances

Thus far in Chapter 6, Solomon has talked about three examples of great folly:

- **Putting up security for others (cosigning) and making other promises you can't keep.**
- **Sleeping, resting, or waiting for direction when you know what you need to do.**
- **Plotting to create dissension.**

With each of those, Solomon added some explanations, including the outcomes from pursuing those great follies. Now, he switches to a list of seven follies that are so great, Solomon doesn't feel the need to go into great depth about them. He has talked about each of them before. Let's refresh our memories on each of these:

- **Haughty eyes.** According to the New Oxford American Dictionary, "haughty" means "arrogantly superior and disdainful." The person with haughty eyes looks down on others in a demeaning way. Rather than being humble before the LORD, this person is prideful to the point of arrogance, thinking himself superior to others. This pride is the gateway to the other six detestable behaviors.
- **Lying tongue.** Rather than telling the truth, the person with a lying tongue has to twist the facts or make things up. What's worse, these lies are intended to cause harm of some sort. The person who tells these kinds of lies is using the perverse speech Solomon talked about in Chapter 2.
- **Hands that shed innocent blood.** This isn't referring to those who accidentally kill another. The law provides a manner in which to deal with those situations. This is referring to those who intentionally strike out at those who are innocent. The innocent person can range from the harmless soul discussed in Chapter 1—the killer doesn't know this harmless soul; he just happened to walk by when the killer decides to kill—to a close friend who has never wronged the killer. Whatever the case, the killer has no reason to attack his victim.
- **A heart that devises wicked schemes.** According to the New Oxford American Dictionary, "scheming" is defined as "given to or involved in making secret and underhanded plans." Scheming is bad enough; wicked scheming is in another category of evil. It introduces a truly wicked level of violence toward others.
- **Feet that are quick to rush into evil.** In Chapter 1, we see these wicked people are quick to run into sin and to shed innocent blood. While the two prior behaviors involved waiting or scheming, this person runs headlong into evil. He isn't going to wait for an opportunity to do evil; he is going to commit evil as soon as he can.

- **A false witness who pours out lies.** Witnesses play an important role in our communities. When something of community interest happens, we rely on those who were there to tell us what happened (what they witnessed). So, as a witness, it is a great evil to fabricate a story about what happened, especially if it results in an innocent person taking the rap for a crime he didn't commit. Here, it probably refers to false testimony resulting in the death penalty for the innocent person.
- **A man who stirs up dissension among brothers.** In the prior section, Solomon talked about scoundrels and villains who stirred up dissension. Certainly a bad thing. Now, he talks about a man who goes about trying to cause dissension among brothers. Whether he is talking about blood relatives, men who are as close as brothers (such as David and Jonathan), or a close-knit family, it's an especially evil man who works to create dissension among those who have close relationships.

Because they are detestable to the LORD, these seven great follies are in a special category. Unlike the foolishness of the over-promising person or the sluggard, those who engage in these seven detestable follies do so with an evil intent. The LORD, who is the ultimate good and cannot stand evil, hates to see anyone do evil.

Business Application

What a list of detestable behaviors! Each one in its own right can create grief within an organization.

Take the first one: an employee who arrogantly believes he is superior to others and is dismissive of them. When that employee is right about something, he becomes insufferable. He'll make sure you know all about his brilliance, and he will keep bringing up his brilliance to show how superior he is. When he is wrong about something, it is almost impossible to get him to acknowledge, much less understand, his error. If in a position of power, this employee can crush worker morale or hurt the company through his decisions.

Many of the late-1800s tycoons took fledging companies (Ford, Standard Oil, etc.) and, through their brilliance and audacity, made them the dominant company in their industries. But along the way, some of the founders, because of their arrogant pride, engaged in behavior toward their employees, competitors, and even close associates that proved to be detrimental to their companies.

Justifiably so, much of today's soft skills development training emphasizes the idea of humble, servant leadership. You should be aware of your skills and abilities, but you should not let it go to your head, getting to the point where you think you know it all. You don't. Rather, the company and the employees gain from sharing knowledge and ideas. You never know from where the next great idea will come; drop the haughty eyes and learn.

How does anyone ever get away with a lying tongue? As I think back over the years, I try not to think about how many times bosses, peers, employees, and vendors lied to me. There were certainly times when promises were made and, even though much effort was put in to make the promise come true, someone just couldn't deliver on the promise. I see that much differently than the person who would promise delivery schedules she had no intention of meeting. Or staff members who would submit an agreed-upon project on time saying it was complete, but a quick review, sometimes within a few minutes, revealed there was a lot more work to do and it wasn't close to being complete. Or leaders who said one thing and then did another. The list of purposeful lies goes on and on and on, as does the damage they do. They cause so much wasted effort and hurt so many people.

As we look at the next three examples, let's assume no one in your organization is going so far as wanting to actually kill or murder someone! But they may want to do something that has a seriously harmful effect. I'm thinking about those who don't care about whom they injure to get to the top. If this person sees another employee as a threat to her own advancement, she will take steps to ensure this "competitor" is put into an embarrassing position, one that might endanger his advancement or continued employment. Going further, she might even scheme with others to carry out her plot. And it's an evil plot because the person she is gunning for is doing absolutely nothing wrong; his only fault is he is in the way. This happens a lot in the political world. Just look at all the negative advertising intended to label rather than inform.

Then there is the person who always seems to be involved in whatever trouble is going on. I'm thinking of those who make it their business, even though it is none of their business, to find out about all of the "issues" going on in the company. Of course, finding out isn't good enough; they have to spread it around to their friends. It is like they are addicted; they have to snoop to get all of the dirt they can. I suppose that is one form of rushing to evil. It definitely caused us problems from time to time as upsetting rumors circulated around the company. Often these rumors were dumbfounding; there was no way we were going to do what the rumor said we were going to do. We were forced to take time away from other work to dispel the rumor, only to have another inaccurate rumor come to light a month or two later. It really was remarkable. No matter how many times these busybodies were wrong, others believed them.

False witnesses are truly like a snake in the grass; you never know when you'll get bit. One personnel action comes to mind. As you'll see, it left an indelible imprint. We had conducted an opinion survey of our employees and, in reviewing the results, it was obvious a morale problem existed in one of my divisions. In order to find out what the problem might be, I spent a day interviewing each of the employees individually to get their perspectives. What I heard from half of the employees astounded me. Their descriptions of the supervisor's behavior were unbelievable and clearly outside of the standards we had set. In consulting with our Human

Relations department, legal consultants, and my boss, we agreed termination was the correct action to take. The supervisor appealed, and we all headed to the independent review board to present our cases. My case, as the employer, fell apart as witness after witness changed their testimony from what they had given me in the initial interviews! Rather than being a problem, the witnesses testified their relationship with the supervisor was okay. As you might expect, because we had based our case on these false witnesses, we lost the case and the supervisor was reinstated. As we brought the supervisor back on board, the next few months proved to be quite interesting—another story for another time.

Finally, let's look at the person who stirs up dissension between brothers. This is a particularly nasty behavior within an organization, because it seeks to destroy the closeness among groups you have worked so hard to create. For instance, you may have a cross-functional team of supervisors who have jelled into an incredibly effective group. Not only does the team generate profitable ideas and handle problems as they arise, but the team members also genuinely like each other and look out for each other as well as the company. It's a dynamic team; it exemplifies the culture you want throughout the organization.

But an employee, jealous of that team's success and status, starts to raise doubts in some of the team members' minds. In a side conversation, this employee asks a seemingly innocuous question about a matter, which gets a team member thinking about a possible injustice being done to his department. The dissension-driven employee may take a positive comment a team member told him about a second team member and twist the comment into a negative one that he freely shares with the second team member. Just one whisper won't create the dissension this employee is trying to create. But eventually, if not stopped, this employee can create cracks in the team, reducing its effectiveness and cohesion.

It's especially nasty when the company is a family-owned and -operated business torn apart by dissension. Right now, I'm thinking of a once-prosperous family-owned restaurant with multiple locations.

While the father was alive, he made the decisions and kept harmony in the family. However, after he died, family members—egged on by a spouse or two—created a situation where they couldn't even agree to continue business operations. Overnight, at least it seemed that way, the restaurants closed. Each side brought in attorneys, and all activity came to a standstill. Those buildings sat empty for years before the family members reached a resolution. In the end, they all lost.

Loss is the result you'll get from allowing these behaviors to exist in your company. Each one undercuts and damages a company differently and can bring a company down. Good companies with good business cultures must continually work at ferreting out those who engage in these detestable behaviors. Stay on guard!

Personal Application

This section should catch our attention right away. If the LORD hates or detests some behaviors, wouldn't you want to know what those things are so you can avoid really ticking off God? It's one thing to engage in great follies like false promises and sluggardly behavior, which emanate from the Simple or the Young. It's quite something else to engage in the activities enumerated here. They come from evil intent and are designed to hurt others deeply, sometimes to the point of killing them.

While it is easy to point your finger at others and talk about "them," Solomon is directing his wisdom directly at you. Yes, he is asking you to take stock of yourself. Imagine these few verses as a series of essay questions for you to consider and complete. Each of the seven behaviors would have questions like these:

Section 1:

- Do you have a proud heart (haughty eyes)?
- How have the actions coming from your proud heart hurt others?

- Do you realize how detestable those actions, and a proud heart, are to the LORD?
- Will you turn toward righteous living and give up your proud heart?

Section 2:

- Do you tell lies rather than telling the truth (lying tongue)?
- How have the actions coming from your lying tongue hurt others?
- Do you realize how detestable those actions, and a lying tongue, are to the LORD?
- Will you turn toward righteous living and give up your lying tongue?

Let me suggest you take some time to consider these questions for each behavior carefully. If you are serious about knowing if you engaged in these detestable behaviors, don't be surprised when past actions start coming to mind. God has a gracious way of working with those who seek the truth about themselves.

As I've written about each of these seven behaviors, rest assured I've been reminded of several of my past evil behaviors, more of them than I want to admit. I wish I could go back and get a redo, but life doesn't work that way. So I live with the regret from my past actions. But I also live with the knowledge that God forgives those who confess their unjust and unfair actions, repent of their evil ways, and accept God's ways. God wipes the slate clean of our past actions and remembers them no more—how gracious! His grace extends to being willing to walk with us day by day to help us become the person we can be—one who does what is right, just, and fair.

God took the first step by letting us know He is there and ready to guide us out of our evil ways to the ways of righteousness. The next step is up to you. Won't you take that step toward God and His goodness? He's waiting for you with open arms!

Chapter 26

Let Wisdom Keep You from Great Folly
Proverbs 6:20-29

My son, keep your father's commands and do not forsake your mother's teaching. Bind them upon your heart forever; fasten them around your neck. When you walk, they will guide you; when you sleep, they will watch over you; when you awake, they will speak to you. For these commands are a lamp, this teaching is a light, and the corrections of discipline are the way to life, keeping you from the immoral woman, from the smooth tongue of the wayward wife. Do not lust in your heart after her beauty or let her captivate you with her eyes, for the prostitute reduces you to a loaf of bread, and the adulteress preys upon your very life. Can a man scoop fire into his lap without his clothes being burned? Can a man walk on hot coals without his feet being scorched? So is he who sleeps with another man's wife; no one who touches her will go unpunished.

Background/Circumstances

Having gone over ten examples of great folly in the first nineteen verses of Chapter 6, Solomon takes a few verses to remind his son of the value of Solomon's commands and his mother's teaching (see discussion in Chapter 3) and how these commands and teaching will protect the son if he makes them a part of his life, both internal and external—internal by binding them upon his heart so his heart beats in tune with the commands and teaching, external by wearing the commands and teaching like a beautiful necklace he and others can see and appreciate. If the son handles the commands and teaching as Solomon recommends, his son's pathway will always be well lit; he'll see where he should be going and skip by trouble lurking in the darkness.

But it gets even better:

- Whenever the son starts to walk or take action, the commands and teaching will be faithful guides.
- While he sleeps, resting and defenseless, the commands and teaching keep watch over him, in his thoughts and dreams.
- When he awakes, answers to his questions and directions for that day will be clear.

And if those benefits aren't enough, these commands and teaching serve as a basis of discipline to correct the son should he ever start to venture away from them. The son will need all of this protection to keep away from the smooth-talking immoral woman—also called the "wayward wife." She knows the words to say and things to do to entice and captivate a man. This isn't her first rodeo; she is practiced in her art and sees the son as just another man to conquer. The son will be like a loaf of bread she enjoys and consumes before looking for another loaf of bread to satisfy her hunger. Although her words may make the son feel special, he doesn't really mean a thing to her; he is just a means to put money in her pockets and fulfill her craven desires.

Solomon reminds his son the lust she inspires becomes a blazing fire that consumes whoever goes to her. Holding her and walking in her ways is like holding fire in your lap or walking on hot coals; the person who does it is going to get severely burned!

Business Application

This section makes me recall situations when we had an individual (board member, CEO, staffer, vendor, citizen, media representative, or others) try to entice us to do something that was far from our mission and culture. Many times, the proposal sounded like something we needed to do, but wisdom suggested a different course. I'll discuss two proposals, but first you need a little background about the setting and circumstances.

In the early 1990s, Salina, Kansas, was one of many cities recovering from the economic swoon of the late 1980s caused by the savings and loan debacle. An early indication Salina was going to recover quickly was almost simultaneous announcements by several major retail companies. Each one was coming to town or greatly expanding their footprint. Those companies were anticipating an economic boom for the area rather than a slow recovery. At the same time, Salina was at the tail end of its housing recovery from the 1964 closure of Schilling Air Force Base. That's a long story in its own right, but one result of the closure was the large number of housing vacancies resulting from the 25-percent population loss after the airbase closed. It took more than two decades but the housing glut turned into a housing shortage. The housing shortage and economic recovery converged in the early 1990s to create a red-hot housing and retail market. City revenues soared as sales tax and property tax revenues both grew by more than 10 percent each year for three straight years. A fiscally conservative city suddenly found itself with more revenues than expected. How to use those unexpected revenues was the question of the day.

With that short background, let's look at two proposals that came in at different times.

Proposal 1. The community theater group realized it needed to renovate and expand their facilities to meet the growing demand for seating, as well as provide better educational and performance opportunities. Because the community benefitted from its work, community theater supporters asked the city government to provide capital and operating expenses. The community theater was without a doubt a good cause and benefitted the city's residents. As the governing body and staff considered the theater's request, two key questions came to bear:

- How would providing support to outside groups' capital and operating needs affect the city's long-term ability to fund its primary obligations of police, fire, streets, etc.?
- What expectation should the city set for other community organizations when it came to financing good causes?

After several discussions on the topic, the governing body adopted a policy providing for limited capital funding—one-third of the capital need—for qualifying nonprofit community organizations. To receive city support, the nonprofit community organization needed to demonstrate it had funding in place for the remaining capital as well as the additional operating costs it would incur from the expansion. In addition, the community organization had to demonstrate its facility and programs were available to the general public—even if a nominal fee was involved—and contributed to the greater public good.

Proposal 2. After three years of red-hot tax revenue growth, the city had a decision to make when preparing the 1994 budget on how to apply these unanticipated revenues. One proposal came from tax-revolt adherents. They proposed the city use all extra revenues from one year to reduce property taxes for the next year. (As I recall, the reduction would have been around 25 percent.) In discussing the idea of significant property tax reductions, the governing body wanted answers to two key questions:

- How would reducing the property tax rate and revenues affect the city's long-term ability to fund its primary obligations of police, fire, streets, etc.?
- Is there a better use for these extra revenues?

As the governing body members considered the mix of services the city provided, they felt very confident the service mix was right on the button—not too much and not too little. Small tweaks needed to be made to adjust to changing community needs, but all services were at the appropriate level. As the governing body members looked at future financial projections, they saw a 25-percent reduction in property taxes would require a much larger percentage increase within two years. Rather than making property taxes yo-yo up and down, the governing body adopted a plan to reduce the property tax rate gradually over the next five years. That plan allowed the governing body to check long-term financial stability during the annual budget process. Before adopting the next property tax rate decrease, the governing body had to be satisfied future basic city operations like police, fire, streets, and others could be funded at projected service levels needed in succeeding years.

Besides the actions on these two proposals, the governing body was interested in using the extra revenues to increase the city's financial sustainability. After several discussions, the governing body decided to use a portion of the additional revenues to pay for smaller capital items with cash rather than financing them over ten years. In the course of three years, the city avoided paying 5- to 6-percent interest on millions of dollars of debt.

The overall theme here is the governing body in Salina, Kansas, knew what it was about—providing basic city services at levels desired by the community. The governing body evaluated every proposal made to ensure basic city services could be maintained. The governing body held true to its vision and avoided pitfalls that could have led to future financial problems. Just like the advice from Solomon, the governing body members kept to their "commands and teaching," were guided by them, and used the light from them to stay away from "wayward" proposals. Because the governing body members held to their commands and teaching, they built a solid financial foundation for the city government and future governing boards. Of all the places I worked, that group of governing body members was the best at understanding their charge from the community and fulfilling it.

Many organizations spend a good amount of time and money developing visions, mission statements, and other top-down direction. More is spent on reams of paper explaining Human Resources and other organizational policies. I've worked on my fair share of them. But as I read this section of Proverbs, I can't help but wonder if those all missed the mark. If they had hit the mark, why did we still have to deal with results from bad choices that felt like having fire in our laps or walking over hot coals?

Rather than all of the corporate mumbo-jumbo that seems to change with each new administration, perhaps we can agree on a few basic reasons why an organization exists:

- **Earn a reasonable profit.** Profit expectations can vary dramatically by industry and purpose. Within the world of business, companies in high-volume sales with multiple competitors have different profit expectations than a company in a regulated industry; likewise, they both have different profit expectations than a company in a high-demand, low-competitive market. But they all are in business to earn a reasonable profit that satisfies their owners. Nonprofits also want to earn a reasonable profit; they just measure it differently, usually in changed lives. Like a business that isn't making a profit, a nonprofit that isn't changing lives won't make it.
  Let's not forget all the governmental organizations. Although funded by taxes and fees, they also are expected to generate a "profit" for their communities or constituents. Among those benefits is the provision of police, fire, parks, water, sewer, and other professional services at costs below those an individual would pay for them. For example, it would be pretty expensive

for me to hire police or fire protection for my property on my own. Having professionally trained, well-equipped municipal police and fire forces provides a higher level of service at a much lower cost than I could deliver if trying to do it on my own.

- **Do good.** This standard covers a lot of ground. You can do good for your customers and clients, your staff, yourself, your industry, your community, and so many others. You also can ensure your product is as environmentally sound and sustainable as possible. You can provide fair compensation to your employees and good products to your customers. You can work well with clients to give them the best advice you can for their situation.
- **Act well.** A lot of problems would never occur if we all acted well toward each other. For example, can you imagine how things would operate if people really respected each other? If a decision affected Joanna and her work group, because you respected them, you would involve Joanna and her work group in the discussion. If you respected Julia, you would talk to her about a problem in her workgroup rather than going straight to her boss. If you respected your peers and boss, you would seek out their thoughts on how you could help them and how you could improve your own performance. If you respected your fellow worker, you would avoid committing any offense toward them, and if you did, you would be the first to recognize it and go to them to make amends. Organizations can act well, too, in any number of ways. Do you treat your customers well or are they viewed as revenue sources to be pumped dry of as much money as you can get from them? Do you use your position and influence to lead community efforts?

Of course, these basic reasons for an organization to exist must be balanced. Letting one of these reasons dominate the other puts your organization in peril. Accordingly, the best organizations do an outstanding job balancing these reasons and not letting any one of them dominate the other two for very long.

Whatever you come up with as your "commands and teaching," it has to be crystal clear so:

- All in the organization can "bind" them in their hearts and "fasten" them around their necks.
- They provide guidance and light to every employee.
- They make it easy to determine when someone is going astray so corrective action can be taken quickly.

If your commands and teaching are like those Solomon recommends, you can avoid having fire thrown in your lap or being forced to walk over hot coals!

Personal Application

Did you know there are a few secrets to walking over hot coals? According to a July 8, 2022, *Science ABC* article by Hussain Kanchwaia, the length of the hot coals to be traversed has to be fairly short, never more than fifteen feet. In addition, the person "walking" over them minimizes the amount of time each foot is in contact with the coals, usually just a fraction of a second. The reason someone can make it that far over the coals is due to the moisture feet produce. There is just enough moisture on the bottom of a foot to protect someone for a brief trip over hot coals. But you never see anyone taking a leisurely stroll in a field of hot coals—if you do, I want to know. Why? Because hot coals will burn feet staying in contact with the coals for more than a fraction of a second or over a longer path. Violate those constraints and your feet will be burned.

If walking on coals is foolhardy, someone scooping fire into his own lap is more so. Not only will the person's lap get burned, but his clothes also will catch fire and start burning other parts of his body. Even quick action won't prevent the person's body from being severely burned. Burn injuries are among some of the most painful injuries and, even in our world of medical miracles, burns often leave disfiguring scars.

We all learn at an early age about the dangers of fire. My lesson, not too painful, came from touching the rusted metal barrel we used on the farm to burn trash. One day, I saw a whiff of smoke coming from the barrel. Curious at what was going on, and with the ground around the barrel being uneven, I put my hands on the barrel to steady myself so I could look inside it. Fortunately for me, the fire was a small one at the bottom of the barrel; the barrel's side was too hot to handle but not quite hot enough to burn. My reactions took over, and my hands flew off the barrel even before my mind had time to think, "That's hot; get your hands off it!" I'm sure my parents had warned me about fire and how it could burn, but I had a moment where I either forgot what they had told me or didn't quite realize how it applied to the trash barrel. It's safe to say the warnings about fire became very real to me in an instant; I never had to be taught about the danger of fire again!

So like real fire, the "fire" of adultery and prostitution deserves all of the warning labels we possibly can put on them.

In the case of prostitution, a female prostitute works to inflame a man's passion so he'll forgo what he knows is right. In return, that fire bakes him into something much like a loaf of bread, a commodity of low value, even commonplace and indistinguishable from other loaves. There's no respect; to the prostitute, her client is just another transaction. When the roles are reversed, the man takes the role of the prostitute and the woman becomes the loaf of bread. Love is nowhere to be found in these relationships. Instead, they are empty relationships leading victims astray.

Similar to the prostitute, the wayward wife (or husband) entices her victim with smooth words, sultry eyes, and other indications she is available and interested. She seeks to fire up a man's lust to the point where he forgets all the cautions about sleeping with another man's wife. The fact this relationship happens on the sly should tell you how dangerous it is. No one who touches another man's wife will go unpunished.

One final comment. Did you see the phrase "the corrections of discipline are the way to life"? That tells us two things:

A man who knows the commands and teaching and uses them constantly will be given some sort of discipline—warning, if you prefer—when he starts to consider the prostitute, wayward wife, or other poor choice. Much like my experience with the hot trash barrel, the discipline will cause a man to realize he is dealing with something that can burn him.

A man always has two options after receiving discipline. He can:

- Rush headlong past the discipline, keep on the bad path, and become like a loaf of bread to be consumed by others.
- Come to his senses, turn back to the good path, and enjoy the promised blessings and honor.

While it's best if you can keep on the good path all of the time, should you stray, realize the corrections of discipline are the way of life. Because these corrections and discipline are for your own good, be like the man who came to his senses and returned to the good path. It's much better to enjoy blessings and honor than to be treated like a loaf of bread.

Chapter 27

Disciplining Those Who Lack Judgment
Proverbs 6:30-35

Men do not despise a thief if he steals to satisfy his hunger when he is starving. Yet if he is caught, he must pay sevenfold, though it costs him all the wealth of his house. But a man who commits adultery lacks judgment; whoever does so destroys himself. Blows and disgrace are his lot, and his shame will never be wiped away; for jealousy arouses a husband's fury, and he will show no mercy when he takes revenge. He will not accept any compensation; he will refuse the bribe, however great it is.

Background/Circumstances

Having just talked about how sleeping with another man's wife is like asking for fire to be scooped into your lap or walking on hot coals, Solomon adds some perspective to his statements by doing a comparison between a starving thief, who takes food to satisfy his physical hunger, to the man who commits adultery, who takes a woman not his to satisfy his sexual hunger.

Solomon observed most people didn't despise a starving thief. Many of them may have experienced hunger or had a reason to consider what they would be willing to do if they couldn't feed their family. Deep down, if it came to that, each person knew he would steal to keep from starving. While they didn't despise the person who stole for that reason, the thief was required to make restitution to the party from whom he stole. By law, the required restitution was seven times the amount taken. Knowing if caught he would have to pay back seven times as much as he took gives an indication of how desperate the thief had become. The thief's situation had come down to life or death; people understood why he would steal.

But the man committing adultery wasn't in the same situation as the starving thief. The man committing adultery was far from being in a life-or-death situation from starving. Instead, his own actions put his life in mortal danger.

Notice Solomon doesn't say the thief lacks judgment; rather, he made a reasonable judgment. Unless he acquired food by whatever means available to him, he was going to die. While Solomon isn't condoning stealing, he is saying what the thief did made sense.

Solomon has a different take on the man committing adultery. The adulterer completely lacks judgment. Why? Because he knows the result of adultery, once discovered, will be disgrace, shame, no mercy, and, as required by law, death. The adulterer also knows how he would react if he found his wife in an adulterous affair with another man; he wouldn't show the other man any mercy. Truly, no amount of money could dissuade him from enforcing punishment. He would make the man having an affair with his wife suffer every lawful punishment. While the adulterer knows he would require capital punishment for the one who commits adultery with his wife, he thinks the rules will be different for him when he commits adultery with another man's wife. His thinking shows a complete lack of judgment.

Business Application

Discipline can be a tricky thing. There are times when you have to discipline someone even though you really don't want to do it. Sometimes the offense seems fairly minor or understandable—like stealing a bit of food to keep from starving. As you learn more about the offense, you may find yourself feeling badly for the offender, especially if it's his first offense. While it may be tempting to give the offender somewhat of a pass, that isn't the right thing to do. Whatever the prescribed discipline for the offense, you need to apply it. Otherwise, how will the offender learn?

Although you are discipling the person for his offense, you can include a message affirming him while still correcting him for his actions. If you need help in delivering such a message, you can enroll in a management course specifically targeting how to discipline for an offense while affirming the offender.

I benefitted tremendously from these management classes. The presenters used the course materials and group discussion to challenge the group's understanding of human relations and steer us to a better way of understanding and dealing with others. As I became a more understanding supervisor, I was better able to discipline for the deed while affirming the doer.

As a supervisor, you'll get to deal with a wide variety of offenses and people who commit them. Some situations will be comical, almost like the Abbott and Costello "Who's on First" skit. When everyone involved understands what happened, you all will have a good laugh, fix the miscommunication, and move on. In some situations, your employee already will have realized her mistake and taken actions to self-correct. As the situations become more serious, employees become less willing to admit to their actions. You'll need good human relations skills to show these employees you can affirm them while holding them accountable for their actions. Done well, your employee comes out of the experience a better person and someone you want to retain.

Now and then, you'll run into an employee who is like the man who commits adultery. This employee does things he knows are wrong. In this situation, the egregious nature of his offense and his attitude are so closely intertwined separating the two will be next to impossible. When you approach him about the offense, you'll get a barrage of excuses or accusations. He simply won't recognize his faulty judgment or culpability. After going through a few of these situations, I finally realized dealing with this kind of person was almost impossible. The best course was to end the relationship as quickly as possible.

It reminds me of a story a fire chief told me about one of his firefighters. The firefighters had gone to a residence to put out a fire, which they did with minimal damage. As the firefighters were doing their final checks, this firefighter saw a ring on a bedroom nightstand and, on the way out of the room, pocketed it. When the owners were allowed back into the house, they discovered the ring was missing. They filed a report with the police department. Following their protocols, police department personnel promptly checked with the local pawn shop and found the ring. The police department retrieved the ring and returned it to the rightful owner. But that wasn't the end of their work.

Besides providing the police with the ring, the pawn shop also provided the name of the person who sold them the ring; it was the firefighter. The police chief contacted the fire chief to let him know what had happened. Now, a city can't have a reputation its fire department will steal from you whenever you call them to your house. So, the fire chief called the firefighter in, dismissed him from the force, and told him to clean out his locker.

This firefighter lost his job over the $15 he received for the ring. To this day, I remember how astonished the fire chief was to know a firefighter would risk his job and career over a $15 ring. To make matters worse, the firefighter was doing well financially and didn't need the $15 he received from selling the ring. What astonished the fire chief the most was the firefighter didn't seem to understand why his offense was such a big deal. He expected to be talked to, maybe given a day or two off without pay, and then be reinstated. Instead, because he violated the public trust, he was fired quickly.

Such is the message from this section of Proverbs. When you have someone who demonstrates an intentional lack of judgment, there really isn't any other way to handle it than their dismissal. Literally, you can't get rid of the person quickly enough. Who knows what else they may do? But one thing is sure: By removing them now, you'll only be dealing with their past lack of judgment—not the future troubles they may cause.

Personal Application

There's something within us that makes us want to be seen as a person who makes good decisions, a person who demonstrates good judgment. But we don't always meet that high standard. Like the starving thief, we can get into situations where we do something we never thought we would do. For instance, we would never lie, but somehow, we forget to mention a defect in the car we are trying to sell to a buyer. Let the buyer beware, right? We say we would never steal but we don't correct the grocery clerk's mistake when it is in our favor. After all, it was the clerk's mistake, wasn't it? We say we would never cheat someone, but when we charge someone the bid price for a job even though the bid price contained a double charge for the materials supplied, we tell ourselves it is just too much trouble to adjust the price. After all, didn't he agree to pay the bid price?

Maybe you won't be despised for those kinds of ethical lapses, but don't be surprised how people react when they find out that you lied to, stole from, or cheated them. Depending on the situation some people may be somewhat forgiving. Then again, others may be more determined to make sure you don't get away with the offense. They may file charges and take you to court. For sure, they will want you to cover their actual financial loss. Depending on how much you misled them and how aggrieved they feel, don't be surprised if they pursue, and the court awards, punitive damages as a way to encourage you to change your ways. While the final bill may not be seven times what you took, paying it off could take a long time.

But the man who commits adultery faces a jealous husband who will not let the offender off so easily. Rather than a monetary settlement, an adulterer can expect blows, disgrace, and fury. Because of that fury, no mercy will be shown. The jealous husband is going to insist on the maximum punishment. No matter how large the bribe, he will refuse it.

Knowing this is what happens to the adulterer, you almost can hear Solomon asking those who are toying with committing adultery, "Have you lost your mind?" Having described the beautiful relationship between a husband and wife at the end of Chapter 5 and how his son can achieve it, Solomon stresses the great folly his son undertakes if he seeks to commit adultery. It's an astonishing lack of judgment to forsake something of great value—his wife who adds good things to his life—to be with the adulteress. The adulteress will treat the son like a loaf of bread. When he finds out about the adultery, her husband will have the son beaten and killed for going to bed with his wife. A man committing adultery is taking an incredible risk for momentary pleasure.

Most of us started out our marriages with high hopes, looking forward to sharing life together. Fairly soon, we learned life presents twists and turns that can strain a marriage. Those who are wise use the opportunities the twists and turns provide to build something into their marriage to make it even more valuable. However, too many couples take an opposite approach.

For example, rather than learning to appreciate his spouse in these difficult moments, the husband starts to think, "She doesn't understand me" or "Things do look greener on the other side." He starts to notice the flirty glances from another woman. It's a downward spiral from there. Unless the husband comes to his senses, he'll find himself in the arms of another woman. And he'll pay and pay and pay. His former wife will want her share, including the kids and the house and who knows what else. The other woman's husband will want his pound of flesh, too. The ex-wife and the jealous husband, especially if one or both are deeply hurt, will not be willing to relent in their demands. The man who commits adultery will pay for what he did.

In today's world with no-fault divorce, the stigma of divorce isn't nearly as great as it used to be. But even then, there's always talk. Your friends and associates will see what is going on and form their opinions—and have their discussions—about what happened to your marriage. While still your friends, if you were the one who blew up the marriage by stepping out with someone else, their opinion of you will be diminished. They may not tell you to your face, but you can be certain they know you are someone who is willing to trade allegiances if something "better" comes along. If you were willing to "trade out" your wife, why would you be hesitant to do the same to them?

When you lack judgment, you do things that don't make a lot of sense. You give up your longtime, reliable friends for new friends who strike your fancy. You give up your spouse who stuck with you through difficult years for a new woman who seems more exciting. You give up on your kids when all they really needed was for you to be there and to be an encouragement for them. You give up on the good path to take a path that seems easier or more fun.

Stepping from the good path toward forbidden fruit is a real temptation; that's why Solomon brings it up. Rather than keep silent, Solomon talks to his son about these temptations and compares what happens to the starving thief versus the adulterer. Both do wrong. Others may understand why the starving man stole but have no understanding for the one who stole another man's wife. While the thief may lose all the wealth of his house, at least he is still alive. The adulterer will lose his life, even though he offers all he has as a bribe to keep his life. Either route leads to great loss but, by far, the adulterer sustains the greatest loss.

Once again, knowing all of that is true, why would someone pursue the great folly of adultery? I think Solomon would say he stepped away from wisdom and went on a Fool's errand. As we saw in Proverbs Chapter 1, the Fool despises wisdom and discipline. When temptation comes, the Fool rejects what he knows is right and goes after the temptation—whatever it might be and no matter the outcome.

As he ends this chapter, Solomon pleads with you to understand the wages of adultery and to stay away from the temptation. He continues that plea in Chapter 7 and tells a story of what happened to a young man who became a victim of an adulteress. Because Solomon devotes so much of his letter to adultery and wayward women, tremendous dangers must be awaiting you if you start down that path. If you want to be wise, you'll stay far away from that path!

Proverbs

Chapter Seven

Chapter 28

Using Dramatic Stories to Make Your Point
Proverbs 7:1-27

My son, keep my words and store up my commands within you. Keep my commands and you will live; guard my teachings as the apple of your eye. Bind them on your fingers; write them on the tablet of your heart. Say to wisdom, "You are my sister," and call understanding your kinsman; they will keep you from the adulteress, from the wayward wife with her seductive words.

At the window of my house I looked out through the lattice. I saw among the simple, I noticed among the young men, a youth who lacked judgment. He was going down the street near her corner, walking along in the direction of her house at twilight, as the day was fading, as the dark of night set in.

Then out came a woman to meet him, dressed like a prostitute and with crafty intent. (She is loud and defiant, her feet never stay at home; now in the street, now in the squares, at every corner she lurks.) She took hold of him and kissed him and with a brazen face she said, "I have fellowship offerings at home; today I fulfilled my vows. So I came out to meet you; I looked for you and have found you! I have covered my bed with colored linens from Egypt. I have perfumed my bed with myrrh, aloes and cinnamon. Come, let's drink deep of love till morning; let's enjoy ourselves with love! My husband is not at home; he has gone on a long journey. He took his purse filled with money and will not be home till full moon." With persuasive words she led him astray; she seduced him with her smooth talk. All at once he followed her like an ox going to the slaughter, like a deer stepping into a noose till an arrow pierces his liver, like a bird darting into a snare, little knowing it will cost him his life.

Now then, my sons, listen to me; pay attention to what I say. Do not let your heart turn to her ways or stray into her paths. Many are the victims she has brought down; her slain are a mighty throng. Her house is a highway to the grave, leading down to the chambers of death.

Background/Circumstances

Solomon continues his discourse on the great folly of adultery in this chapter. He starts by telling his son to hold on closely to the words and commands he is teaching him. His urgency is obvious when you consider the son is to "keep," "store," "bind," and "write" them in his heart and on his fingers. In addition, he is to "guard" them as he would his own eyes. Then, Solomon implores his son to position wisdom and understanding as close to him as a sister or a kinsman. After this, he illustrates his point with a story of a young man who fails to follow these commands.

In the story, the young man takes actions demonstrating his poor judgment. Knowing where a wayward wife lives, he "happens" to walk down her street, toward her house, as it is getting dark. One gets the impression the young man likes the idea of playing with fire but he doesn't really want to get burned. It's almost like he is being egged on by his friends, so he heads toward her house thinking nothing will really happen.

Imagine his surprise when she comes out to meet him. She is dolled up and says she was waiting just for him. Of course, the truth is she was ready to accept just about anyone who was foolish enough to come her way—it meant she didn't have to go out looking for someone with whom to spend the night. She promises a great night of great food from the fellowship offering, a seductive setup and a full night of lovemaking, and they won't get caught because her husband is away on a trip. By the time she ends her well-practiced speech, the young man is entranced and, on what sounds like a whim, "all at once followed her." All resistance was gone. Solomon compares him to animals and birds that are enticed into snares that result in their death. The young man truly has no more judgment than a wild animal.

After this illustration, Solomon implores his sons to avoid the folly of turning their hearts toward wayward women. Too many men have fallen to wayward women and the certain death that folly brings. Solomon describes that death four different ways: "brought down," "slain," "highway to the grave," and "chambers of death."

Business Application

Good stories are effective when trying to make a point. Look at the story above. The characters are vivid. You almost can see the unsure young man as he slowly walks down the street and toward the house of temptation. Knowing what is coming, didn't your mind start to feel badly for the young man? Didn't you want to tell him to turn away before it was too late? But, like Solomon, we can't help the young man in time. Instead, the woman jumps out, seduces him, and escorts him over her threshold. His choice is a bad one and will end up costing him dearly. It's the kind of story meant to shock the listener, so he will remember it when he faces a similar circumstance.

Although there are plenty of stories about what not to do, the best stories are about what to do. Many companies have great stories of how they came into being and how they care for their customers. Do you know why your company exists? Most likely, your company started to meet some customer need, maybe one the customer didn't realize he had! Whatever it was, have you turned it into a story that gets told and remembered?

Although lots of long-remembered stories are out there, let's look at one from 1831. In this story, a young clerk in a village store realized he accidentally overcharged a customer six pennies. Rather than keep the pennies, the clerk walked five miles to return the money to the customer. The clerk became known for his honesty and the moniker stuck with him; he became known as "Honest Abe." He eventually became one of our most-revered presidents. Although there are many reasons why we might remember Abraham Lincoln, the story of his honesty in 1831 still rings true to us today.

While you may not have as dramatic a story as this to tell, if you look for them, you'll find employees who have gone the extra mile to help each other or your customers. If you haven't done it in a while, take some time to hang out with a group of employees and work your way into a conversation about people in their group who have helped others. You may find they are reluctant to brag, but with a little persistence, stories will start to emerge. Once the stories start, you might be surprised at how many times your employees step in to help others in ways you never realized. Talk to enough groups within your company and you'll gather a lot of really good stories.

As you think about which of these stories you want to use, you'll want to make sure the story is really tight and makes the point you want it to make. Let's review a good story that made the wrong point.

At one city where I worked, management was using a story to show the value of cross-functional teams. The story was about a cross-functional team that came together to address a payroll software failure. The team had a very short timeframe to resolve the problem. If the team failed to meet the deadline, payroll would not go out on time, a result no one wanted. The team worked well together and managed to resolve the problems, test the software fixes, and get payroll processed and out the door with ten minutes to spare. It was a good story.

But it had a weakness: It was only a good story because they met the deadline. If the team had missed the deadline by only a few minutes, rather than being a story about great cross-functional work, it would be a story about failure. As a result, instead of the desired focus of encouraging cross-functional work, the real focus of the story turned out to be how important winning was to upper management. With that interpretation becoming well known, instead of jumping into more cross-functional work teams, several department heads hedged their bets.

Department heads wanted to evaluate the likelihood of success before they would permit their employees to join a cross-functional team. Furthermore, if their individual department's success might be hampered by allowing their employees to participate on cross-functional teams, it was nearly impossible to get their department's participation on a cross-functional team. The department heads wanted to see how cross-functional work would be considered in their annual evaluations. As they suspected, department wins counted almost 100 percent toward a department head's annual evaluation; cross-functional work and wins barely were noted. Scoring was the same for all administrative positions; department wins counted while cross-functional work and wins didn't. You can predict the result: While cross-functional teams did continue, the enthusiasm for being on one melted away.

As you consider which stories to use, you need to make sure it aligns with how you want to run your company. Organizational structure, evaluations, incentives, and daily decisions all need to align or the story—no matter how good it sounds—will become another mixed message that causes confusion or joins the trash bin of good stories gone bad.

Take a hint from Solomon: The stories you use should be vivid and press home the point you want your employees to remember. Make them unforgettable stories and employees will recite them from memory and be proud to be a part of keeping the story alive. The more wisdom and understanding you can include in the stories the better, because you are creating a company and workforce that strives to do good, using good judgment to do what is right, fair, and just.

Personal Application

What story better illustrates how temptation and sin works in your life than this story? We have a young man, who knows better, leaving his friends to take a closer look at a wayward wife. Instead of doing the wise thing and walking away from temptation, he shows his lack of judgment by walking closer and closer to the wayward wife's home. He even times his journey so he arrives when there will be shadows so no one can see if he falls to temptation.

It is no mystery sin, in the form of this wayward woman, comes out to meet him. The evil one is ready to pounce when a person is at their weakest point and temptation is at its greatest. Oh, how good the evil one makes it all look! This young man can be full of food and make love all night long in a place prepared especially for him without anyone else ever knowing. And isn't that how the evil one presents his offers to us—all upside without a downside?

Those lacking judgment fall for it every time. In this story, the young man puts away judgment and believes all the lies he is told. Though a little bit of judgment would have shown him the trap into which he was walking, he goes right ahead and walks into the trap. He never sees, until it is too late, that he is caught and cannot escape.

Sin works the same for us today. How many people do you know who walked right past all the warning signs and ended up trapped in a mess they couldn't get out of easily? Lack of judgment leads to so many troubles in so many areas. Adultery is one of the more obvious and most painful due to the betrayal of oaths taken. But lack of judgment can affect you in financial, family, and work matters just as badly. For instance, spending more than you make every month is a lack of judgment on your part. You are headed toward financial disaster. Focusing on your spouse's negatives rather than her positives is a lack of judgment on your part. You are headed toward marital disaster. Giving a half-hearted effort at work is a lack of judgment on your part. You are headed toward poor job performance and disappointment.

Solomon gives us quite a list of actions that show a clear lack of judgment:

- **Putting up surety for your neighbor**
- **Making promises you can't keep**
- **Acting the sluggard (refusing to take control or sleeping instead of working)**
- **Plotting evil with deceit in your heart**
- **Stirring up dissension**
- **Having a proud heart (haughty eyes)**
- **Having a lying tongue**
- **Shedding innocent blood**
- **Devising wicked schemes**
- **Being quick to rush into evil**
- **Being a false witness**
- **Stirring up dissension among brothers**
- **Falling in with the wayward woman (adultery)**

As you look at the list, it's a good time to examine your own life. Are you showing wisdom or a lack of judgment in these areas? If you have any doubts about how you measure up to wisdom in these areas, it's in your best interest to ask a wise friend—even better a wise Christian friend—how you are stacking up in these areas. Ask her to tell you the truth. And when your friend gives you the truth, you have to be willing to hear the truth and deal with it. Having a lack of judgment in any of these areas for very long suppresses the good and brings the bad to the fore. The bad can be really, really bad and leave you hurting, lonely, and thinking there is no way out. Using good judgment in these areas brings really, really good benefits: a life full of good friends and family and blessings. You can't help but be a blessing to others.

Some of you may think, "It's too late for me. I'm so far in I can't get out. I'm so lost." Solomon does paint a damning picture for those who get off the wisdom path. He doesn't offer much hope for them, because the Good News hadn't been revealed to him. That Good News came a thousand years later, when Jesus said about himself, "For the Son of Man came to seek and to save what was lost" (Luke 19:10).

If you're feeling lost, I have good news. Jesus is looking for you and wants to save you. Whether you are lost, hurt, lonely, or seeking, all you have to do is ask Jesus and he will come walk beside you. He offers the blessed life Solomon talks about, for Jesus is LORD and the source of all wisdom. All you have to do is call on the name of Jesus and believe.

Why wait?

Proverbs

Chapter Eight

Chapter 29

Can You Hear Wisdom's Voice?
Proverbs 8:1-11

Does not wisdom call out? Does not understanding raise her voice? On the heights along the way, where the paths meet, she takes her stand; beside the gates leading into the city, at the entrances, she cries aloud: "To you, O men, I call out; I raise my voice to all mankind. You who are simple, gain prudence; you who are foolish, gain understanding. Listen, for I have worthy things to say; I open my lips to speak what is right. My mouth speaks what is true, for my lips detest wickedness. All the words of my mouth are just; none of them is crooked or perverse. To the discerning all of them are right; they are faultless to those who have knowledge. Choose my instruction instead of silver, knowledge rather than choice gold, for wisdom is more precious that rubies, and nothing you desire can compare with her."

Background/Circumstances

Having spent a few chapters talking about great follies, Solomon turns his attention back to wisdom. As in Chapter 1, Solomon reminds his son Wisdom is active not passive. Wisdom is calling out and raising her voice. Wisdom wants to be heard! To increase the likelihood Wisdom will be heard, Wisdom goes to those places where people will be. If he only will listen, Solomon's son will find Wisdom calling out from the heights, along the paths, beside the gates and at the entrances to the city. Essentially, wherever the son chooses to go, Wisdom will be there calling out to him. Because he will become king of Israel someday, knowing wisdom is all around him and available to him should be a comforting thought.

As a literary device, Solomon lets Wisdom speak for herself. Wisdom starts her speech by saying her message is for all men (and women). Rather than being reserved for one special group, wisdom is available to anyone who will listen. Since wisdom is for everyone, Wisdom says she raises her voice so all can hear. She wants to be heard above the daily hustle and bustle of life.

From there, Wisdom narrows her message to speak directly to those who are simple and foolish, including Solomon's son. Because those who fall into these categories are at great risk, Wisdom points out exactly what they need to gain if they are going to stay on the good path. It's a repeat from Chapter 1: The Simple needs to gain prudence while the Fool needs to gain understanding. After all the descriptions of the traps and snares awaiting the simple and foolish, there's a definite sense of urgency to Wisdom's command.

That urgent command is followed by another command: Listen to what I, Wisdom, have to say. The implication is clear. By listening to Wisdom, the simple and foolish—and Solomon's son—will learn what they need to know about living life well. Her words truly are worthy, because Wisdom will:

- **Speak what is right.** Wisdom has a purity that always requires her to speak up for what is right and worthy of our attention.
- **Speak what is true.** Wisdom detests wickedness, so she would never lie to anyone.
- **Speak what is just.** Wisdom always points the way to the good path a person should follow. She never will lead someone to a crooked or perverse way of living.

If the simple and foolish doubt Wisdom's testimony about herself, she points them to the testimony of those who are discerning and those who have knowledge—the two things the Simple and the Fool are lacking. It's especially interesting the discerning find her words to be right while the knowledgeable find her words to be faultless—true and just, respectively.

The final command in this section is to choose between two things. We might have expected the choices to be between right and wrong. However, Solomon's son is given the choice between 1) instruction and knowledge or 2) silver and choice gold. Wisdom urges him to choose instruction and knowledge, because the wisdom he will gain is more precious than silver, gold, and rubies. If that reason for choosing instruction and knowledge isn't enough, Wisdom tells Solomon's son nothing else he may desire—power, women, land, or anything else—comes close to the value he will find in wisdom. Wisdom is of supreme value.

Unsaid in this section, but just as true, is the thought that without discernment or knowledge the listener will find Wisdom's words to be wrong and full of error. To this listener, her words are simply foolishness or too simple. Given the choice, this person will choose silver, gold, and rubies, or whatever the other options might be, over wisdom every single time.

Wisdom calls out all day long to anywhere and everywhere mankind lives. The question isn't whether Solomon's son will hear her. Rather, the question is whether his son will use his discernment and knowledge in considering Wisdom's words. If he does, he will gain what is invaluable and worth much more than anything riches can buy.

Business Application

I've found it true that Wisdom calls out, sometimes with a voice so loud or a feeling so strong I can't ignore it. While her call comes in various situations, her call has been especially strong when two choices were in front of me and I was undecided about which one to choose.

It happened to me during two different job searches. In each job search, I made it through the long and extensive interviewing processes, with two agencies offering me their CFO position within days of each other. In both searches, each agency and its job offer had their strong points. Any of the agencies would have been a great place to work. The difficulty in my decision related to two things:

- **Each offer would require me to uproot my family and move to a different state.** Moving from one house to another in the same city is hard, but much of your life stays the same—same doctors, barbers, friends, church, etc. Moving to another state would mean we would have to start over with everything. In addition, the locales of each offer would mean new climates, geography, and cultures. It was hard to know which one would be best for my family.
- **There are lots of unknowns when taking a new job with an unfamiliar agency.** While job ads, research, and interviews can provide some background, issues needing immediate attention, expectations and other crucial matters won't be known until after employment starts. Those include the real culture of the organization, the real power structure, the skills and personalities of staff and consultants, and simmering problems yet to come to the attention of upper management. Because of these unknowns, I wasn't sure which agency would be the best match of my talents to its needs.

After my indecision stretched over several days, I suddenly felt a strong, unmistakable urging to take one job offer rather than the other. In an instant of revelation, I knew which offer I should accept. Along with that revelation came a peace I find hard to describe. I *knew* which offer was the right choice and everything would work out well.

Both times, I ended up working for an agency where my skillsets matched the agency's needs exactly. Did that mean there was smooth sailing? Hardly. Both agencies were facing substantial financial challenges. With great leadership at the governing body and CEO levels, both agencies developed solid financial plans and moved toward better financial positions.

While it felt good to be a part of both of those success stories, each situation turned out to be good for me, too. Although I thought my governmental finance and management skills were good, I found out I needed to know so much more. In each situation, I learned a great deal from the governing board members, my bosses, staff members, consultants, and citizens. Their perspectives and suggestions helped grind away some of my sharp edges and gave me more insight into what it meant to be a professional CFO at a governmental agency.

Each situation turned out to be good for my family, too. Each time, they found a great group of friends and activities that worked well for them and expanded their horizons.

But I should tell you about another job search. An outstanding government CFO job became available. The job had some tremendous personal advantages for me, so I applied for it. Although the first interview went very well, as I returned to my hotel room I had a strong sensation this wasn't the job for me. While preparing for the final interviews to be held weeks later, the sensation only grew stronger. Focusing on the advantages I thought the job would give me, I ignored the sensation, went to the final interviews, and gave the three worst candidate interviews of my entire career. Of course, I didn't get the job. Although disappointed, I also was relieved. I *knew* that job wasn't for me; my next job was going to be somewhere else.

In all three of these situations, Wisdom was calling out—even shouting out—to me, telling me the right thing to do. In two situations, I heard her calling, listened, followed the direction, and profited. In one situation, I heard her calling, listened, ignored the direction, and almost walked into what I later learned would have been a bad situation for me. When I followed Wisdom's advice, I gained understanding and showed prudence. When I didn't follow her advice, I was being foolish and simple, looking at my advantage—a form of silver, gold, and rubies—rather than wisdom.

Because we don't always listen may be why Wisdom has to continue to call out and raise her voice everywhere. Although we may use prudence and understanding most of the time, situations will occur when you and I are likely to revert back to simple and foolish behavior. It's only too easy to do.

Everyone, including you, has at least one area of weakness—a place where the right approach by the right person can grab your attention and lead you astray. While riches—silver, choice gold, and rubies—can be one place of weakness, pay attention to the other areas that Solomon mentions. Those areas include:

- **Discounting the worth of wisdom.** How often have you received good advice, rejected it, and then wished you had followed it?
- **Ignoring what is right.** While you might not engage in wrongdoing, instead of standing up and addressing it, you turn your back to the wrong and hope it will go away.
- **Ignoring what is true.** At times, you may wish what is true wasn't true. To get what you want, you may be willing to stretch the truth or plunge ahead anyway.
- **Engaging in wickedness.** Whatever the approach, the allure of the gain is so great you're willing to cross the line from what is allowed to what is unethical or illegal.
- **Being crooked or perverse with your words.** To get what you want, you are willing to mislead others through a form of double-talk or spread untrue accusations about your competitors.

- **Failing to gain knowledge.** Without checking to find out if other information is available, you grab information that aligns with your thinking and run with it. Even when it becomes apparent other conflicting information is available, you refuse to listen to it.

Because you have at least one weak area, the most reliable defense is to sharpen your ability to hear Wisdom and gain the prudence and understanding needed to protect your weak areas. The good news is Wisdom is calling out. Can you filter out the other noise in your life to listen to her?

Personal Application

If you had a genie who could make all your wishes come true, what would you wish for? A posh place? Wealth? A gorgeous spouse? A fit body with great athletic ability? Fantastic food and lots of it? While there is nothing wrong with any of those wishes, they pale in comparison to what is of real value—wisdom. Think about it. How many times have you read stories about the foolishness of those who are well-to-do but lack discernment and understanding? There is no shortage of stories about those who seem to change spouses when a new "love" comes along or who get caught up in behaviors leading to poor health or early death.

It's easy to throw stones at those who are in the news. Their lives are played out before the public, often because they want them to be. Many seem to be running from one wish to another without finding what they seek. It can be hard to watch. But they aren't the only ones who run from one wish to another trying to find satisfaction. Although news coverage may be lacking, you can fall into the same pattern as those "newsworthy" people. If your answer to the question about the genie making things come true is all about things, then you really are no better off than the newsworthy people who make bad choice after bad choice.

Let's be honest. Most of us were brought up to think in terms of things and achievements. In my family, I remember two themes that dominated our conversations: 1) graduating from college and 2) doing better than my parents. It's no surprise those themes played out in my life. Being a top student at our small high school, a state college awarded me a large enough scholarship I could go there directly from high school rather than first attending junior college for two years. Still, finances were tight, so summers were spent working to earn enough money to get through the next academic year. Working summers and the scholarships allowed me to concentrate on studies, student government, and other achievements during the school year. As graduation approached, my attention turned toward finding a great job and starting to work on the second theme of doing better than my parents. One job led to another and another. With each change, we (I was married by then) could afford nicer and nicer things. Mission accomplished!

But there was another theme Mom and Dad promoted. That theme was about character. There was a right way to live—work hard, be honest, help others, show good sportsmanship, etc. I was expected to follow all of them. While my parents were happy when I graduated from college and did well in the world, looking back they were happiest when I displayed character traits they wanted me to have. Deep down, they knew having character would be worth more to me than things.

Solomon makes the same case: Obtaining wisdom and understanding is supreme. They are worth more than anything else we might desire—gold, silver, rubies, power, fame, and so on. Earlier Proverbs sections emphasized you have to be willing to gain wisdom and understanding. Gaining them starts when you hear Wisdom's voice and listen to her instructions.

We all have experiences that give us glimpses of this truth. Think of the times you were getting ready to do something you knew was wrong. Did you hear a little voice or feel something inside telling you not to do what you were about to do? Sometimes, especially if you are getting ready to do actions that are going to hurt others or yourself, that voice becomes a shout and the feeling overwhelms you. That shout or overwhelming feeling is Wisdom trying to get through to you. In that moment, Wisdom's call has reached you and you are faced with a decision: Do you follow Wisdom or folly?

While you may experience some consequences of following Wisdom or folly in your lifetime, the ultimate consequence occurs after you die. The things of this world are left in this world, and you will stand before the LORD, who will judge rightly, fairly, and justly. Because the LORD is interested in what is right, fair, and just, He will be interested in how well you listened and obeyed Wisdom. Of greatest importance, did you listen to Wisdom's words about Jesus and accept Jesus as your savior? While you may have some idea of how the LORD's judgment should be made, when all is said and done your perspective doesn't count. God is the one who will judge your life and the decisions you've made.

Wisdom calls out and raises her voice from many different platforms so she can be heard above all the noise around you. Will you listen to her and seek prudence and understanding? Do you want what is of great value or will you accept the things of this world, which in the end hold little value? As always, the choice is yours. What will your choice be?

Chapter 30

The Value of Loving Wisdom
Proverbs 8:12-21

> *"I, Wisdom, dwell together with prudence; I possess knowledge and discretion. To fear the LORD is to hate evil; I hate pride and arrogance, evil behavior and perverse speech. Counsel and sound judgment are mine; I have understanding and power. By me kings reign and rulers make laws that are just; by me princes govern, and all nobles who rule on earth. I love those who love me, and those who seek me find me. With me are riches and honor, enduring wealth and prosperity. My fruit is better than fine gold; what I yield surpasses choice silver. I walk in the way of righteousness, along the paths of justice, bestowing wealth on those who love me and making their treasuries full."*

Background/Circumstances

Wisdom began to call out to man in Chapter 8, Verse 4 of Proverbs saying she had precious things for mankind to hear. In this section, Wisdom reveals what she loves and hates as well as what she can do for the one who listens to her.

The "things I hate" list is short:

- **Pride is first on the list for good reason; it's a big flaw.** According to *AV1611.com*'s KJV (King James Version) dictionary definition, "pride" is "inordinate self-esteem; an unreasonable conceit of one's own superiority in talents, beauty, wealth, accomplishments, rank or elevation in office, which manifests itself in lofty airs, distance, reserve, and often in contempt of others." Pride doesn't come close to aligning with the signs of wisdom: prudence, knowledge, discretion, sound judgment, and understanding.

- **Arrogance, showing an offensive attitude of superiority or exaggerating or disposed to exaggerate one's own worth, is pride's close cousin.** Arrogance and pride usually go together creating a package that keeps a person from acknowledging the LORD had anything to do with the good in his life.
- **Evil behavior and perverse speech reflect the inner heart; the person who does evil and causes dissension has let evil control his heart.** A person's actions are a natural flow of what is in his heart. As with pride and arrogance, evil behavior and perverse speech don't reflect prudence, knowledge, discretion, sound judgment, and understanding.

In a bit of a surprise, the "things I love" list is even shorter. In fact, the list includes only one thing: **Wisdom loves those who love her**. While that sounds simple, there is a clear if/then implication: If you love Wisdom, then you will seek her. As seen in Chapter 2, Verses 1-8, this seeking is intense. Solomon says his son has to desire wisdom enough that he strongly will verbalize his need for it. His son also will need to dig for it as he would for silver or hidden treasure, throwing away the impure to find the pure.

The good news is Wisdom says those who seek her will find her. Those who find her will find out she owns or dwells with a lot of good things—like prudence, knowledge, discretion, counsel, sound judgment, understanding, power, riches, honor, enduring wealth, prosperity, fruit better than fine gold, righteousness, and justice. Wisdom promises she will take from her unlimited wealth, bestow wealth on those who love her, and make their treasuries full. While that wealth may well include financial prosperity, the real focus is on character qualities, things that are better than gold or silver. Gold and silver pass away, but the enduring wealth Wisdom provides lasts forever.

Inserted into this are a few verses that talk about those who reign and govern. Those who do so with Wisdom at their side make just laws. They can do so because Wisdom brings counsel, sound judgment, and understanding with her. Those who rule with Wisdom also enjoy a power that comes from being right, just, and fair. Although not stated, the implication is those who rule and govern without Wisdom will enact unjust laws and use power to act in ways that are wrong, unjust, and unfair.

Business Application

It's an interesting thought: Those who reign and govern with Wisdom by their side make just laws. As you think about your company or the group you supervise, would you be able to say the rules you put in place are just? According to the New Oxford American Dictionary, to be just means to be "based on or behaving according to what is morally right and fair." In today's world, there is no shortage of opinions about what is morally right and fair. Because we know Solomon was extremely wise, let's see what he has to say on that topic.

As we've seen in previous chapters, Solomon has said a lot about what is just, fair, and right. Rather than go back and review previous chapters, Solomon summarizes them in this section.

There is something basic about fearing the LORD that is crucial to gaining wisdom. As you may recall from the article on Proverbs 1:7, I have chosen to use "a loving reverence for the truth" in place of the phrase "fear the LORD." With that substitution, Proverbs 8:13 would read, "To have a loving reverence for the truth is to hate evil." Loving truth and hating evil is a really good place to start.

Start loving truth and ferreting out evil in your workplace and great things will happen. You may ask, "How do I know what evil looks like?" Solomon tells us it shows up in attitudes and actions. While pride makes the top of the "things I hate" list, arrogance, evil behavior, and perverse speech are other indicators. When those attitudes and actions begin to crop up in your business, you have to deal with them. Frankly, "deal with" is too soft of a phrase. Because Wisdom hates them, you should hate them, too. As a leader, you have an obligation to drive these things out of your organization. A halfhearted try isn't going to cut it. You have to be clear, insistent, and persistent.

In addition to hating evil, you need to develop a love for wisdom and seek it. You are used to the idea of seeking out knowledge. You probably have your own example when you were so focused on getting an answer to a technical question that you willingly spent many more hours than you intended to get the right answer. In other words, your love of the truth drove you to spend time to get the right answer.

Love of truth in technical matters is one thing; what about loving the truth when it comes to wisdom? Developing that love is a crucial step in gaining the wisdom of which Solomon talks. If you don't have a loving reverence for the truth, you won't be interested in wisdom. This passionate love of truth will drive you to listen actively for Wisdom's voice and dig deep to understand how you and the organization need to change. The seeking may involve lots of reading, discussion, and reflection on past actions before you can find Wisdom and her treasures and toss aside the crud you held on to before.

Let me give you an example. In the early 1990s, I worked for Salina, Kansas, a North-Central Kansas city with a population of 44,000. The governing body, the city manager, and a talented staff had the city humming along. All seemed to be going well, but there was a problem. The city's workforce didn't mirror the diversity of the city's population. The city manager identified this diversity issue and determined he would address it.

He did so by inserting an additional step in the city's hiring process. The previous process had Human Resources staff collecting all the applications for a position after the application deadline and giving them to the hiring authority. The hiring authority reviewed the applications and selected those he wanted to interview. The hiring authority set up the interviews, conducted the interviews, and selected the applicant he wanted to hire. In the new process, after the hiring authority's interview selections but before setting up the interviews, Human Resources staff reviewed minority applications. If the applicant met minimum qualifications, the applicant was added to the pool of applicants to be interviewed. This one step increased the number of minorities interviewed and hired by the city—a step toward more diversity.

While the city benefitted from this change, so did I. Prior to this process change, I would have told you I was unbiased in my review of applications. None of the applications included the applicant's race, so it wasn't a factor in my selection of whom to interview. However, what I soon learned was there was a noticeable difference in how minorities completed applications compared to other applicants—minority applicants generally, but not always, provided much less information about their relevant experience on their applications. Although I wasn't trying to be biased, I gravitated toward those applicants (white) who provided more information on their applications and selected them for interviews.

Going through this process change was an eye-opener for me in two ways:

- Although no one was pushing the city manager to work toward workforce diversity, he understood the organization needed to change. In his wisdom, he implemented a hiring process change to achieve his desired results.
- I learned I wasn't as wise as I thought I was when it came to unbiased hiring practices. I gained knowledge and wisdom and

> used them not only in future hiring processes but also in other interactions with people not like me.

Those who love and seek out Wisdom are promised Wisdom will love them back and let the seeker find her. (Read that last sentence again for emphasis.) Looking at the list in these verses, you can see Wisdom has much to give to the one who loves and seeks her. While she may give a one-time answer to your urgent need, Wisdom wants to give you heaping helpings of prudence, discretion, sound judgment, and understanding. Those gifts are extremely valuable ones; she is willing to give them in abundance to those who love and seek her. Note the reverse is true, too; she is willing to, and will, withhold all of those valuable things from the person who doesn't love or seek her.

Withholding of wisdom is what happens when a company and those within it really don't love Wisdom and seek her. While those in the company may create a façade of wisdom, if they don't love and seek Wisdom, the façade is only hiding the pride, arrogance, evil behavior and perverse speech permeating the company. Even though the company may be financially successful, working there will be tiring and unrewarding. If you actively are seeking to find Wisdom, working at that company will be even more unrewarding for you. The values clash between you and the company will be severe enough you'll either need to find a way to change the company or find another place to work that aligns with your values.

Walking in the ways of righteousness and along the path of justice has never been easy. But if you love Wisdom and seek her out, you'll find Wisdom abundantly rewards those who walk in her ways. You'll gain prudence, knowledge, and discretion. Because Wisdom loves those who seek her, she will give you good gifts, just like we do to those whom we love.

Again, Solomon challenges you. Will you hate evil and love Wisdom? Will you choose to be prideful and arrogant taking evil actions and speaking perversely or will you run away from those into the loving arms of Wisdom? Choose Wisdom!

Personal Application

Do you know someone who loves Wisdom and seeks her out? We have been fortunate to have known several people who fit that description. I'll talk a little bit about Mary.

Mary and her husband moved to the small town where we were living and came to the church we were attending. Although there was a decade difference in our ages, we became good friends and took turns entertaining in our homes. That good friendship and Mary's wisdom came into play one day as Mary and my wife were talking about our plans to sell our house.

The house was one we had built for us when we were in our mid-20s. In our minds, it was a dream house, one we would stay in for a long time. But that dream house required monthly payments. We managed to make the monthly payments and pay our other bills, but little money was left after all the bills were paid. Knowing that situation wouldn't work in the long term, I pushed for selling the house and buying a less expensive house to lower our monthly house and utility payments. To say the least, the idea of selling the house caused some tension in our house for a while. Because of our financial situation, my wife agreed to put the house on the market.

But my wife wasn't at all happy about it. As she was talking to Mary one day, my wife complained about putting our dream house on the market. But she went beyond that. She started making accusations about my motives. Rather than the sympathetic ear she thought she was going to get, my wife was talking to someone with real wisdom. Mary reviewed the reality of the situation with my wife. Then she set the record straight about my motives. Rather than seeing bad motives in my actions, Mary told my wife she always should look for the good motives behind my actions. My wife never forgot that wise advice. Over the ensuing years, my wife had other conversations with Mary, gaining more wisdom and understanding from her.

Several years later, my wife told me about her conversations with Mary and how they saved me from a lot of grief I otherwise would have gotten! In those conversations, Mary used her wisdom to pass on some of her wisdom to my wife. Those conversations set a pattern for my wife; she learned to listen to wisdom and apply it. In the short time we knew Mary, she passed on a great deal of wisdom to both of us.

Wisdom, although spoken or staring us right in the face, is only of value if we accept it and let it change our lives. Changing our lives is the hard part; often, we want to keep our lives as they are. We want to complain and get sympathy about how badly life is treating us. We like the pride, arrogance, evil behavior, and perverse speech option. Although acting these ways may make us feel good for a while, if we take an honest look at ourselves, we will see none of these actions make us or our life any better. At best, we're still in the same old pit we were in before, except we may have dug the pit a little deeper, making it harder to climb out. Until we seek and listen to Wisdom, we will be in the pit for a while.

But if you seek Wisdom, you'll find wisdom is all around you. It's in the heavens with the sun, moon, and stars as they run their assigned courses. It's in nature as even the ant knows it needs to work to provide for the colony and store provisions for winter. It's in the plants, animals, birds, fish, and everything else that inhabits the Earth. We marvel at creation's creativity and learn from it to create our "inventions." And there are those, like Mary, who have sought and acquired wisdom they freely share with others. If you look around, you can find someone like Mary, a person Wisdom gifted with prudence, knowledge, discretion, and sound judgment.

But you have to seek. It's like looking for a valuable ring you've lost in your house. You will look in every room, nook, and cranny of the house to find it. If you still haven't found the ring, you will turn the place upside down until you do find it. Having looked so hard, and knowing the value of the ring, you will put the found ring in a special place where you always can find it.

It's the same with seeking Wisdom. You have to have a driving passion to find Wisdom, a passion that will take you wherever you need to go to find her. Then, having found Wisdom, you will use her teachings to change how you live your life. Things that were important before will become less important as you seek the most important thing—having a loving reverence for the LORD and following in the ways of Wisdom.

One more thing. Some people believe they are paying attention to Wisdom when they really are paying attention to other voices—voices from the Evil One. One way to know the difference between the two is whether the voice is directing you toward a loving reverence for the truth. If the voices are directing you to do what is right, just, and fair in the LORD's eyes, you are on the right path. However, if the voices are directing you toward pride, arrogance, evil behavior, and perverse speech and leading you away from a loving reverence for the truth, those voices are leading you down the wrong path.

Let me encourage you to apply this simple test to the voices you are hearing and your current actions. This test will help you know whether you are seeking Wisdom or listening to the voices trying to drown out Wisdom's voice. Ignore those voices trying to drown out Wisdom's voice and tune in to Wisdom's voice. Love her, seek her, and enjoy the wealth she provides!

Chapter 31

Keep Wise Counselors Close
Proverbs 8:22-36

"The LORD brought me forth as the first of his works, before his deeds of old; I was appointed from eternity, from the beginning, before the world began. When there were no oceans, I was given birth, when there were no springs abounding with water; before the mountains were settled in place, before the hills, I was given birth, before he made the earth or its fields or any of the dust of the world. I was there when he set the heavens in place, when he marked out the horizon on the face of the deep, when he established the clouds above and fixed securely the fountains of the deep, when he gave the sea its boundary so the waters would not overstep his command, and when he marked out the foundations of the earth. Then I was the craftsman at his side. I was filled with delight day after day, rejoicing always in his presence, rejoicing in his whole world and delighting in mankind.

"Now then, my sons, listen to me; blessed are those who keep my ways. Listen to my instruction and be wise; do not ignore it. Blessed is the man who listens to me, watching daily at my doors, waiting at my doorway. For whoever finds me finds life and receives favor from the LORD. But whoever fails to find me harms himself; all who hate me love death."

Background/Circumstances

In this chapter, Wisdom has been calling out the truth to all people everywhere. Wisdom pleads for everyone who hears her voice to listen to her words as she has much to offer—prudence, knowledge, discretion, sound judgment, understanding, and power. Wisdom declares she will bestow these things on those who seek her wisdom. The seeker of wisdom will find these things are worth far more than gold or silver. In this final segment of her speech, Wisdom reveals a crucial truth: She was the first work of the LORD.

As the first of the LORD's works, Wisdom states she was there when the world was created. In fact, she was the craftsman at the LORD's side during Creation. The phrasing in this section is extremely interesting. First, Wisdom talks about the tangible things that didn't exist before her birth—oceans, springs, mountains, hills, earth, fields, and dust. Then, she talks about the actions the LORD took after her birth—heavens set in place, horizon set, clouds established, fountains of the deep fixed, the sea given its boundary, and the foundations of the Earth marked. Because these all took place after she came into being, Wisdom was right beside the LORD during the wonder and excitement of Creation, assisting as new things were created.

Being there during all of Creation must have been incredible! Wisdom says she was filled with daily delight as the LORD spoke new and wonderful things into being. She rejoiced to be in the LORD's presence. She rejoiced in the world He created. Finally, Wisdom expresses her delight in mankind, the capstone of the LORD's creation.

After describing Creation and her delight in it, Wisdom says anyone who listens to her will find life and receive favor from the LORD. Anyone who listens, watches and waits for Wisdom and keeps her ways will receive tremendous blessings. Rather than receive tremendous blessings, anyone who fails to find her only will be harming himself. Those who choose to hate Wisdom are in much worse shape; they love death rather than life.

Business Application

What a difference it makes to have a wise person by your side!

Over my working years, I was pretty good at coming up with unusual ideas and I appreciated having wise bosses, legal staff, elected officials, staff, and technical experts who were willing to review them. Once these wise counselors started asking questions, the worst ideas collapsed pretty quickly. Their questions exposed potential problems I completely had overlooked or minimized. Their insightful questions and comments revealed a particular idea wasn't ready for prime time and saved me from pressing forward with an idea that was going to waste resources and cost me political capital. If I had failed to listen to their wisdom, I would have proceeded with my idea and harmed myself.

But some of the unusual ideas were good ones. With these ideas, as the wise counselors received answers to their penetrating questions, I could see their excitement rise as they began to grasp the potential behind the idea. A good example is my suggestion for a city representative to attend and participate actively in the county's tax sale of vacant residential properties with unpaid property taxes and special assessments on them.

The first goal was to ensure the one hundred residential properties were sold for at least the amount of unpaid property taxes and special assessments. For most properties, those unpaid taxes and assessments were around $450. If someone was willing to pay at least that much for the property, the city representative stopped bidding. If no one was willing to pay the amount of unpaid taxes and assessments, the second goal was for the representative to buy the properties for the city, which then would sell them directly to citizens for the amount of unpaid taxes and assessments. Because there was a housing shortage, I believed individual citizens would jump at the chance to buy for only $450 an 80-

by-120-foot lot on which to build a house. Besides recovering thousands of dollars of past-due taxes and assessments, the city would receive future taxes and assessments.

As we explored this idea, the growing excitement in the room showed. As others became more excited about the idea, they rolled their chairs close to the table and leaned in to participate. Smiles began to emerge as we worked together to refine the idea. One good thought triggered another good thought, and the group had fun crafting the good idea into a great idea. Their wise counsel and questions helped shape it into a project that ended up being profitable for the city's taxpayers as well as the new property owners.

Having wise counselors in the room makes a dramatic difference in outcomes. Wise counselors help achieve a good outcome. Taking a good idea into a room with less-than-wise counselors can feel like rolling dice. If this group is having a good day, the good idea can move forward and achieve good results. But it is more likely this less-than-wise group will look at a good idea and find ways to tear it apart or modify it to their individual advantages. A group of less-than-wise counselors can't help themselves because they are focused on other things than the good of the company—their status versus your status, how it affects the size of their group, how it impacts one of their favorites, and more. Strangely enough, this group will do the same thing with a poor idea. Instead of dismissing it through a few wise questions, this group may use the idea as a vehicle to get what they want. The beauty of it is: Because it was someone else's idea, they can blame the eventual failure on the person who came up with the idea while reaping the benefits they wanted from the deal.

If possible, you want wise counselors around at the beginning of your company and career. It's good to keep those wise counselors around as long as you can. Because they know you and your company's history, when problems arise they quickly can help you get to the root of the problem. These counselors always will take your call and do what they can to help advise you. Because they have invested so much of their life helping you, they gain pleasure from seeing you succeed, rejoice with you, and gladly let you receive all of the accolades for your success.

As you think about your current counselors, can you say they all fit the bill as wise counselors? If so, rejoice! You are among the lucky few who have only wise counselors advising them. But it is more likely your circle may include some less-than-wise counselors who may be holding you back. Find a few minutes, an hour, an afternoon, a day, or whatever time you need to think about the kind of advice you are getting. If changes need to be made, then resolve to make those changes as soon as possible. The little time spent now regaining wise counsel will serve you well.

If you believe you are lacking wise counsel, you should address the situation right now. Look around for one of your peers who is getting good advice. Pay attention to whom she talks with to gain wise advice and ask if your peer would be willing to introduce you to her wise counselor. Whether it is official or unofficial, find out if your firm has a mentor program and ask for a mentor who is interested in providing wise advice to you. Professional consultants are another possibility. Your company may have professional consultants delivering programs in your workplace. Ask to be included.

Opportunities outside your company abound. Professional consultants conduct online and in-person seminars. Look for one that interests you and join in. Civic clubs and professional organizations exist to introduce people to each other and create lasting friendships. Join one, become active, and get to know others in the group. You are likely to find a wise counselor or someone who can direct you to a wise counselor he knows.

Many options are available to explore. Once you find your wise counselor, listen to his advice and become wiser. Whatever you do, don't ignore your wise counselor's wise advice!

Personal Application

We can spend our days many different ways. Some like to be super busy, running from one thing to another from the time they get up until it's time for them to lie down for the night. Some like a more leisurely pace, one with chunks of time available for friends, contemplation, an extra nap or two during the day, or whatever comes up. Some look forward to the new day while others dread it. While each of us have our own twist on how we go about spending our days, it may be instructive for us to take a look at how Wisdom has, and does, spend her days.

As the LORD's first work, Wisdom:

- **Was a craftsman at the LORD's side.** As you may remember from an earlier chapter, "the LORD" is used to describe a very personal relationship with God. That personal relationship is evident as Wisdom is working side by side with the LORD. This portrays an intimate working relationship where Wisdom is using her skills to help the LORD fashion the world. It's easy to imagine they talked about what the LORD was doing and why.
- **Was filled with delight day after day.** As Creation is occurring, you can feel the excitement building. As each new thing is created, Wisdom is there and watching. Her reaction is pure delight. Rather than a momentary feeling, Wisdom is filled with delight all day, every day of Creation. Each new day's work brings about a greater feeling of delight.
- **Rejoiced in the LORD's presence.** Wisdom was with the LORD every day; she rejoiced she was in His presence. A similar example we experience is the rejoicing we feel when our loved one has been in extreme danger for a long time (e.g., war combat zone) and he arrives at our doorstep unannounced and unharmed. The pure joy of that moment describes the level of joy Wisdom knows from being in the LORD's presence.

- **Rejoiced in His whole world.** As the LORD completed the creation of the world, Wisdom rejoiced at what the LORD had done. It was perfect! Oceans, springs, mountains, hills, fields, dust, heavens, clouds, fountains of the deep, sea boundaries, and the very foundations of the Earth—from the largest to the smallest, all were perfect. We rejoice in the same way at the birth of a healthy baby. Our unique baby is examined and found to be perfect in every way. Nine months of work—thanks to all the moms out there—brought forth a bundle of joy, smiles all around, and pure joy at this new "creation."
- **Delighted in mankind.** As the LORD kept creating, Wisdom must have marveled with each addition. With the world created and everything in place, Wisdom must have thought the LORD was ready to "rest." How much better could it be? Then, in His crowning Creation achievement, the LORD creates mankind in his own image. And Wisdom is absolutely delighted!

As we think about how we spend our time, we would do well to consider Wisdom's model. In today's words, the model goes like this:

- **Join God in what He is doing and work with Him.** Do what He wants, not what you want.
- **See the results of this work and delight in it.** Be glad in the results and your part in achieving them.
- **Be happy you are in God's presence.** The LORD is present. It's your choice whether you acknowledge His presence.
- **Look at the world around you and rejoice in it.** Rejoice in the good and remember who made it.
- **See those around you for what they are, God's special creation.** Delight in the uniqueness of others. Get to know them.

Making these five things a part of your life certainly will draw you closer to God and allow you to see things in a completely different way. You also can apply this in your relationships with others. How would your marriage change if you:

- Joined in your spouse's work?
- Delighted in the results?
- Were happy to just be around your spouse?
- Rejoiced about the things in your life, even though not always easy?
- Saw your spouse as a special creation?

How would your relationship with your kids change if you did these five things with them? Give it a try and see. I think you will be very happy with the results! After your successes with your spouse and kids, following this model may become the standard in all your relationships.

The good news is Wisdom didn't stop working when Creation was completed. She stands ready to give you all the instructions you need to become wise. If you take the time to look, you can see her in the way the universe fits together, plants and seasons, and creatures around you. She resides in books, on airwaves, and in the hearts of the wise. With these sources speaking wisdom, it's quite obvious Wisdom is trying very, very hard to reach out to you.

Wisdom wants to know: Will you be wise and seek her? Will you watch and wait for her until you find her? Are you willing to listen to her and follow her instructions? Are you one of the few who will become wise?

Those who won't seek her out or who listen but won't follow her instructions are doomed to a dismal fate. Wisdom says these people are choosing to harm themselves. By hating her, they are blocking out any favor they might have received, and death awaits them.

Rather than suffer the fate of the unwise, Wisdom wants you to find her and the life she gives. She gives true life, not the artificial and foolish existence we come up with to satisfy ourselves. This true life is a life full of wisdom, a life spent seeking to be beside God, working with Him, rejoicing in Him and the world He created, and delighting in others. The LORD favors those who live a true life and grants them eternal life with Him.

Proverbs

Chapter Nine

Chapter 32

Creating an Inviting Environment
Proverbs 9:1-6

Wisdom has built her house; she has hewn out its seven pillars. She has prepared her meat and mixed her wine; she has also set her table. She has sent out her maids, and she calls from the highest point of the city. "Let all who are simple come in here!" she says to those who lack judgment. "Come, eat my food and drink the wine I have mixed. Leave your simple ways and you will live; walk in the ways of understanding."

Background/Circumstances

Having finished her "why men should listen to me" speech in Chapter 8, Wisdom starts speaking about what she has done to prepare a place for those who seek her. In the Bible, the number seven represents completeness. With her house having seven pillars, Wisdom is telling her audience that the house is complete. A house with seven pillars would be a large house. Thus, Wisdom is proclaiming there is room for all who want to come.

Besides providing a wonderful gathering place for the Simple, she is providing food, too. While it is tempting to see this only as physical food to satisfy physical hunger, Wisdom is talking about food that brings understanding to the Simple. To meet both needs, her meat and wine have been prepared specially. Take note the wine is "mixed" wine.

That means regular wine has been mixed with spices to create an exceptionally tasty drink. Only the best will do for those who come to Wisdom's house! As the good host, Wisdom's table is set and ready; those who come can feast on her good food right away.

Rather than wait for people to show up, Wisdom sends her maids out into the streets to invite people to come to her banquet. But Wisdom does more. She goes to the highest point of the city and calls out her invitation. Her call is to a specific audience—those who are simple and lack judgment. She calls to them because she has prepared food specially for them. When the Simple come to her house and eat Wisdom's food, their eyes and minds will be opened to the way of understanding. They will have what they need in order to live.

Wisdom knows she can provide the Simple with understanding and will go to great lengths to get the Simple to come to her. Reading this passage a few times, you can feel her urgency, her pleading with the Simple to just come to her house. If the Simple will just listen and act, they will gain a treasure they never knew they needed. As the gracious host, Wisdom will take care of their material needs and provide wisdom and understanding; their lives will be changed forever.

Business Application

If you want to know how to create an inviting atmosphere, take a look at what Wisdom does. She provides a great space, prepares for her guests, sends an open invitation to all, and describes why they should come. Although her arms are open to all, she makes a point of issuing an open invitation to those who will benefit most by coming.

Wisdom is onto something. If you want to reach your workforce, especially those who may be most reluctant to gain wisdom and understanding, you have to create an inviting environment for them. That is easier said than done. With today's workforce diversity, creating an inviting environment for all employees is a difficult task. Accordingly, you have to be as intentional as Wisdom was. You intentionally have to prepare your place, food, and teachings to meet your employees' needs. Because your employees may not be aware of their needs or your company's provisions to meet their needs, your invitation must be so compelling they will come, ready to listen and learn. While creating an inviting environment takes a lot of work to pull it off, the results of a well-planned, inviting environment yields tremendous benefits to you, your workforce, and your company.

Other ways to pass on "wisdom" and "understanding" to a workforce certainly exist. Many of them have negative aspects. You may get your point across to someone by embarrassing them in front of others with a question like "How could you be so stupid?" But a question like that leaves an imprint on an employee, giving him permission to interact with other employees in the same way. You also can get your point across by firing employees for minor infractions. Seeing such a dismissal take place, other employees understand they need to avoid earning your ire, keep away from you, or limit the information they provide you.

Employees learn a lot by watching their bosses. What you say—and especially what you do—tells your employees what is acceptable in your company. Rather than using a negative work environment to teach lessons, wouldn't it be better to create a positive one?

And Wisdom shows us how to do it. Look at the preparations she makes:

- **A place has been built allowing her to meet with all who come.** As you think about your work environment, space is always a consideration. It costs to have facilities. But there is also a cost to having inadequate facilities or equipment. It makes me think of the struggles we had at the transit agency to upgrade bus maintenance facilities.

  To help address local pollution episodes, the agency changed from an all-diesel bus fleet to a fleet with a mixture of diesel, electric, and compressed natural gas ("CNG") buses. In addition, some standard-length buses were being replaced with longer, articulated electric buses. As the bus fleet changed, the agency needed to update its bus maintenance facilities to comply with new CNG and electric bus service requirements and provide bus bays to handle the longer buses. Because relocating a bus maintenance facility is expensive, the agency did its best to upgrade facilities on its current properties.

With finances tight, the agency was able only to update one of its six bus facilities for the incoming CNG buses. Moving to CNG buses was a plus, but having only one maintenance facility renovated to handle the unique CNG buses' service needs meant the CNG fleet had to be assigned to that one maintenance facility and the service area it supported. Until financing became available for upgrades to other facilities, the agency couldn't expand the CNG fleet.

The longer, articulated electric buses required modifications to a different bus maintenance facility. In addition to extending the bus bays at this facility, the bays needed to be modified to address the special maintenance requirements for electric buses. Without the benefit of unlimited funding or a new site, the transit team met minimum electric bus maintenance bay requirements and left other needed renovations for another day. Transit staff worked wonders to maximize the number of buses and employees their facility could handle. They made the facilities work, but the facilities fell short of being the kind of "place" the agency really needed.

- **Basic needs are addressed.** It's hard for someone to listen to Wisdom when they are hungry. We hear it all the time: Children who come to school hungry have a much harder time learning. Because of that truth, governments and nonprofits have funded programs to provide food to those children so they can listen to their teachers rather than their complaining stomachs. The same wisdom applies to how you compensate your employees. Now, I'm not advocating for wages that ensure your employees can eat steak and lobster every night. But there is wisdom in making sure your employees are paid fairly, allowing them to put nutritious food on their tables and take care of their basic needs.

- **Those who need help are invited.** Isn't it interesting Wisdom invites in the Simple and those who lack judgment? What does her invitation tell us about whom we should be inviting into our companies? To me, this points out a fallacy in current hiring practices. It is certainly okay to try to seek a person who has all the talent and experience you would desire for a position. But do you miss out on a great talent when you hire the candidate who has reached her potential rather than the candidate who needs help developing her potential? Think of the second candidate as a person with rough edges who, if those edges were rounded off, would become a dynamo. In the end, with which person would you be better off?
  At times, hiring the most accomplished candidate makes sense, especially if you have an immediate crisis at hand. When a crisis isn't at hand, you likely will be better served by hiring the high-potential candidate, developing her, and giving her room to create. Hire and develop a few of these dynamos and you'll be creating an inviting environment for those who want to join a dynamic company.

Let me encourage you to spend a little time considering what you could do to make your work environment more inviting. Let me encourage you to ask your employees to provide their ideas about an inviting environment. Rather than big-ticket items, my employees wanted inexpensive changes like replacing a broken microwave, replacing an old office chair, painting the breakroom, or letting them attend professional training. Do everything you can to take care of those inexpensive items as quickly as possible. Morale will improve and you'll have taken steps toward having the inviting environment your employees need.

Personal Application

Did you catch how much trouble Wisdom went through to be ready to help those who needed to leave their simple ways and gain understanding? Before she invited them in, she made sure she had a welcoming place for them. Her house was prepared with plenty of room. She had ample and tasty food ready to serve. The table was set with anticipation her guests would come. Wisdom had done everything she could think of to create a welcoming environment for whomever would come in.

My wife and I do something very similar when we have guests over to our house. We scurry around to make sure our home is set up to handle the number of people we anticipate coming. We straighten the house up, clean, and do what we can to have it spic and span for our guests. If we are having guests for a meal, we usually buy and prepare a special meat. To go along with the meat, we prepare side dishes as well as scrumptious dessert offerings. As important as the food, we give some thought to what our guests may be interested in talking about and have a few questions ready to start table conversation. We do everything we can think of to create a welcoming environment.

While my wife and I make those arrangements for a small group, Wisdom makes her special, and better, arrangements for a much larger group. While our invitations to our guests are low-key and limited to a few, Wisdom takes a much broader approach:

- **Wisdom goes to the highest point in the city to invite others in.** As the leader of her group, she is involved in reaching out to others. If you want to be a leader of a group, you have to lead from the front, exposed but courageous.

- **She sends her maids out to help.** Even the best leaders can't do all of the work; others in the group need to help out. Some group members may be standing next to the leader as he does his work; more likely, most will be in the trenches, talking to those around them, persuading and asking others to come join in. Their work of guiding others to join in is just as important as their leader's work.
- **Wisdom uses an easy-to-understand message.** Wisdom doesn't leave anyone guessing; her message is for two groups: 1) the Simple and 2) those who lack judgment. The rest of her invitation is unambiguous, too. She invites the Simple and those who lack judgment to come to her prepared place—where there is abundant food and drink, where they can find and live life in a new and full way.

What does Wisdom's actions tell us about what we should be doing?

Let's take it to an individual level first. If you know someone who could use guidance in his life, perhaps you should be the one who prepares an inviting place where you could meet to talk about the things of life, share your wisdom, and steer him toward a better life. It may be a hassle for you to prepare the place and a challenge to have the discussion, but wouldn't it be worth it all to see his life changed? And you don't have to do it alone. It is okay to have others standing beside you to help with preparations and discussions.

Now, if you believe you are a person who could benefit from gaining advice from another person, it's okay for you to invite them someplace where you can talk. You certainly don't have to go through all of the preparations Wisdom made. If you've invited a wise person to talk with you, she won't really care about the house or the food; she only will care about you and what you need. You'll find those wise counselors if you just take some time to look around and listen. If the worldly noise is too loud for you to pick out a wise counselor, then let me recommend you seek out a Bible-believing church near you and talk with the pastor. You'll find someone who cares about you.

While there are individual applications, I think there is a great application for our churches. I hope church leaders will take a close look at what Wisdom did to reach those who needed help. Look how she prepared. Her place was clean and inviting. She made sure her food—the worship service, Sunday school, Vacation Bible School, small groups, counseling, etc.—was sustaining food and that it was ready. She had her table set and was ready for the guests to arrive. The message is clear: An inviting church purposefully prepares and welcomes all who come into the church's orbit.

Although the church is prepared, it's important it has as clear a message as Wisdom's. There needs to be a call out to those who are struggling or who have shown a lack of judgment. Rather than a finger-pointing exercise, this call is akin to a mother opening her arms wide to accept and comfort her hurting child. That compassionate call needs to be broadcast as widely as possible. Shouting from the highest point of a city worked well then. Today, the church needs to use every available method to transmit its message.

Finally, don't miss this: She promised they would "live." Wisdom was pretty direct: "I know you have a problem. Come and I'll help you. Come and you'll find true life!" Jesus had the same message. He knew we had a problem. He invited people to come to Him so He could help them. He promised abundant and everlasting life to those who would come and believe in Him.

Although we aren't told how many actually acted on Wisdom's invite, I think it is safe to assume some did. Knowing some would come, Wisdom gladly went through all of the work to prepare and invite them in. As you and the church prepare to invite others in, make sure you follow Wisdom's example and create an inviting place with great "food" ready for your guests and be ready with the message that imparts true life.

Chapter 33

Be Wise and Grow Wise; Be a Mocker and Suffer Proverbs 9:7-12

"Whoever corrects a mocker invites insult; whoever rebukes a wicked man incurs abuse. Do not rebuke a mocker or he will hate you; rebuke a wise man and he will love you. Instruct a wise man and he will be wiser still; teach a righteous man and he will add to his learning. The fear of the LORD is the beginning of wisdom, and knowledge of the Holy One is understanding. For through me your days will be many, and years will be added to your life. If you are wise, your wisdom will reward you; if you are a mocker, you alone will suffer."

Background/Circumstances

After going through great pains to prepare for and invite the Simple and those who lack judgment, Wisdom ends her speech comparing the Mocker to the wise man.

A Mocker doesn't want to listen to correction. Rather than listen, understand, and accept the correction, the Mocker takes a different tack. He will insult the person who tried to provide correction, putting this person down as effectively as he can. Giving a rebuke to a Mocker draws an even stronger response. Going beyond insults, now the Mocker resorts to abuse. How far this abuse will be taken is hard to know because the Mocker hates the person who rebuked him. Although the Mocker strikes out at those who tried to help him, in the end Wisdom says the Mocker is the one who will suffer.

A wise man takes a completely different approach. He is open to rebuke, instruction, and teaching. Rather than hate the person who chastises him, the wise man loves him. He realizes the person who is reprimanding him is doing him a great favor by caring enough to give the reprimand. After the reprimand, the wise man is open to instruction knowing he will be wiser for listening. And he is ready to be taught what he needs to know. He not only listens, but he also adds this teaching to his prior learning. He remembers this teaching and uses it in his life. In the final analysis, Wisdom says the wise man will be rewarded for his wisdom.

The key to whether one is a Mocker or a wise man is whether the man fears—has a loving reverence of—the LORD, the personal God. The person who has that loving reverence is at square one of obtaining wisdom; it's the beginning of gaining a knowledge of God. Through gaining the knowledge of God and His ways, the wise man comes to understand the big picture, what life is all about. With that understanding, the wise man readily welcomes Wisdom into his life. In return, Wisdom promises to add years to the wise man's life. When all is said and done, the wise man will have his reward. So will the Mocker; his reward is to suffer and suffer alone.

Business Application

Isn't it a joy to work with someone who listens and learns? Whether in a formal classroom, on-the-job discussion, or private conversation, the person who listens and learns wants to talk to you about overall strategy as well as operation details. His curiosity and openness lead to fulfilling discussions on a wide variety of topics. His willingness to listen and learn extends to the area of discipline, too. When you correct or rebuke him, he appreciates the correction or rebuke and shows a desire to make things right. He will learn from that conversation and not make the same mistake, or anything similar to it, again. You know his heart is in the right place.

It's easy to be drawn to people who listen and learn. Because they truly appreciate your expertise and wisdom, you'll find yourself wanting to take every opportunity you can to help them. In their pleasant way, they will seek to understand how their duties and skills fit into the company and the areas in which they could improve. Employees willing to listen and learn are especially open to teaching, instruction and, if deserved, rebukes. As you may have experienced, finding someone like this is fairly rare. Many people can be pleasant and not really care about the business. It's a much smaller number who want to learn, excel, and become wise. If any of that small number works for you, hold on to them! These good folks will be beneficial for your company.

But another group—the Mockers—are not good for your company. While a Mocker may do his job, don't try to correct him unless you want a sharp retort coming back at you. You know how this works: You point out a minor thing he did wrong and he starts a stream of nasty remarks directed at you. But he doesn't stop there. He also shares his unfiltered opinion about you to his coworkers. Rebuke him in a private or public setting and you'll have a war on your hands. What may have been an okay relationship before becomes a life-and-death matter for the Mocker. He will do whatever he can to make you look bad. It's been rare, but I have had this happen to me.

In my position, I conducted annual reviews of higher-level managers. When going over their performances, the managers who aligned with the "wise man" approach listened intently to my feedback for them. While my feedback was usually about their stellar performance, they mostly were interested in hearing about hard or soft skill areas in which they could improve their performance. They would ask questions to clarify my feedback. They wanted to know the truth. Once they had a firm understanding of an area in which they could improve, they shifted the conversation to what they could and would do to improve in that area. Our discussions covered a lot of ground: training they could take, obstacles I could help remove, and review dates for progress reports. Participating in those annual reviews was a pleasure.

The annual review went differently for those who aligned with the "Mocker" approach. Those managers wanted to focus on only the good things they had done during the year. They resisted, and in some cases rejected, all my comments related to hard or soft skill improvement. No matter what evidence I provided, their responses ran the gamut from denial to excuses to loud and long diatribes about how unjust I and the company had been to them.

I wish I could say the "Mocker" managers eventually came to their senses and changed their tune. I can think of one or two who did. But most went the other direction and saw me as their enemy. Some even went so far as to engage in behaviors they knew could result in their dismissal. Once those behaviors were discovered and reviewed, the company had no choice but to expedite their departure. While they had to go, it was always a sad situation. Except for their unwise behavior, they could have stayed and contributed greatly to the company. Instead, they acted like the Mocker Solomon describes. Even though those managers caused me a lot of anguish, to this day, I wish they would have taken the wise man's approach.

In the first part of Chapter 9, Wisdom called out to those who are simple and lack judgment. It must be a large group; Wisdom said she had to build a large house to accommodate them. However large the "simple and lack judgment" group may be, it is flanked by Mockers on one side and wise men on the other side.

An employee who has chosen the Mocker's path will be a pain to deal with for a long time. If you keep him around, be prepared for ongoing insults and abuse. No matter what you do to help him, he will be one of those employees who hates and despises you.

An employee who has chosen the wise man's path will make everything easier. You'll be able to count on her and her work. She will strive to learn and better herself and the company. She will be a joy to work with and her coworkers will love her. You'll be glad she is around and wish your company was filled with employees like her.

While it's good to think about others, the wisdom Solomon provides always is directed toward the individual. That begs the question: "Which of these categories do you fall into?" It's worth your time to consider your answer carefully. The camp with which you associate will have an effect on how you are seen within your company and your opportunity for advancement. If you choose to be a wise man, you will have a much easier path than a Mocker. You actively will work to build bridges and create positive relationships while learning about the work and other employees.

While a Mocker may do all the same things, he always has a certain nastiness about him. The little negative comment here and the edgy joke there are the first indications someone is a Mocker. But the bad behavior really shows up—and often surprises the top brass—when the Mocker is challenged or corrected. The nastiness rises to a new, ugly level. No matter how hard a Mocker works to hide how he really feels, circumstances always will come around to expose him.

Again, the choice is clear. If you choose the path of the wise man, you will be rewarded and have many days and years added to your life. If you choose the path of the Mocker, you will miss out on wisdom and get to suffer for it.

Personal Application

Of all the verses quoted from Proverbs, the one I hear the most is the first half of Chapter 9, Verse 10: "The fear of the LORD is the beginning of wisdom." It is certainly true, but quoting it without understanding the context in which it is used loses the urgency of the message. By itself, the verse is more like a platitude—a good saying, a good thing we should do. By using it that way, we lose what Solomon is saying: What is at stake for us is our very lives.

In this chapter, Solomon's summary of the Mocker's fate is he will "suffer." That suffering seems rather mild until you go back to Proverbs Chapter 1 and read the list of things a Mocker will "suffer." The list includes disaster, calamity, distress, trouble, and destruction with no relief. It truly is a case of "You made your bed, now lie in it."

Because that outcome isn't what the LORD wants for any of us, throughout the first nine chapters of Proverbs, Solomon describes numerous ways to know if you are a Mocker. In this chapter, Solomon says how you respond to a well-deserved correction or rebuke is a surefire tell.

Now is a good time to think back to a situation when others tried to correct your bad behavior or rebuked you for something you said or did. How did you respond? When I was younger, too many times I responded with an insult or smart remark intended to hurt the other person. While I don't recall "hating" a person who corrected or rebuked me, I do remember friendships that changed because of my actions—some to the point where my smart remarks ended them. In every case, those who were giving me well-deserved corrections or rebukes had the very best of intentions; they were looking out for me. My incredibly stupid response was to lash out or blame others. Looking back, lashing out and blaming others was foolish on my part; I was more Mocker than wise man.

But at some point, I realized I should value other's feedback, no matter how hard it was to take or how poorly it was delivered. I resolved to listen, evaluate the criticism, and respond to what I needed to change. My first step was to listen intently to what the other person was telling me. Once I heard their feedback, as the next step I asked clarifying questions. Many times, the clarifying questions brought out the real reason for the feedback, allowing us to zero in on the specific incident they wanted to discuss. Once I understood the other person's specific feedback, I would hold up their feedback to the "light of day" and ask myself, "Is there any truth in this feedback?"

Let's not skip too quickly past this last question. Asking to see the truth in feedback requires you to be a humble truth seeker. When I was less than a humble truth seeker, it was too easy for me to discount the feedback, shrug my shoulders, and go on with my life. Like the Mocker, I didn't learn anything. But when I humbly sought the truth in their feedback, I had to take the last step; I had to deal with the truth of the wrong I had committed. I found the best way to address my wrongdoing was to "repent" of it. Repenting meant I had to be truly sorry for my wrongdoing, realize how wrong my actions were, and then make changes to ensure I never did it again. Let me give you an example.

For years, the places where I worked used the phrase "throw someone under the bus" to indicate one person was putting the blame for something they had done on someone else. It was a shorthand phrase we all understood. However, when I went to work for a transit agency, I soon learned using the phrase "throw someone under the bus" wasn't at all welcomed in the workplace. The first mild correction I received made me realize how inappropriate it was to use that phrase in the transit environment. I repented and never used the term again (until now).

Let's go back to the question about how you respond to well-deserved correction or rebuke. One way is to lash out, abuse, and hate the person who corrected or rebuked you. If that is what you do, beware! You are on a path leading to disaster, calamity, distress, trouble, and destruction. It's a bad path, and you should do everything you can to get off of it and on the path of the wise. You'll know you're on the path of the wise when you find yourself loving the person who pulls you aside to correct you on some point. You'll know you're there when you willingly listen to instruction and learn from it. When you compare the different paths of the wise man and the Mocker, isn't it much better for you, and those around you, if you to choose the path of the wise man?

There's one other way you'll know you are on the path of the wise man; you'll have a loving reverence for the LORD. As that loving reverence grows with knowledge of the Holy One, you'll gain wisdom and understanding. Although other rewards may come along, the reward of knowing the Holy One is so great the others pale in comparison. For the reward of knowing the Holy One—and His Son Jesus—is an abundant, overflowing life now and an eternal life with the author of wisdom. What other reward could ever compare to that one!

Chapter 34

Following Folly Spells Disaster
Proverbs 9:13-18

The woman Folly is loud; she is undisciplined and without knowledge. She sits at the door of her house, on a seat at the highest point of the city, calling out to those who pass by, "Let all who are simple come in here!" she says to those who lack judgment. "Stolen water is sweet; food eaten in secret is delicious!" But little do they know that the dead are there, that her guests are in the depths of the grave.

Background/Circumstances

Solomon's letter to his son ends with a new person, Folly, speaking. Although Solomon has talked about folly before, this is the first time folly is personified. It is less than a flattering portrait. Like the adulteress in Proverbs Chapter 7, she is loud. One gets the sense her loudness is also vulgar. But that loudness is no surprise because Folly is also undisciplined and without knowledge. In describing her that way, we also know Folly lacks good judgment, prudence (she is undisciplined), and the fear of the LORD (knowledge). Solomon makes it clear in the first verse of this section Folly is not someone to whom one should listen.

Solomon goes on to show how Folly and Wisdom compare to each other:

- **Wisdom seeks while Folly waits.** Wisdom and her helpers go throughout the city looking for the Simple and those who lack judgment. Wisdom goes to the highest point of the city to call out to those who need her message. Now we find out why she went there; Folly has built her house at this highest point. A battle for the minds and hearts of the Simple will be taking place for all those who come by Folly's house.

- **Both call out to the Simple and those who lack judgment.** Wisdom and Folly are calling out to the same group of people. Both understand the Simple and those who lack judgment can take the path toward wisdom or stumble onto the path leading to great folly.
- **Wisdom offers good food while Folly offers stolen food.** Wisdom has prepared meat and mixed special wine for her guests. The table is set and ready for them. What Wisdom offers is wholesome and can be consumed with others in an open setting. It satisfies and brings life. Folly is offering stolen water and food to be eaten in secret. It's a nice way of describing the disgusting life Folly offers. She and her followers will steal their pleasures from others and enjoy them in secret, but Folly won't share the deadly outcome awaiting those who succumb to her call. An example of this is the adulteress Solomon described in Proverbs Chapter 7. Preying on the weak, she lures her victim in for a night of pleasures without the victim realizing he has forfeited his life.

The results from choosing Wisdom or Folly are dramatically different. While those who listen to Wisdom's voice leave their simple ways and begin a journey leading to understanding and true life, those who go into Folly's house will join all the others who are marching toward death.

Thus, Solomon ends his letter to his son with a summary of the prior eight chapters:

- **Don't be one who mocks God.** You surely will suffer horribly.
- **If you are simple and lack judgment (maybe how Solomon saw his young son), you have one of two paths to follow.** You can seek and listen to Wisdom and enjoy a good life full of good things, including true life. You can listen to Folly and follow her. While your life may seem good, you are on a path leading to death.
- **How blessed it is to be a wise man who seeks and gains knowledge, understanding, and discernment!** Long life and many good days are his.
- **Learn and keep two guiding principles and all will go well with you.** The first guiding principle is "The fear of the LORD is the beginning of wisdom." The second guiding principle is "Knowledge of the Holy One is the beginning of understanding." If Solomon's son will make these two principles the primary focus of his life, he will be a successful person and king.

For those who don't know what happened when Solomon's son became king, here is a brief summary.

Solomon's son, Rehoboam, became king when he was forty-one and reigned for seventeen years. As Solomon feared, Rehoboam listened to Folly. Early in his reign, Rehoboam listened to foolish, rather than wise, advisors. Ten of the twelve Hebrew tribes broke away and formed a nation they called Israel. Rehoboam was left with the two remaining tribes, thereafter called Judah. Israel turned away from the LORD. Following a series of bad kings, Israel was destroyed by the Assyrians in B.C. 722. Egypt invaded Judah in Rehoboam's fifth year of reign and took all the treasures—the great wealth Solomon had accumulated—from the temple and royal palace. Although there were good and bad kings in Judah, the evil kings of Judah became too much for the LORD to withstand. Judah and Jerusalem were destroyed by the Babylonians in B.C. 586 and the nation went into exile (cutoff from the land). Rehoboam's failure to pursue Wisdom was the beginning of the demise of the kingdom David and Solomon had built.

Business Application

You would think most business people would see red flags when someone approaches them with a proposition that sounds like Folly's proposition of "Stolen water is sweet; food eaten in secret is delicious!" Rather than accepting these assertions, a prudent business person asks questions: "Why is this water so sweet?" "Why do I have to steal it to get it?" "What are the consequences for me if I go along with you?" "Why do we have to do this in secret?"

While it would be nice to have bad propositions presented as bad propositions, let's acknowledge most dubious propositions are covered with an attractive veneer designed to appeal to the business person being targeted. I experienced something like this several years ago when I was the CFO at the transit agency.

Air quality was, and is, a seasonal concern along the Wasatch Front in Utah. With a high percentage of diesel buses in its fleet, the agency was interested in replacing its buses with CNG (compressed natural gas) buses. Financial restrictions limited how quickly the buses could be replaced; at best, the agency was looking at fourteen to fifteen years to move to an all-CNG fleet. In addition to the CNG buses, maintenance facilities needed to be renovated to handle the different maintenance requirements for CNG buses. The agency was stuck; the money wasn't there to make the kind of modifications needed or accelerate CNG bus purchases.

Then a high-ranking state official who was very concerned about air quality introduced the agency's CEO to a group who said they could help the agency quickly move to an all-CNG fleet. Because this was a financial proposition, I was asked to provide financial information to the group so it could better analyze the agency's needs and present its best proposal. In the first meeting, I told the group I was willing to provide it with relevant financial information and answer clarifying questions. Because I was also the agency's chief procurement officer, I made it clear if the agency decided to move toward an aggressive bus replacement plan, the agency would develop and issue a public request for proposals (RFP). The RFP would include the same public information the group was receiving from me and competition for the contract would be completely open to all vendors. While the group heard what I said and made the appropriate acknowledgments, it also started to bring forward arguments why the agency could receive and accept their proposal without issuing an RFP. The first meeting ended with assignments for each of the parties.

At our next meeting, we reported on our assignments and then rehashed the need for a public RFP. The group had sharpened its arguments and presented them. The group believed the agency could accept a no-bid, twenty-year agreement to acquire hundreds of CNG buses and upgrade all bus maintenance facilities. In addition, the agency would agree to purchase CNG from the group's company for the next twenty years at a price sufficient to pay for the CNG, CNG buses, facility improvements, financing costs, and their profit. Although we still disagreed on the RFP, we scheduled another meeting to refine the financial assumptions.

The next meeting was in the evening at the group's offices. While we discussed financial assumptions, the real purpose of the meeting was to convince me an RFP wasn't needed. After some discussion, the group understood my position regarding the RFP was firm. Because we were all professionals and had handled ourselves accordingly, we agreed to disagree and ended the meeting on good terms. It was the last thing I ever heard about this CNG proposal.

Now, let me make sure you understand the group's concept was innovative and had quite a bit of merit to it. The group had done enough homework to develop an interesting proposition. But its insistence the proposal had to be kept secret and go straight to the board of directors for approval raised suspicions and I proceeded cautiously. I provided only publicly available financial information, insisted RFP requirements be followed, and prepared summaries of the meetings, specifically noting discussions about RFP requirements. My prior experience allowed me to understand the situation and act appropriately.

Experience and judgment are your good friends when evaluating a proposition. You need to ensure those with experience and judgment are key members of your evaluation teams. Even then, be aware bad actors will attempt to find the area where these key members lack judgment. Whether it's power, money, position, fear of losing, or any number of other things, the saying "every person has their price" has validity.

You likely know someone, or have heard about someone, who stole a substantial amount of money from their employer. In most cases, this happens because the employee was in a tough financial spot and found a way to steal. Once he started stealing, he couldn't stop stealing. Confronted with a tough financial spot—this employee's weakness—he displayed his lack of judgment by stealing rather than looking for another option. Because lack of judgment isn't limited to stealing, you need to develop effective safeguards to catch someone's lack of judgment while the damage done is still minor.

It is entirely appropriate Solomon ends his letter talking about the dangers awaiting those who are simple or lack judgment. Others will find out where the Simple and those who lack judgment are vulnerable and seek opportunities to take advantage of those vulnerabilities. It may come as "an offer you can't refuse," a slick way for you to get ahead, or any number of "sweet" or "delicious" suggestions. However the sweet proposition comes, the person who lacks judgment won't do his due diligence and may accept the proposition. But the wise, prudent, and discerning person will take time to investigate thoroughly and understand the proposition and, seeing the danger, reject the bad proposition and save himself many, many heartaches.

Personal Application

Have you walked along the midway at your state or county fair and noticed the loud cries from the barkers imploring you to try their games? As you watch the games, throwing a ring onto one post in a field of posts or tossing a ball into a basketball hoop looks easy. The barker makes it sound easy, too. All you have to do is put three rings onto three posts or three balls through the basket and the gigantic, prominently displayed prize is yours. Because it looks easy and the prize looks wonderful, you lay your money down and start anticipating how great it will be to win that big prize.

But, as you play the game, you find the game isn't as easy as it first appeared. The rings you toss land between the posts or your basketballs hit the hoop and bounce out. You know you can do better, so you lay more money down and give it another try with the same results. "Bad luck," says the barker. "Surely your luck with turn with your next try!" Determined to win the big prize, you keep laying your money down and throwing rings and balls, believing your luck will change.

At some point, you realize the games aren't as simple as they look or as easy as the barker made them sound. Rather, the games are set up with the posts too close to get a ringer except by a perfect throw and the basketball rim small enough only a perfect shot goes in. The games are tilted so far in favor of the barker that almost every time he wins and you lose. With that realization, you turn away from the games and walk along the midway a smarter and wiser fairgoer.

Of course, playing these games at a state or county fair usually isn't a big deal, unless you spend that week's family food or rent money playing them. These games are intended to be a fun diversion. However, in these passages, Solomon is not talking about fun diversions; rather, he is talking about the reality of life.

As you go through life, you will encounter a barker, Folly, who will try to entice you into "sweet" and "delicious" ways. Though these ways look sweet and delicious—and they may be at first—they are really traps. Unlike the midway games where you can walk away, once you have walked into Folly's trap it's hard, if not impossible, to get out. Once in, you will tend to become like Folly herself—loud, undisciplined, and without knowledge.

You probably know someone who swallowed Folly's bait—hook, line, and sinker. He went after that beautiful lure and ended up caught and reeled in. His life began to change, subtly at first, then with greater and greater departures from whom he used to be.

Someone who chooses to take drugs usually comes to mind. Those who take that path often become addicted to the drugs they take and will cheat, lie, and steal so they can get their next fix. Their appearance and their demeanor change as the drugs do their dirty work to their bodies. While some escape, many don't. But there are others—and let me submit many more—who take other kinds of bait and end up just as caught. That list is long, but some baits that come to mind include: greediness in all its forms, calling wrong right and right wrong, sexual perversions, power, popularity, having a critical spirit, becoming bitter, and gossiping.

Folly is sinister in her dealings. As you pass by her house, she will offer you whatever bait is most attractive to you. She'll place the sweet and delicious stuff around the bait so she can hide the sharp hook in the middle. She will tell you all sorts of lies and half-truths to get you to take a bite, just like the wicked queen persuading Snow White to take a bite of a poisoned apple. But Folly won't tell you the truth about what will happen to you when you take the bite; she only wants to destroy you.

Wisdom is just the opposite; she tells the truth and calls you to walk the righteous path. Even better, Wisdom will walk with you as you walk along your life journey to become right, just, and fair. If you seek, listen to, and follow her, she will provide wisdom, knowledge, and understanding. She will ensure you have a superior life and enter into the courts of the wise.

The question Solomon leaves with you is: "Will you hear and heed Wisdom's call and walk to her house or listen to Folly's call and step into her house?" With all of his being, Solomon implores you to choose Wisdom. Will you?

Final Thoughts

Solomon stays true to the purpose he stated at the very beginning of the letter. He wants his son, and you, to attain wisdom and discipline, understand words of insight, and acquire a disciplined and prudent life so you will do what is right, just, and fair. Solomon goes about it in an interesting way.

He starts by talking about the types of people you'll find in this world. While observing these are the types of people with whom you will have to deal, he also sets the stage for the drama that will take place in the rest of the letter. Will you choose Wisdom?

After that brief and weighty introduction, Solomon goes through five cycles hitting the same points. The points in each of these cycles are:

- You need to have the wisdom I'm offering you to successfully handle an upcoming threat.
- Here is the threat, evil or folly trying to lead you astray.
- The consequences are real. If you follow my wisdom, your life will be good. Ignore my wisdom, and you will head toward destruction.

While these discussions follow a familiar flow, the complexity of the threat escalates with every cycle. Therefore, the level of wisdom needed must escalate in the same or greater proportion.

These cycles point out a fact many of you know: Just when you think you have the wisdom you need to handle whatever comes your way, a new and confounding situation shows up, one that requires you to seek out new wisdom. Although following instruction and teaching (cycle 1), understanding what is right, just, and fair (cycle 2), keeping commands (cycle 3), and walking along straight paths (cycle 4) are good and protect you from so many threats, the best protection is found through living with Wisdom (cycle 5). Only through her instruction can you have the wisdom, understanding, and knowledge that makes you wise enough to turn away from Folly's "sweet and delicious" temptations.

At the end of each cycle, you can almost hear Solomon asking, "Will you choose Wisdom?" Having seen the benefit from choosing Wisdom and the consequences of ignoring it, it's no wonder Solomon wants you to choose Wisdom and live with her every moment of your life. As Solomon tells us: Nothing else we may desire comes close to what she is worth.

From here, the book of Proverbs suddenly switches from Solomon's letter to hundreds of pithy wisdom sayings. Most of them refer back to one of the types of people Solomon introduced in the first few verses of Proverbs. For instance, we were introduced to the sluggard in Chapter 6, but there is more to say about him. You'll find twelve proverbs more fully describing him from Chapter 10 on. But that is for another day in another book....

Acknowledgments

I would like to thank the many people without whom this book would not have been possible. As I began this project, my friend Vaughn Robison and my son, Jeffrey Biles, helped me formulate the nature of the project and shape the eventual product. My wife, Deanna Biles, provided me with the time and support to pursue my search for wisdom. Many thanks to my brother, Rick Biles, my sister, Jan Biles, and Deanna Biles for their careful editing, content questions, and on-spot advice. I also want to thank the fine people at Dorrance Publishing Company for their help in putting the final product together.

Thank you to the numerous business leaders, coworkers, and consultants who demonstrated and shared their wisdom with me. Their remarkable wisdom in the moment left a lasting impression on me. I've had the pleasure of having many wise personal acquaintances. Their down-to-earth wisdom had its positive effect on me, too. Combined, their wise advice helped me go through life with a minimal number of stumbles and directed me back to the path of the wise many, many times. While there are too many to list here, I hope they will recognize their contributions to my development.

Finally, I want to thank those who over the years so carefully preserved and translated Solomon's letter to his son. Retaining Solomon's wisdom and making it available to everyone was well worth their efforts.

Appendix 1

Business Application Questions

Chapter 1:

- David chose Solomon over his other sons to become the next king. When it comes to choosing your successor, how will you go about making that choice and letting others know?
- Why is it important that wisdom and discipline go together?
- Can you think of a situation when you heard what someone said but didn't understand it? What did you do? How did the situation turn out?
- If it is true the Wise speak in proverbs, parables, sayings, and riddles that aren't always easy to understand, how do you go about gaining understanding?
- Solomon describes four types of people and their weaknesses. Did Solomon get it right?
- How will you go about restructuring your work teams to ensure a wise person and a discerning person are always on every team?
- As you look at your company, are your wise and discerning folks actively involved in teaching the Young discretion?
- Do you provide the kind of direction your workforce needs so they can do a good job for you?
- What other points in these verses do you want to discuss and understand?

Chapter 2:

- Solomon's description of the Fool is blunt. In your experience, is Solomon's description accurate?
- The Fool doesn't care about gaining knowledge and despises wisdom and discipline. Do you have someone like that in your company?
- Do you have an example of where you successfully counseled or disciplined an employee who was acting like the Fool?
- Do you agree that you need to provide an early exit path for every fool in your organization?

Chapter 3:

- How would you describe the distinction between teaching and instructing?
- What actions is your company taking to imprint its principles upon its employees? Would you say the principles are imprinted? How do you know?
- Do your employees know how you want your principles implemented? Are your instructions clear enough to achieve a consistent result? How do you know?
- What is your company's commitment to developing your employees?

Chapter 4:

- How might "sinners" successfully appeal to your employees? What firewalls have you put in place to address these potential appeals?
- What teachings and instructions have you given your employees to help them reject a "sinner's" enticement?

- What is your first reaction when someone throws an enticement your way?
- Do you have examples you can share with others about times when you turned away a "sinner's" enticements?
- Are you aware of where you might be vulnerable to a "sinner's" enticements? What have you done to protect yourself?
- Are there areas in which you've compromised and need to make things right, just, and fair?

Chapter 5:

- Wisdom is pretty clear that certain types of people are headed for disaster. What examples have you seen that aligns with Wisdom's predictions?
- Change is very hard for some people. How do you help those who are resistant to needed changes adjust their attitudes and efforts?
- How do you prepare to deal with vocal critics of proposed changes?
- When have you had a sense that the "good" advice you were given really wasn't good advice? What tipped you off and what did you do to find the best advice?

Chapter 6:

- Solomon describes six steps one has to take to obtain wisdom. Which of these steps do you find most difficult for you? Why?
- Think about a time when you've had to dig to obtain wisdom and knowledge. How have you used what you learned about obtaining wisdom and knowledge since then?
- Would you say you and your company have been following the

course of the upright, blameless, just, and faithful? Please point to an example in each area that supports your answer.

- What steps do you need to take to help your company become upright, blameless, and just? List them.
- How do you know that your employees are being faithful in carrying out your policies?

Chapter 7:

- We usually think of wisdom relating only to our minds. If wisdom also can enter our heart, how does that change your thinking about wisdom?
- According to these verses, there is a connection between understanding what is right, just, and fair and having wisdom enter your heart. How have you seen this truth in your own life or in your fellow employees' actions?
- How has wisdom guided you in establishing a good business path?
- Do you have a story to tell your coworkers about a time when wisdom helped you avoid a disastrous path?
- Discretion protects; understanding guards. How have discretion and understanding protected or guarded you or your company?

Chapter 8:

- It's interesting to note the concept of needing more tools in the toolbox in order to meet new challenges at higher levels. How is your company doing at adding tools to your employees' toolboxes?
- As you think about the characteristics of wicked men and the

adulteress, are you and your company equipped to identify those who exhibit these characteristics and restrict their influence?

- How do you exercise due diligence when a "too good to be true" proposal comes your way?
- How do you use discretion when considering a "too good to be true" proposal?
- Some proposals are so seductive, you'll be tempted to go for them. What safeguards do you have in place to ensure seductive proposals are subject to a full due-diligence process?

Chapter 9:

- What does "living and remaining in the land" look like for your company?
- How do you and your company "walk in the ways of good men" and "keep to the paths of the righteous"?
- What do you do to develop high moral character and high business acumen for yourself?
- In what ways do you need to modify your interview process to gauge an applicant's moral character as thoroughly as her business acumen?
- What are your processes to identify internal candidates who desire to achieve high business acumen and high moral character?

Chapter 10:

- How closely do your outward displays match your company's values? Be prepared to give examples to support your answer.
- How close are the departments or divisions within your com-

pany to having a 100-percent commitment to love and faithfulness?

- What would it take for you and your company to move toward a 100-percent commitment to love and faithfulness in every area? Be specific.
- Having a good name and favor with your customers is a valuable asset. What are you doing now to earn a good name and favor with your customers?
- "Flashes of brilliance" are fairly common. What stories do you have in your company when someone in a "flash of brilliance" made an invaluable contribution to the company?

Chapter 11:

- What story do you have about a time when you or a business associate you know became over confident and, because of that over confidence, made a mistake?
- What do you do to remind yourself to be humble?
- What have you done recently to sincerely thank those who helped you become the person and success that you are today?
- Provide examples when direct reports provided wise advice or warnings to you. Did you give heed to the wise advice or warnings? Explain your answers.
- What is your attitude when someone corrects or disciplines you?

Chapter 12:

- People have different thoughts about whether it is proper to gain wealth. Please articulate your thoughts on the propriety of gaining wealth.

- How have wisdom and understanding come into play in your wealth gaining actions?
- How has your company helped its employees find work-life balance? Point out examples where your company has made allowances to meet an employee's business or personal needs.
- When confronted with a work problem, it's usually best to seek to understand the problem before proposing a solution. What percentage of the time would you say you seek to understand a work problem before providing a solution?
- Do you have a preference for developing home-grown solutions or importing outside solutions? What evidence can you provide to support your answer?
- How open are you to others' feedback or advice? Provide examples where you received feedback or advice, processed it without bias, used it to develop solutions, and communicated back to the person(s) who gave you the feedback or advice.

Chapter 13:

- What have you and your company done to ensure every decision is made through the filter of sound judgment and discernment? List some examples.
- Have there been a few instances when sound judgment and discernment were not employed in a decision? What did you have to do to recover from those unsound decisions? What did you change to preserve sound judgment and discernment thereafter?
- As you review the attributes of an amazing workplace, which ones apply to your workplace? Which one best exemplifies your workplace?
- In your hiring/promotion process, what steps do you take to determine whether a candidate possesses and uses sound judgment and discretion?

- Are you willing to make the commitment to have an amazing company? What are the first three steps you will take to achieve it?

Chapter 14:

- What do you and your company do to stress the importance of and teach sound judgment and discernment? Be specific.
- What systems do you have in place to alert you when sound judgment and discernment aren't being used? How well are those systems working?
- What minor annoyances are you putting off addressing? Make a list and allocate time or resources to address them within the next week.
- Are you constantly putting out fires rather than doing the work you were hired to do? How can you use your sound judgment and discernment to change the situation so you can go back to performing high-value work?

Chapter 15:

- When have you set aside your regular duties to take advantage of a teachable moment for one of your coworkers? Provide a short outline of the circumstances and what you did. What was the result?
- Solomon uses advice from a highly respected source to reinforce the wisdom he is providing to his son. How do you and your company use wisdom from a highly respected source to reinforce the wisdom and understanding you provide to your employees? Bonus question: How do you know your workforce sees the source you want to use as one they highly respect?
- Using only knowledge in your decision-making process leads to sterile, what's-best-for-the-company decisions. Do you have an example of this you can share?

- What difference does it make to include knowledge, wisdom, and a discerning heart when making decisions? Describe a situation when all three were used in the decision-making process.
- What steps will you take to include wisdom, discernment, and knowledge in your future decisions? Who can help you keep your eye on the ball?

Chapter 16:

- How do you know the counsel you are receiving is wise?
- Give an example of wise counsel you have received. What made it wise? Was it hard to take?
- Give an example of less-than-wise counsel you have received. Why was it unwise?
- Wise counsel only makes a difference if you embrace it. Tell us about a time when you fully embraced wise counsel. How did your actions or attitude change?
- It's easy to forget wise advice. What have you done to remember wise counsel?
- Have you established a stable of wise advisors? Take some time to list your wise advisors. If you haven't sent them a note of appreciation lately, consider taking time to contact them now. If your stable is a little thin, consider who you would like to enlist as additional wise advisors.

Chapter 17:

- What systems do you have in place to determine what is going on with your key personnel? Are there subtle signs that some problem may be brewing?

- Many corporate trouble stories relate to a trusted employee who decided to do wrong. What checks and balances have you implemented to regularly verify that your trusted employee is in fact an employee who can be trusted?
- What actions do you take when an employee's previously stellar performance begins to fluctuate? What successful approaches have you used?
- As you read about Solomon's six indicators, did any employees come to mind? What actions do you need to take to learn more about whether they are acting on one of the six steps?

Chapter 18:

- What responsibility do you have to new employees, especially those new to the workforce?
- Is learning taught or caught in your company? Give some examples.
- Every company has work that requires its employees to be more exacting to ensure quality requirements are met or employee safety is maintained. Name some of those areas in your company. What precautions have you put in place to make sure your employees know what to do?
- How do you prepare your work team for a new project so that the win percentage for your team will be high and include several big wins for your company?
- Employees can have flaws that become more obvious as they advance in a company. What efforts do you and your company make to identify and correct an employee's flaw early in their tenure?

Chapter 19:

- How do you and your company communicate the boundaries of what is illegal or unethical to your employees? How do you know your efforts are effective?

- Have you had the experience of someone bringing an illegal or unethical business opportunity to you? How did you know the opportunity was illegal or unethical? How can you pass on your wisdom to others in your company?
- When has a wise counselor given you advice that helped you see the business opportunity you wanted to undertake was a poor one? How did that wise advice help you?
- How receptive would you be to another employee, especially a subordinate, pulling you aside to tell you the great business opportunity you were pursuing was heading for trouble?
- Do you seek wise counsel on a regular basis or does wise counsel have to force itself on you?

Chapter 20:

- In your business dealings, have you ever become so captivated by one thing that you lost sight of your goals or purpose? What was the situation? How did it end?
- Have you lost sight of the value of your team members? Take a few minutes to think about each member of the team and list what they bring to the table. How do you know this list captured all of their value? How might you go about finding out what other skills and talents your team members could bring to the table?
- Do you have team members who undervalue themselves? Make a list of whom they are. What steps will you take to help these team members gain an appreciation of their value to the team? When will you do this?
- Would your customers and employees say your company is captivated about its purpose and service? What testimonials do you have that show your customers are delighted in your company? What value do your customers see in your company?

Chapter 21:

- What happens in your organization when someone asks a question like "Why go down that path?" Provide examples to support your answer.
- Does your organization have masterful plans that can't be questioned? What are they and why can't they be questioned?
- Give an example of when someone's, maybe your, plan was questioned and the questions kept the person and the company from suffering loss. What was the situation and how did it unfold?
- When you are good at your job, it's easy to "tell" more than "listen." How do you maintain the right balance between telling and listening?
- Does your company place a premium on people speaking up when they sense the company is venturing off course? What examples do you have when speaking up was rewarded rather than quelched?

Chapter 22:

- What promises have you made to your customers? Which ones will be the most difficult for you to fulfill? Why?
- What promises have you made to your employees? Which ones will be the most difficult for you to fulfill? Why?
- How do you ensure all of your written and verbal commitments are taken into account in your business and financial planning? As you look at your current plans, are there any commitments that need to be included?
- Are you serving as a guarantor for another person or entity? How do you monitor their performance? What reserves do you

have available to meet your guarantee?
- For those who have stepped in as a guarantor, what transpired? How well were you prepared to meet the guarantee?

Chapter 23:

- Do you find it true that sluggardly employees are likable and popular? Why do you agree or disagree?
- How have you tried to deal with a sluggardly employee? Did your actions change the employee's sluggardly ways? What was the end result?
- When do you find yourself engaging in sluggardly behaviors? What do you do to escape that behavior?
- How does a self-starter add value to the team's work? When have you taken the lead on getting work done?
- When was the last time you were caught unprepared for a work assignment? What events caused you to be unprepared?

Chapter 24:

- Name those employees, vendors, or customers you find most dynamic and invigorating. What sets them apart from other employees, vendors, or customers?
- Think of those employees, vendors, or customers who always seem to be throwing monkey wrenches into things. How do your feelings about them differ from those you identified in the previous question?
- What can you do to deal a "villain" out of your major decision-making processes? If you can't, how can you manage the process to minimize the damage from monkey wrenches he may try to insert into the process?

- Is there someone in your company who leaves a trail of conflict, dissension, and problems behind them? How will you determine their motives? Are you willing to move quickly to address the situation via coaching or an invitation to leave the company?
- Take a moment to evaluate your leadership team. Does anyone on the team leave a trail of conflict, dissension, and problems behind them? What effect is that having on the company? When will you address this issue?

Chapter 25:

- When have you seen an example of arrogant pride in your company? What was the situation? How was it addressed? Do others see you as a servant leader or a proudful person?
- In your company, is lying or fudging the facts with each other or vendors and customers a common occurrence? What types of lies are taking place? What happens to those involved when a lie is discovered?
- Can you think of an instance when 1) one employee sabotaged another employee, 2) an employee made it his business to spread false information, or 3) an employee falsely testified about what happened? Did the employee get away with it? How did the outcome affect organizational culture?
- What do you do to create and maintain dynamic teams? How do you keep dissension from tearing your teams apart?
- What are you doing to stay on guard against the seven detestable behaviors described in these verses?

Chapter 26:

- What is your company's purpose? Are there projects or programs that aren't aligned with your company's purpose? How can you adjust to either bring them closer to your company's purpose or jettison them?

- When contemplating a new program, project or venture, what base questions help you and your organization determine whether you should pursue the proposal? Have these questions been effective? How do you know?
- Did you agree with the three basic reasons for an organization to exist? Explain your answer. Are there other basic reasons for a company to exist? Please give them and your reason for including them.
- Describe a time when your company focused on one of the three basic reasons at the expense of the other two. Why did that happen? Did the change become permanent?

Chapter 27:

- Have you had to discipline an employee even though you were reluctant to do so? What were the circumstances? Why did you go ahead with the discipline?
- Think about a time when you failed to discipline an employee when you should have. How did that situation turn out?
- When giving discipline to an employee, what do you do or say to discipline for the deed while affirming the employee?
- Have you found it true as situations become more serious, employees become less willing to admit to their actions? Provide examples that support your answer.
- How have you handled a situation in which an employee has demonstrated an incredible lack of judgment but wouldn't recognize his faulty judgment?

Chapter 28:

- Have you turned the story of how your company came to exist into a memorable story? What is it? If not, who can you ask to help create that memorable story?
- What memorable stories do you have about an employee going above and beyond to help a customer or another employee? Which ones are part of the folklore of your company?
- Do your memorable stories make the point you want to make? Do any need to be modified or taken out of circulation? What do you do to ensure your good stories make the right point?
- How well does your memorable story align with your organization's structure, evaluations, incentives, and daily decisions? What changes do you need to make to align them?
- Does your story provide your workforce with more wisdom and understanding of how to do what is right, just, and fair?

Chapter 29:

- Wisdom shows up everywhere. Think about a time when you received wisdom from an unlikely source. What was that wisdom? Why was the source an unexpected one?
- When faced with a business decision, when have you felt a strong, unmistakable urge within yourself that one option was the best option to choose? Did you choose that option? How did things turn out from that choice?
- When have you followed Wisdom's advice and consequently gained understanding and showed prudence?
- Solomon provides seven areas where you may have a weakness. Take some time with each area and consider whether you are weak, strong, or somewhere in between. Which of your wise

counselors will you use to help with your evaluation?

- Using the information you gleaned from the preceding question, what will you do in your weaker areas to ensure you filter out the other noise in your life and listen to Wisdom?

Chapter 30:

- What examples do you have when a person's pride, arrogance, evil behavior, or perverse speech impacted your work group? What was the impact?
- How do you drive pride, arrogance, evil behavior, and perverse speech out of your workplace? Would you say your efforts are halfhearted or clear, insistent, and persistent? Explain your workplace answer.
- Do you have a passionate love for gaining wisdom? How has that shown up in your work actions or policies? What areas in your workplace would benefit from gaining and using wisdom?
- When have you gained wisdom from a change someone else recommended? What did you learn and why was it important?
- When has Wisdom abundantly rewarded you because of your passionate search for wisdom? What valuable gifts did you receive? How did those gifts benefit you?

Chapter 31:

- When has it profited you to have wise counselors around to review one or more of your ideas? How did these counselors improve your idea or help you see the idea needed to be put on the shelf?
- Think about a time when your wise counselors realized the gem of an idea you had and worked to improve and implement the

idea as quickly as possible. Describe how the mood in the room changed from the time you suggested the idea to the end of the discussion.

- Have you seen less-than-wise counselors ruin a good idea (yours or someone else's)? What points did these counselors make that ruined or sabotaged the idea?
- Do your current counselors qualify as wise counselors? Which of your current counselors need to be replaced? How will you go about finding more wise counselors and adding them to your counselor group?

Chapter 32:

- What have you intentionally done to create an inviting environment for your workforce or work team? What improvements could you implement to make the workforce or work team more inviting?
- How are wisdom and understanding passed on in your workforce? Would you rate the methods being used as mostly negative, mostly positive, or a mixture? Please provide examples.
- Do your facilities and equipment create an inviting environment for your workforce? What needs to change to make it a more inviting workplace?
- Does your compensation package create an inviting environment? Have you made sure your employees are paid fairly, allowing them to put nutritious food on their tables and take care of their basic needs?
- What have you done to seek out those rough-around-the-edges candidates who could be developed into dynamos? How could you do a better job at seeking high-potential candidates?

Chapter 33:

- Have you worked with someone who was attentive to your teaching and instructions, demonstrated they were learning, and responded positively to correction? How willing were you to work with this person again? What did you do to help retain this person in your organization?
- Have you worked with someone who falls into the Mocker category? What happened when you tried to correct him? How willing were you to work with this person again?
- Do you have employees who fall into the Mocker category? How are those employees negatively impacting your company or work team? What action do you need to take to change their impact on the company or work team?
- How about you? Do you fit in the Wise, the Simple, or the Mocker category? What examples can you provide to support your answer? Do you know in which category your supervisor or coworkers would place you? Are you willing to talk to them to find out?

Chapter 34:

- Describe a time when you received a shady business proposition that was covered with an attractive veneer. What prudent questions did you ask?
- How have your experience and judgment helped you when evaluating a proposition?
- Do your evaluation teams include employees who have the appropriate experience and judgment to make a prudent evaluation? How do you ensure the evaluation team includes those with different perspectives? How do you protect the team from

bad actors who may attempt to sway one or more members of the team?

- What safeguards do you have in place to catch someone's lack of judgment while the damage done is still small?
- Are you prepared to be wise, prudent, and discerning when "an offer you can't refuse," a slick way for you to get ahead, or any number of "sweet" or "delicious" suggestions comes your way? What safeguards do you have in place to ensure you act wisely?

Appendix 2

Personal Application Questions

Chapter 1:

- Why is it important that wisdom and discipline go together?
- Can you think of a situation when you heard what someone said but didn't understand it? What did you do? How did the situation turn out?
- If it is true the Wise speak in proverbs, parables, sayings, and riddles that aren't always easy to understand, how do you go about gaining understanding?
- Solomon describes four types of people and their weaknesses. Did Solomon get it right?
- If you had to choose, which of the four categories best describes you?

Chapter 2:

- Solomon's description of the Fool is blunt. In your experience, is Solomon's description accurate?
- The Fool doesn't care about gaining knowledge and despises wisdom and discipline. Do you have someone like that in your personal life?
- Do you have an example when you successfully counseled or disciplined someone who was acting like the Fool?
- If a loving reverence of the LORD is the beginning of knowl-

edge, would you say you have a loving reverence for the LORD? How do you know?

- How do you respond to wise counseling and discipline?
- Are you choosing to associate with those who lead toward wisdom? How do you know?

Chapter 3:

- How would you describe the distinction between teaching and instructing?
- Can you identify teachings and instructions onto which you have held? How did they help you?
- Can you identify teachings from which you strayed or instructions to which you didn't listen? Were you harmed when you strayed from the teachings or failed to listen to the instructions?
- What are you doing to provide wise teaching (life principles) and instructions to young ones around you?
- What underlying principles do you want to imprint upon the young ones in your life? Will those principles and your instructions lead them to an honored and beautiful life?

Chapter 4:

- How might "sinners" successfully appeal to you? What have you done to keep from accepting their appeals?
- What teachings and instructions have you used to reject a "sinner's" enticement?
- What have you done to keep your underlying values and instructions before you?
- What is your first reaction when someone throws an enticement your way?

- Can you provide an example of when you were tempted but refused to give in to those who wanted to lead you astray?

Chapter 5:

- Have you had an experience when you waited too long to listen to wise advice? What consequences did you experience?
- Have you gotten past loving simple ways, delighting in mockery, and hating knowledge? How do you know?
- When and where did you hear Wisdom speaking to you? How did that clear wisdom change your actions and resulting outcomes?
- Do you find yourself living in fear of harm or living in safety and being at ease?
- How do you intend to begin listening more often to Wisdom's voice?

Chapter 6:

- Solomon describes six steps one has to take to obtain wisdom. Which of these steps do you find most difficult for you? Why?
- Think about a time when you've had to dig to obtain wisdom and knowledge. Since then, how have you used what you learned about obtaining wisdom and knowledge?
- Do you seek for wisdom and knowledge as intentionally as Solomon describes? How do you know?
- It can take some time to align our hearts and minds with wisdom, knowledge, and understanding. What has your journey been like?

Chapter 7:

- We usually think of wisdom relating only to our minds. If wisdom also can enter our heart, how does that change your thinking about wisdom?
- According to these verses, there is a connection between understanding what is right, just, and fair and having wisdom enter your heart. How have you seen this truth in your own life?
- As you think about the path your life has taken, what are some of the good choices you've made?
- As you think about the path your life has taken, what choices have you made that were less than right, just and fair?
- Have you become better at making decisions that are right, just, and fair? Write down some examples.

Chapter 8:

- It's interesting to note the concept of needing more tools in the toolbox in order to meet new challenges at higher levels. As you've matured, what new wisdom tools have you added to your toolbox?
- As you think about the characteristics of wicked men and the adulteress, have you identified those in your life who exhibit these characteristics and taken steps to restrict their influence on you?
- Do you have family or friends who have been devious with you? What have you learned about dealing with them?
- Have you had a wayward person try to lead you astray? Give an example or two, including how and when you identified the methods the wayward person was using to entice you.

- "Is this person trustworthy?" and "Why am I being presented with this?" are great questions to gain understanding. What questions have you used to increase your understanding or exercise discretion?

Chapter 9:

- What does "living and remaining in the land" look like for you?
- How do you "walk in the ways of good men" and "keep to the paths of the righteous"?
- Think about a recent "fork in the road" with which you had to deal. How did you determine which fork to take? When making the decision, were you more like an apprentice or an accomplished tradesman?
- Do you have wise men or wise women who help you gain wisdom? Name them and determine to do something this week to express your appreciation!

Chapter 10:

- How closely do your outward displays match your values? Be prepared to give examples to support your answer.
- Are there areas in your life where you have less than a 100-percent commitment to love and faithfulness?
- Solomon commands his son to never forget his teachings. Please list some of the valuable teachings that drive your outward acts.
- As you look at your list of valuable teachings, which ones do you believe you keep in your heart? How do you know?
- How would you characterize your trust level with God? Do you trust Him with all of your heart or is your trust in Him conditional?

Chapter 11:

- It's hard to rightly judge one's own wisdom. Describe a time when you thought you were wiser than another person but later found out the other person was much wiser than you in some way.
- Have there been times when you thought you were wiser than the LORD? Explain.
- What does it mean to "honor the LORD with your wealth"? How do you demonstrate that in your life?
- You may have felt the LORD's rebuke or discipline at some point in your life. Did you despise or accept it? Please be ready to tell your story.
- Which one of Solomon's five commands would you like to discuss in greater detail?

Chapter 12:

- People have different thoughts about whether it is proper to gain wealth. Please articulate your thoughts on the propriety of gaining wealth.
- How have wisdom and understanding come into play in your wealth-gaining actions?
- Would you agree with Solomon that wisdom and understanding are more profitable than silver, yields better returns than gold, are more precious than rubies, and that nothing else you desire compares with them? Please give an example where your actions have reflected your answer.
- Solomon provides six additional benefits that come with seeking and finding wisdom and understanding. Which ones are you experiencing in your life?

- How does knowing the LORD used wisdom, understanding, and knowledge to lay the Earth's foundations, set the heavens in place, divide the deep, and let clouds drop the dew change your perspective about the importance of wisdom, understanding, and knowledge?
- Keeping Solomon's commands can be hard. Which one is most difficult for you to keep? Why?

Chapter 13:

- Most of us, most of the time, know what we need to do and we do it. List some areas in your life where you know what you need to do and have done it. Explain how you have steadfastly used sound judgment and discernment in these areas.
- Have there been a few instances when you put sound judgment and discernment aside? Did you realize the results from unsound judgment or lack of discernment immediately or after some time? What did it take to recover from your poor choice?
- There are plenty of distractions around us. Which distractions tend to interfere with you using sound judgment and discernment? What do you do to regain your focus and preserve your sound judgment and discernment?

Chapter 14:

- Solomon says you should not withhold good from those who deserve it, when it is in your power to act. What criteria do you use to determine whether someone deserves help? What criteria do you use to determine whether it is in your power to act?
- As you consider this section, would you say you regularly provide to or withhold from a deserving person who needs help? Give some examples to support your answer.

- Do you have a friend or relative who has asked you for help? Based upon Solomon's teaching, what should you do with their request?
- Solomon lists four other "Do not" activities. Have you done any of them? If so, how did you keep from going down the entire spiral to becoming a wicked person?
- Are you close friends with someone who consistently uses sound judgment and discernment? How has that person affected your life for the good?

Chapter 15:

- Solomon uses advice from a highly respected source to reinforce the wisdom he is providing to his son. How do you use wisdom from a highly respected source to reinforce the wisdom and understanding you provide to others? Bonus question: How do you know others see the source you want to use as one they highly respect?
- When raising children, your relatives or friends who exhibit wisdom, discernment, and knowledge can be a big help. How could these wise relatives and friends be of a greater help to you?
- What unbelievable blessings can you provide to your children, grandchildren, relatives, and friends?
- Which of the wise parent practices are you determined to implement? Why that one?
- Are there any areas where your actions before your kids and grandkids don't match what you are telling them? What will you do to align them?

Chapter 16:

- If a movie were made of your life, which of the three movie script examples would most closely match your life story? Explain.

- Do you agree with the statement "Those who follow good advice get good outcomes while those who follow bad advice get bad outcomes"? What experiences have you or a close friend had that validates the statement?
- When you hear good advice, how do you know that you have heard it, accepted it, clung to it, and guarded it? Give an example.
- Good advice leads you on straight paths, lets you walk unhampered, and keeps you from stumbling. What one piece of good advice has stuck with you through the years?
- How skilled do you believe you have become at determining what is wise counsel?

Chapter 17:

- Are you on guard against the six unwise actions Solomon describes? How do you know?
- Looking back at a fall you've had, did you go through all six steps? Explain your answer.
- Describe a time when you immediately kicked an evil thought from your mind/heart and put up a "no admittance" sign.
- Who is the trustworthy person(s) you use as a checkpoint? How has this person helped you stay on the good path, neither swerving left or right?
- No matter how much wise advice you receive, in the end it comes down to you and your willingness to follow Solomon's commands. How willing are you to follow Solomon's commands?

Chapter 18:

- Think about a time when you fell for a practical joke. What did the prankster do to make his story believable?

- On a more serious vein, have you fallen for a "too-good-to-be-true" story? How did the too-good-to-be-true story differ from what actually happened?
- How good have you become at spotting too-good-to-be-true stories? What events helped you become good at spotting them?
- How have you used your wisdom in this area to help instruct others who are less experienced, especially your children and other family members? How do you change your instruction as your children mature?
- What did you think of Solomon's model for discussing topics with young adults? How might it be useful for you?
- Did someone come to mind with whom you need to have a discussion about a certain topic? How will you prepare for the discussion and when will you have it?

Chapter 19:

- Solomon advises his son to stay away from the path to the adulteress. What similar advice have you received? Who gave you that good advice?
- Think about a time when you received good advice but didn't follow it. What cost (financial, relational, etc.) did you incur from not following that advice?
- Have you ever found yourself in a position where you were under the thumb of a cruel person? What was that like? How did you escape?
- Are you currently going down, or contemplating going down, a path that you know you shouldn't be taking? What will it take to convince you to change direction?

Chapter 20:

- What actions have you taken to enrich your relationship with your spouse? How are you watering and feeding that relationship? How are you taking care to ensure weeds never enter it?

- What are you doing to keep your marriage fresh and beautiful? What areas have you neglected and allowed to become ragged, dull, or dry? What will you do to change the situation?
- What would it look like if you really rejoiced in, and was captivated by, your spouse?
- Do you have other relationships that have lagged and could use some care and feeding? List three relationships you want to refresh and make beautiful again. Contact them this week.
- Do you focus on how green the grass is on the other side of the fence rather than focusing on making your own yard green? What will it take for you to turn your attention to making your own yard green rather than being captivated by and coveting what others have?

Chapter 21:

- What have you examined closely? What did you learn from your close examination?
- What is your response to knowing all you do, including your motives for doing them, are known by God and examined by Him? Does that frighten or comfort you? Explain your answer.
- Because God sees and examines all, Solomon recommends leading a life of discipline. How are you seeking to lead a life of discipline toward what is right, just, and fair? What do you understand are the benefits of seeking a disciplined life?
- Because God sees and examines all, Solomon also recommends rejecting folly. As you consider your life, what folly have you already rejected? What folly is before you now that you need to reject? How can your wise counselors help you?
- Past actions can bind us. Are you feeling bound by a past folly in which you engaged? Do you want help in being freed from those bindings?

Chapter 22:

- When did you make a promise you didn't keep? What was the situation and who was involved? How did it impact your relationship with the person to whom you made the promise?
- Have you ever made a promise you wished you hadn't made? Did you keep it or wiggle out of it? What did you have to do to get out of that promise?
- When has breaking an ill-advised promise cost you a friend, damaged a relationship, or set you back financially? What did you learn from that painful experience?
- Have you made financial guarantees for others? What are you doing to ensure they are making the scheduled payments? Do you have sufficient resources to make payments in their place? When do your obligations terminate?
- Do you find yourself overcommitted—double- or triple-booked at times? What will you do to stop overcommitting yourself?

Chapter 23:

- Have you observed ants going in and out of their anthill or a bird gathering materials for a nest or food to feed its young? What observations and conclusions did you make? How did they differ from Solomon's conclusions?
- What things during your day distract you from doing what you need to do that day? How can you better manage those distractions so you can complete your work more efficiently or earlier in the day?
- Your financial future is your responsibility. What are you doing

to prepare for your future financial needs once you cease working?

- Are you determined to meet your financial, spiritual, and other goals? What changes do you need to make to ensure you stay focused on your goals?
- What lessons are you teaching your children, grandchildren, and other youngsters about financial matters? What resources are available to help you teach them financial literacy?

Chapter 24:

- Do you have a friend who is constantly stirring up dissension? How does this person go about creating dissension? Do you encourage or discourage your friend's activities?
- When have you inadvertently caused dissension? Who alerted you to the dissension you had caused and how did they tell you? How did you react to knowing you caused dissension?
- When have you deliberately interjected dissension and havoc into a peaceful situation? What were your reasons? How did the situation turn out for you and others who were involved?
- If you were to grade yourself, would you say you never gossip, gossip infrequently, gossip quite a bit, or gossip most of the time? Why did you grade yourself that way? If a good friend were grading you, would they give you the same grade?
- What glances or motions do you use to let others know what you think about another person or what that person is saying? What is your intent when you do this?
- Have you said or done things to create dissension within your family? How can you make amends? What changes will you make to say and do things to build up your family?

Chapter 25:

- Did it catch your attention when the LORD said He detested these seven behaviors? Did it make you question if you had engaged in any of them?
- Take some time to consider the four questions you should ask yourself about each of the seven detestable behaviors. What did you learn about yourself?
- Although you can't get a redo on what you may have done before, if you ask and turn toward God's ways, God is willing to forgive you for the unjust, unfair, or evil things you have done. Will you take that step toward God and His goodness?

Chapter 26:

- What commands and teachings have you received that helped you see the right way for you to go? Did they seem to guide, watch over, and speak to you when you needed it?
- What lessons have you learned the hard way rather than through previously provided instructions and teachings? What made these lessons more memorable than the instructions and teachings?
- Describe a time when a wayward person tried to convince you to follow his leading. When and how did you come to understand the end result of following his leading would be like having fire scooped into your lap or walking on hot coals?
- Solomon says the corrections of discipline are the way to life. What does he mean by that statement?
- When did the corrections of discipline turn you from a poor path to a good path?

Chapter 27:

- When have you gotten into a situation where you have done something you never thought you would do? How did you and others react to you being in that situation?
- Have you been required to make restitution for your actions? How did it come about? Were you assessed some sort of punitive charges, too?
- What high hopes did you and your spouse have as you began to share life together? How have the twists and turns of life affected those high hopes? How did you use the twists and turns to build something into your marriage to make your marriage more valuable?
- When has your lack of judgment led you to do something that didn't make a lot of sense? Were your actions more like the starving thief or the man committing adultery? What did you learn from the experience?

Chapter 28:

- How does Solomon's story illustrate how temptation and sin work in someone's life? How did a lack of judgment affect what the young man in the story decided to do?
- When have you walked past all the warning signs and ended up trapped in a mess that proved to be hard to escape? What did you learn from that experience?
- Solomon presents us with thirteen actions that show a clear lack of judgment. Are you showing wisdom or a lack in judgment in one or more of these areas?
- Which of your wise friends can you ask to give you their perspective whether you are showing wisdom or a lack of judgment

in these areas? Are you willing to hear the truth and deal with it?
- If you are lost, hurt, lonely, or seeking, are you willing to ask Jesus to come walk beside you? Will you call on His name and believe in Him?

Chapter 29:

- As you were growing up, what themes dominated your family discussions? How did those discussions affect which life goals you pursued? How did those life goals affect your subsequent decisions?
- As you were growing up, did your family discuss character traits they wanted you to have? What were they? Did you end up exhibiting those character traits or go a different direction?
- Solomon makes the case that obtaining wisdom and understanding is supreme. How do you agree or disagree with Solomon's statement?
- Describe a time when you heard a little voice or felt something inside of you telling you not to do the wrong you were about to do. What did you decide to do? How did it turn out? What did you learn?
- Have you listened to Wisdom's words about Jesus? Are you ready to believe in Him and follow His teachings?

Chapter 30:

- Do you know someone who loves Wisdom and seeks her out? How has that person's wisdom been of benefit to you and your family?
- Has there been a situation when you knew Wisdom was speaking to you but you didn't want to accept Wisdom's guidance? What did you decide to do? How did the situation turn out?

- When you have found wisdom, how have you kept that wisdom in a special place where you can find it?
- Are the "voices" to which you listen leading you toward a loving reverence for the truth and doing what is right, just, and fair in the LORD's eyes? What changes, if any, do you need to make to listen more closely to the voices leading you toward a loving reverence for the truth and doing what is right, just, and fair in the LORD's eyes?

Chapter 31:

- How do you approach your days? Are you super busy all the time or do you operate at a more leisurely pace? Do you look forward to or dread tomorrow?
- In her speech, Wisdom gives us a model of how we could spend our time. Which parts of the model are you already using? How do you know? Which parts of the model do you need to implement?
- If you implemented Wisdom's model in your life, how would your marriage and the relationship with your spouse change? Are you willing to give it a try? Are you willing to give it a try with others?
- Have you closely observed Wisdom's work in creation? How have you seen her at work in the universe, plants and seasons, and the creatures around you? Are you delighted by what you find?

Chapter 32:

- What preparations do you undertake to create an inviting place for your guests?

- When you've known a person who could use guidance, how did you go about creating an inviting place where you could meet to talk about the things of life, share your wisdom, and steer that person toward a better life? How did meeting in an inviting place further the conversation?
- Could you benefit from some wise advice? Give your wise friend a call and talk or set up a time and place to talk.
- What does your church purposefully do to create an inviting environment to welcome all who come into the church's orbit? What else do you need to do to be an inviting church? Is your call out to those who are struggling or who have shown a lack of judgment akin to a mother opening her arms wide to accept and comfort her hurting child?
- Wisdom's message was: "I know you have a problem. Come and I'll help you. Come and you'll find true life!" How does your church's message compare to Wisdom's?

Chapter 33:

- Did you pick up on the urgency of Solomon's message in these verses? What else is at stake besides your very life?
- Is it really fair the Mocker gets to lie in the bed he made? Explain your answer.
- How do you respond to a well-deserved correction or rebuke? Do your internal and external responses more closely align with the Wise or the Mocker?
- A humble truth-seeker holds feedback up to the "light of day" and asks herself, "Is there any truth in this feedback?" When have you been a humble truth-seeker? What did you learn from seeking the truth?
- Are you on the path of the Wise? How do you know?

Chapter 34:

- When have you encountered a barker who tried to entice you into "sweet" and "delicious" ways? When and how did you realize the barker was leading you into a trap?
- Folly offers many kinds of bait. Which one(s) have you taken? Were you able to spit the hook out before you were caught? What happened?
- Have you found it to be true that Folly is sinister in her dealings with you? Have you found it to be true that Wisdom tells the truth and calls you to walk the righteous path? Reflect on your answers.
- The question Solomon leaves with you is this: "Will you hear and heed Wisdom's call and walk to her house or listen to Folly's call and step into her house?" What is your answer to Solomon's question?